I0029316

Jules Michelet, Vicenzo Calfa

The Bible of humanity

Jules Michelet, Vicenzo Calfa

The Bible of humanity

ISBN/EAN: 9783742899910

Manufactured in Europe, USA, Canada, Australia, Japa

Cover: Foto ©Suzi / pixelio.de

Manufactured and distributed by brebook publishing software
(www.brebook.com)

Jules Michelet, Vicenzo Calfa

The Bible of humanity

THE
BIBLE OF HUMANITY

BY

JULES MICHELET,

TRANSLATED FROM THE FRENCH

BY

VINCENZO CALFA.

WITH A NEW AND   INDEX.

NEW

J. W. BOUTON,

LONDON: B. QUA

Copyright by

J. W. BOUTON,

1877.

John F. Trow & Son,
Printers and Stereotypers,
205-213 *East 12th St.*,
NEW YORK.

TO

CHEVALIER PIETRO CENTÉMERI,

WHO, IN 1848 AND 1849,

FOUGHT FOR THE INDEPENDENCE

AND

RELIGIOUS LIBERTY OF ITALY,

This translation is inscribed

BY

HIS COUNTRYMAN AND FRIEND,

VINCENZO CALFA.

TABLE OF CONTENTS.

Part First.

THE CHILDREN OF THE SUN.

CHAPTER I.

INDIA.

CHAPTER II.

PERSIA.

CHAPTER III.

GREECE.

Part Second.

CHILDREN OF THE TWILIGHT, OF THE NIGHT, AND OF THE LIGHT REFLECTING AGAINST THE DARKNESS.

CHAPTER I.

EGYPT.—DEATH.

CHAPTER IV.

THE INCARNATION OF SABAZIUS.—MILITARY ORGIES.

CHAPTER V.

THE JEW.—THE SERVANT.

LIFE AND WORKS OF MICHELET.

JULES MICHELET, the celebrated French historian, was born at Paris, on the 21st of August, 1798. His father was a printer, and had his printing-office in the chapel of an abandoned monastery. One of his uncles, Narcissus Michelet, was in 1867 the oldest typographer. The early youth of the future historian was full of hardships : he had to struggle against the straitened circumstances that had fallen upon his family, already half ruined under the Consulate. He became a compositor in order to aid his father, while at the same time he began, in the best way he could, his literary studies, under the guidance of an old bookseller, who had formerly been a schoolmaster. It was proposed to his father to obtain work for the young man at the Imperial printing-office ; but Michelet's father refused, and devoted his last resources to educate his son at the *Lyceum of Charlemagne.* Young Michelet made gratifying progress under the tuition of Villemain and Victor Leclerc, and was chosen an assistant to a professor of the University, after a brilliant competition (1821), and was afterward elected to the professorship of history at *Rollin College*, where he taught till 1826.

His first works : *Chronological Table of Modern History* (1825), *Synchronical Table of Modern History* (1827), though they are only elementary, show the tendencies of the historian, and establish his place in the school which regards history first of all as a course of philosophical training. Michelet, in 1827, was appointed Master of the debating society at the Normal School. He declared his views more emphatically in his *Introduction to Universal*

History (1831), in his translation of the *Selected Works of Vico* (1835), in his *Roman History, The Republic* (1839), and especially in his *Origin of French Law* (1837). This last work shows him to be master of the subject, endowed with rare faculties and possessed with vast knowledge. The *Origin of French Law*, written in a sober, concise, and vigorous style—which was his first manner of writing —pointed out what interest it is possible to give to apparently the driest subjects, and what glimpses of light may be thrown upon the obscurest chaos of ancient institutions. All the past is, as it were, revivified in his pages, which are full of inspiration.

After the revolution of 1830, his professors, Villemain and Guizot, having been raised to power, Michelet was appointed Chief of the Historical Section at the record-offices, and afterward Assistant Professor of the course of history by Guizot at the Faculty of Letters. In 1838 he succeeded Daunau in the Professorship of History and Morals at the College of France, and began his celebrated lectures, to which the younger students eagerly flocked. This professorship was the foremost platform for the advocacy of democratic ideas, and the vivacity with which Michelet attacked the Jesuits, and denounced their underhand practices and encroachments, contributed not a little to win for him the most lively sympathies. Three great books were the result of this teaching. They are the summing up of it under different points of view : *The Jesuits*, written conjointly with Edgar Quinet (1843) ; *Priests, Women and Families* (1844), *The People* (1845). The clergy were powerful enough to silence the professor. The lectures were suspended, and Michelet's public career was momentarily broken. The revolution of 1848 was at hand, and, after the events of February, the choice was given Michelet to be reinstated in his professorship. He declined, and even refused an election as Representative (which honor was offered him), in order that he might devote himself exclusively to study.

Michelet, in 1833, first laid the corner-stone of the great memorial, to which he consecrated the best part of his life—I mean his *History of France* (1833-1867). This work, often interrupted by other undertakings, taken up again heartily, conceived at first on a comprehensive plan, and in its continuation dealt with in large episodic pieces —which are only connected together by the thread of facts, so as to exhibit the culminant point of each epoch —this work, I say, contains the entire writer and thinker, with various modifications which his manner of judging and his style have undergone.

The first six volumes (1833-1846) are a model of be-witching narrative ; facts are interwoven, deducted, and set off with that magic style of which Michelet is the supreme master. The geographic description of France, at the beginning of the second volume, is a masterpiece. Geography—an arid science—becomes in his hands as in-teresting as a masterly painting ; the enumeration of re-gions, of bays, of rivers, of mountains, is transformed into a succession of charming and magnificent landscapes.

As to events and persons, Michelet gives to history a new form. " Augustin Thierry," he says, " has styled his-tory a narrative ; Guizot defines it an analysis, and I call it a resurrection." Men, facts, manners—everything, indeed, revives under his hand, the smallest details of character or costumes are studied thoroughly, though often sketched at one bold stroke ; and carry the reader into the very scene where those personages acted, and make him live in their life and share their passions. Michelet first of all touches the heart : his way of con-vincing is by the emotions. The painstaking annalist lays open before the reader the facts, places in juxtapo-sition the testimony, compares one view with another, and gives a clue that enables him to distinguish truth from falsehood. Michelet, on the contrary, keeps the hard work to himself alone. When he has once compre-hended a fact and a personage, he throws upon them a vivid gleam of the same light in which he saw things and men in his fervent imagination and ever-quick sensibility.

Notwithstanding the success Michelet had obtained in the first part of his *History of France*, he interrupted it when he reached the reign of Louis XI. He left it alone for so long a time that people thought that he would never finish it—for he let himself be led away by other works capable in themselves of absorbing the activity of a life-time. The first of these intervening works I refer to was the *History of the French Revolution* (1847–1853, 7 vols. in 8vo.). The great epopee of the revolution had then for the first time a poet worthy of it. Lamartine, in his *Girondins*, had only written an episode of it, with insufficient historical research, and the book of Thiers, though remarkable from several points of view, was far from giving the proper conspicuousness to the characters of that unique era. Louis Blanc has afterwards more carefully analyzed the same facts and the same characters, throwing on them new light; but although the divergencies of opinion occasioned many sharp polemics between the two historians, and although Louis Blanc has pointed out several inaccuracies in Michelet's work, yet the latter continues to be a powerful, sincere history ; it has cleared the ground which a partisan spirit had obstructed with absurd legends, and above all things it vibrates with a communicative emotion.

After this great effort Michelet wrote some works of lesser importance : *Democratic Legends of the North* (1854), a series of studies on Poland and Russia ; the *Prosecution of the Templars*—a simple collection of the Latin manuscript documents of that mysterious affair—(1851, 2 vols.). Michelet had published the first volume of it in 1841, and had promised to elucidate the second with an introduction ; but he did not keep his word, although ten years elapsed before publishing the second volume. He doubtless thought that he had not yet examined deeply enough into that mystery. He then again took up his *History of France.* The second part was issued without interruption in twelve years (1855-1867), under different titles : *Renaissance ; Reformation ; Wars of Religion ; The League and Henry IV. ; Henry IV. and Richelieu ; Richelieu and the Fronde ; Louis XIV. and the Revocation of the Edict of Nantes ; Louis XIV. and the Duke of Burgundy ; The Regence ; Louis XV. ; Louis XV. and Louis XVI.* Although these volumes exhibit the sequel of history without a break of continuity, their very manner of publication and their titles show the method of the writer, who, taking hold of a culminant point of an epoch, or rather considering its predominant physiognomy, works around it until he makes every part luminous. In this way he embodies the whole Renaissance in Michael Angelo, as he had embodied the whole French Revolution in Danton. To this second part of his history, rather than to the first, must be applied the word " resurrection." " Men and facts are so vividly pictured in his inflamed imagination," H. Taine says, " that the writer at last believes them to be real ; he views them alive, he speaks to them, and hears their answers ; the dialogue and the drama are brought into history on every side. The circumscribed frame of the narrative is broken ; apostrophes, exclamations, dithyrambs, curses, personal confidences throng together ; history becomes a poem, and even when he keeps within the limits of a pure narrative, his vivid imagination is not slackened. The images are so lively, the manner so rapid, the quick invention so happy and so wild that the objects appear to be born again with all their colors, motions, and forms, and pass before our eyes as a phantasmagoria of luminous pictures. The flame of his imagination animates his style, and elevates it even to passion. Michelet writes as Delacroix paints, venturing on the harshest tones, searching in the slums for passionate expressions, borrowing, from medicine and the popular idioms, details and words which strike and frighten, and clothing the whole with splendid metaphors, which put a purple tinge on all the stains he has unveiled." Michelet, on account of his sensibility, possesses above all the faculty of suffering and rejoicing in contact with the past, and he communicates full well this emotion to the reader. Under his guidance there is no more analysis, no more doubt, no more circumspection ; the reader is led on. Some critics have wished to oppose this manner —to them very strange—of writing history. Indeed his method disturbs positive minds that like to place their foot deliberately and only on solid ground ; they have asked themselves if they had to believe those inductions, those hypotheses, those physiological analyses which are so new, and those portraits outlined at two strokes of a pencil, those characters conjectured from a phrase of a chronicler, a portrait or an engraving ; those conclusions which disconcert, those insights which had escaped all other historians, and which all at once set at naught every received opinion. There is, indeed, something confusing in this kind of divining of the historian. H. Taine says : " Must we believe Michelet? As for me, after making the experiment, I say, Yes. In studying the records of an epoch which he has studied, one feels a sensation like his, and finds, after all, that his conclusions of divinatory lyricism are nearly as exact as those of the painstaking analysis and slow generalization. But this verification has power only with those who have made it, and so far only as they have gone."

The mannerism of Michelet has, in his last works, undergone a new transformation ; a decided feminine influence is felt in it. Having failed to find in his first marriage all the happiness of which his tender soul dreamed, he had some years afterwards formed a purely intellectual connection with a young French school-teacher (Miss Mialaret, daughter of Toussaint Louverture's secretary), who was engaged in the remotest part of Poland as a governess. Having become a widower, he married her, and after this second marriage, the books of the illustrious historian seem to have been written under the influence of an uninterrupted honey-moon. We are indebted to this influence for *The Women of the Revolution* (1854)—a work containing detached sketches of his great history ; *The Bird* (1856) ; *The Insect* (1853) ; *Love* (1859) ; *Woman* (1860) ; *The Sea* (1861). Each of these books is somewhat peculiar, and full of an exaltation which is at times unhealthy, but the magic of their style is matchless.

On the whole, Michelet always held fast to his system of psychological studies, and carried into science, physiology and natural history, the same method he had formerly applied to history. He sought after the *soul of birds* as he had previously done for the soul of facts ; relating their sufferings with the same emotion with which he had unfolded those of the people.

His *Bible of Humanity* is a large epic in prose. The artist-historian, in the manner of inspired men and prophets, sings the evolution of mankind. There is no doubt that he throws brilliant glimpses of light on the long course of events and periods which he unfolds; but at the same time he carries away the reader with such rapid flights of imagination, as almost to make him giddy.

At length Michelet again took up his great history. In uniting, through the volume of Louis XVI., his *History of France* to his *History of the French Revolution*, he had run the whole cycle of French annals, as he had at first outlined it in his mind. He wished to continue his work up to our own time, and so began the *History of the XIXth Century*, of which only a few volumes have been published (1872–1873, 3 vols. in 8vo.). The title of the first volume is *The Directory, Origin of the Bonapartes ;* the two other volumes deal with the Consulate, and the first part of the Empire.

The personality of Michelet stands forth pre-eminently in the works he wrote in his old age ; his style is as picturesque and brilliant as ever, and his manner is as original. Some of his faults as a writer, however, are more prominent, and the boldness of his statements, as well as the fierce onslaught upon acquired beliefs, cannot fail to offend many a reader.

Even after what LANFREY had written on Napoleon, Michelet has been able to show the world a Bonaparte still unknown, by exhibiting the uncle through the nephew. Never was a hero so completely overthrown.

Michelet is one of the most sympathetic characters of our time. Standing aloof from parties, for he has never followed any into the arena of active politics, he is nevertheless one of the bravest champions of democracy. He has accomplished more for it than if he had served it in the world of political life, since he has served it so well in the field of thought, by unfolding its history and giving due prominency to the legitimacy of its aspirations. At the time of the second empire he sided with the moderate opposition, but his warfare was always bitter, such as history itself wages against despotism ; he applied to that time the same divinatory proceedings which he so well made use of in such a masterly way as to the past ; and seeing clearly the approaching end of that detested government, he entreated active men to become organized in advance, and think of what they ought to do on the morrow of its falling to pieces. His letter of August, 1869— a year before the overthrow of the second empire—is the voice of a prophet. He was an implacable adversary of the war of 1870, and he immediately published at Florence (where he was at that time) a patriotic appeal to the brotherhood of nations, which cannot be understood. The title of this book is *France before Europe* (1870). (Pierre Larousse's Large Universal Dictionary, 1874.)

Besides the works above mentioned, Michelet wrote *The Memoirs of Luther* (1835); *The Sorceress* (1862); *The Mountain;* and *Our Children* (1869)—a plea for compulsory education. His green old age gave hope that he might write several good books yet, or at least finish his *History of the XIXth Century*, which would have been the crowning of the edifice. But it was not to be, and although his energy never failed, his heart-disease gained ground day by day. He died on the Isle of Hyères on the 9th of February, 1874, and was buried in its little cemetery, but after a short time his remains were transferred to Paris.

Michelet was a great historian and put his heart in what he wrote. He was also a thoroughly upright man, and inured to the buffets of fortune. What he wrote about himself, in an address to his readers prefixed to the first volume of his last work (*History of the XIXth Century*), gives the best idea of the man and his works. Here are his immortal words : " I manifested my sympathies for Germany, and in general for all Europe, at the College of France. I was there surrounded by those young men who liked me, and I spread there the *Round Table*, to which all nations, asking of me the *food of life*, came and sat down. As long as *Cæsar* ruled I did not think of returning there, but I devoted myself to complete the memorial I owed to France."

When, after the fall of Napoleon III., he claimed his professorship, not so much on his own account as for the honor of the College of France, the professors of which hold their positions for life, according to its charter, and also according to the decisions of many a Secretary of State, Jules Simon, then Minister of Education, answered him that the place was regularly occupied by another incumbent. But such was not the case, and Michelet exposed the true state of things.

His books for public instruction, and even his *Abridgment of Modern History*, were proscribed, notwithstanding that they had been previously approved by the University. Michelet, in speaking of this injustice toward him, says : " So much do they fear even the impartial books which ought to take the place of those employed under the empire. But it is not a complaint I am making. I was suspended in 1847 by the Ministry of Guizot ; I was

2

expelled from my professorship, without pension or compensation, after the *coup d'état* of the 2d of December, 1851; the Communists set my house on fire, and the Versailles Government turned me out again from my professorship. But I make no complaint. I have had all I wanted. Rulers and parties have agreed to reward me, by publishing, in the best way that they were able, that I am an independent man. I have deserved such a testimonial. I never forsook my principles. Though I am deprived of my professor's chair, yet I have my platform. It is of sufficient height. I can survey from it the tempests, the winds of revolutions, by which the world is now being shaken and overturned. The last judgment is there —the final conviction, the sentence, the great sword about to fall on the neck of kings and of nations—the revolutions themselves!''

PREFACE.

MANKIND have incessantly deposited their thoughts in a common *Bible*. Every great people writes there its peculiar records.

These records are very clear, but different in form, and in a very free handwriting ; here in the form of great poems and historical accounts ; there in the form of pyramids and statues. A god sometimes, or a city, express much more than books, and, without a word uttered, they express the very soul. Herculès is a verse. Athens is a poem as much and more than the *Iliad*, and the high genius of Greece is entirely in Pallas.

It happens frequently that they have forgotten to write the most profound verse, the life which they lived, through which they acted, and in which they breathed. Who aspires to say, "My heart has beaten to-day ? " They acted like heroes. It is our duty to write their life, to find out their soul, their magnanimous heart, which the coming generations will feed upon.

Our century is a happy one. Through the electric telegraph it tunes the soul of the earth united in its present. By the means of history and the concordance of times, it gives the world a fraternal feeling, and the joy of knowing that the past and the present life is at one, of the same spirit.

All this is new and of this century. The means were wanting till now. These means—sciences, languages, travels, discoveries of every kind—culminated in the present all together. All at once what was impossible has become easy. We have been enabled to pierce through the abyss of space and time, and see skies beyond the skies, and stars beyond the stars. On the other hand, from century to century, going always backward, we have become acquainted with the prodigious antiquity of Egypt in its dynasties, of India in its gods and its successive and superposed languages.

This enlargement, in which we might have expected to meet with more discrepancy, has, on the contrary, led to more and

more harmony. The stars, the very metallic composition of
which has been revealed to us by the spectrum, seem to differ
little from our earth and solar system. The historical ages,
to which languages have enabled us to reäscend, differ very
little from modern times in the great moral things. Especially
in the home and the affections of the heart, as in the elementary
ideas of labor, of right, and of justice, the remotest antiquity is
repeated in us. The primeval India of the *Vedas*, the Iran of the
Avesta, which might be called the Dawn of the World, are by
far nearer to us, in the so strong, so simple, so affective types
they have left us of the family and creative labor, than the
sterility and asceticism of the Middle Ages.

There are no negations in this book of mine. It is but the
living thread, the universal woof which our forefathers have
woven with their thoughts and their hearts. We are continuing
it in a way unknown to us, and our soul to-morrow will be there.
It is not, as it could be imagined, a history of religions. Such a
history cannot be isolated and written separately. This book
passes altogether over classifications. The general thread of the
life which man pursues is woven with twenty united threads which
cannot be isolated but by tearing them down. The links of love,
of family, of right, of art, of industry, are incessantly mingled
with that of religion. Moral activity includes religion, but is not
included in it. Religion is a cause, but it is much more an effect.
It is frequently an arena where true life is acted. Frequently
it is a vehicle, an instrument of active energies.

When faith creates the heart, it is because the heart itself has
already created faith.

My book originates in broad sunlight, among our forefathers,
the sons of light, the Aryas, Indians, Persians, Greeks, of whom
the Romans, Celtes, and Germans have been inferior branches.*

* This book is infinitely simple. A first attempt of this kind must contain only what is very clear, and pass over, 1st, phases of savage life; 2d,
the semi-civilized world, China, etc. ; 3d, the nations which have left little
record and the age of which is yet in discussion ; 4th, the abstract doctrines,
which have never been popular, even among enlightened societies. Philosophers are much spoken of, but their books, even in Greece, were little read.
With great pertinency Aristotle laughed at that foolish Alexander, who complained that his *Metaphysics* had been published. It remained as it had been
unedited, and was for a very long time forgotten.

Their high genius consists in having from the very first created the type of things essential and vital to humanity.

The primeval India of the *Vedas* gives us the *family* in that natural purity and incomparable nobleness which no age has surpassed.

Persia gives us the lesson of heroic labor, in that greatness, strength, and creative virtue which our own century, though powerful, might envy.

Greece, besides her arts, possessed the greatest of them all, *the art of making man.* Wonderful power, enormously fruitful, which lords it over, and sets at nought all that has been done afterward.

If man had not had betimes these three *causes of life*—breathing, circulation, and assimilation—he certainly could not have subsisted.

If, from the most ancient time, man had not possessed his great social instruments—home, labor, education—he could not have endured. Society, and even the individual, would have perished.

Therefore its natural types have existed betimes and in a wonderful and incomparable beauty.

Here we have purity, strength, light, innocence. The whole is INFANCY, but there is nothing greater than this.

Come, girls and boys, take boldly the *Bibles* of light. Everything is there wholesome and very pure.

The purest of those Bibles, the *Avesta*, is a ray of sunshine.

Homer, Aeschylus, together with the great heroic myths, are full of young life—the vigorous sap of March, the effulgent azure of April.

The dawn is in the *Vedas*. In the *Râmayana*—excepting five or six pages of silly, modern interpolation—there is a delightful evening, where all the infancies, the maternities of Nature, spirits, flowers, trees, and beasts sport together and bewitch the heart.

The gloomy genius of the south, through Memphis, Carthage, Tyre, and Judea, quite naturally contrasted, and set itself against the Trinity of light. Egpyt in its monuments, Judea in its *Scriptures*, have written down their *Bibles*, which are gloomy and of profound meaning.

The sons of light had opened life gloriously and made it fruitful. But the sons of Egypt and Judea walked in death. Death and love commingled together work deeply in the worships of Syria, which have been diffused everywhere.

This group of nations is undoubtedly the secondary side, the small half of mankind. Their influence, however, has been great through commerce and the art of writing, through Carthage and Phœnicia, through the Arabian conquest, and still more through the strange conquest which the Jewish *Bible* has made of so many nations.

This venerated book, in which mankind long sought their religious life, is valuable for historical information rather than for edification. It bears evidently, as might be expected, the marks of many centuries of the different conditions of the Jewish nation, as well as of the various states of mind that inspired it. It is assumed to be dogmatic ; but it cannot be so, because it is very incoherent. The religious and moral principle fluctuates infinitely from Elohim to Jehova. The fatal effects of the fall, the arbitrary election, etc., which are to be found in it on every page, are in violent disagreement with the beautiful chapters of Jeremiah and Ezekiel, who promulgated the Right as we understand it at the present time. In its morality there is the same discord. To be sure, the great heart of Isaiah is far, very far from the equivocal skill, and the petty prudence of the so-called *books of Solomon.* The *Bible* is strong for and against polygamy and slavery.

The variety and the elasticity of this book has been nevertheless of much use, when the father of a family—a severe Israelite or a staunch Protestant—read certain chosen fragments and expounded them to his family, pervading them with an inspiration which is not always in the text. Who would put this text in the hands of a boy ? What woman, without casting her eyes down, will dare say she has read it throughout ? It often presents all at once the unveiled impurity of Syria, and many a time the exquisitely calculated and relished sensuality of gloomy and subtle minds which have gone through everything.

The day in which our kindred *Bibles* have appeared in the literary world, it has been better observed how much the Jewish *Bible* belongs to another race. It has a value which will always remain ; but it is dark and full of cumbrous ambiguity—beautiful but unsafe, like the night.

Jerusalem cannot remain, as in the ancient maps, just in the midst—an immense point between Europe, scarcely visible, and Asia Minor—eclipsing all the world beside.

Humanity cannot sit down forever in that landscape of ashes to admire the trees " which formerly may have been there." Humanity cannot stay like the thirsty camel, that, after a day of travelling, they lead to a dry torrent, and say, " Drink, camel, this has been a stream. If you wish to have a sea, hard by there is the Dead Sea, and on its shores there are salt and pebbles for pasturage."

Coming back from the immense shades of India and the *Râmayana,* returning from the Tree of Life, where the *Avesta,* the *Shah-Nameh* presented me four rivers, the waters of Paradise,—here, I confess, that I am thirsty. I appreciate the desert ; I appreciate Nazareth and the small lakes of Galilea. But, to speak frankly, I am thirsty. I could drink them off at a draught.

Allow rather, allow that mankind, free in their greatness, may go everywhere. Let them drink where their forefathers drank. With their enormous works, their task extended in every direction, their wants of Titan, they have need of much air, much water, and much sky ; nay, the whole sky, all space and light, the infinity of horizons—the earth for promised land, and the world for Jerusalem.

OCTOBER 16, 1864.

Part First.

THE CHILDREN OF THE SUN.

——:o:——

CHAPTER I.

INDIA.

The Râmayana.

THE year 1863 will always be to me dear and blessed, for in it I was privileged to read, for the first time, the great sacred poem of India—the divine RÀMAYANA.

"When this poem was first sung, Brahma himself was ravished with it. Gods, geniuses—all beings, from birds to serpents—men and holy anchorites—exclaimed : 'Oh, the sweet poem which we would always gladly hear! Oh, enrapturing song! How it imitates nature! How clearly we see this long history! It lives under our very eyes."

"Happy he who reads this book entire! Happy he who has read but the half of it! It makes the Brahman wise, the soldier brave, the merchant rich. If, by chance, a slave (Pariah) hears it, he becomes ennobled. He who reads the *Râmayana* is absolved from all his sins."

This last expression is no delusion of the fancy. This great stream of poetry sweeps away our abiding sin ; the dregs, the bitter leaven, which time brings and leaves in us, it washes away, and thus makes us pure. Whoever feels his heart dry, let him drink of the *Râmayana*. Whoever has lost what was dear to him, and is plunged in sorrow, let him draw from it the sweet comforts and sympathies of nature. Whoever has labored too much and wished too much, let him drink from this cup a deep draught of life and youth.

Man cannot always work. Every year he must rest, take breath, and renew himself at the great living springs which preserve their eternal freshness. But where are these to be found except at the cradle of our race—on the sacred summits whence descend on one side the Indus and the Ganges, and on the other the torrents of Persia, the rivers of Paradise?

Everything is narrow in the West. Greece is so small that I am stifled in it; Judea is so dry that I pant in it. Let me glance at the side of high Asia, towards the deep Orient. There I have my immense poem, as vast as the Indian Sea, blessed and adorned by the sun—a book of divine harmony, where nothing jars. A calm peace pervades it, and even in the midst of the battles described in it, we perceive an infinite sweetness, a boundless brotherhood, which extends to every living thing; an ocean without bottom or shore, full of love, pity, and clemency. I have found that for which I was looking—the *Bible of goodness*. Receive me then, great poem! Let me plunge in thee, O sea of milk!

It is only quite recently that the whole of this poem has been translated. It had always been judged by an isolated part or an interpolated episode directly contrary to its general spirit. Now that it has appeared in all its truth and grandeur, it is easy to see that, whoever was its last compiler, it is the outgrowth of India—the product of its ages. During perhaps two thousand years the Hindoos gave utterance to the *Râmayana* in the different songs and recitals which constitute this epic; and for the last two thousand years they have enacted it in the popular dramas, which were, and are still represented at the great national festivals.

It is not a mere poem. It is a kind of *Bible* which, with the sacred traditions, contains nature, society, the arts, the Indian scenery, vegetation, animals, and the changes of the year in the peculiar enchantments of the different seasons. We cannot judge such a book as we would of the *Iliad*. It has never undergone those expurgations and corrections to which the Homeric poems have been subjected by the great critics of Greece, the greatest of the world. It has had no Aristarchus. It comes to us unaltered. We see this in its numerous repetitions, and in some of its descriptions, which recur two or three times, and even oftener. We see this also in the many additions which have been made to it at sundry times. Here we meet with facts of such antiquity as to reach back to the cradle of India, and again with things comparatively modern and of such delicate sweetness and fine melody as would seem to be Italian.

It has not been arranged with that skill which characterizes the literary works of the West. No one has taken such trouble with it. Every one has relied on the unity which such an immense diversity receives from a vague harmony in which the shades, the colors, and even the opposite tunes are blended. It is like the forest and the mountain which it describes. Under gigantic trees there is a superabundant life, which springs up from smaller trees and from an infinitude of shrubs and humbler plants, which those wood-giants permit to exist under them, and over which they pour down their showers of blossoms ; and these great vegetable amphitheatres are full of life. On high soar and flutter birds of a hundred kinds and colors; apes swing from the intermediate branches, and now and then the mild-eyed gazelle is seen beneath. Is this totality a chaos ? By no means. The agreeing diversities deck themselves with a commingling charm. At evening, when the sun extinguishes his overwhelming light in the Ganges, when the noises of life are silent, the skirt of the forest exhibits all this animation, so diverse and yet so well blended, in the peace of the sweetest twilight, in which all things love each other and sing

together. A common melody emerges. This is the
Râmayana.

Such is the first impression. Nothing so great, nothing
so sweet. A glorious ray of the *all-pervading* * goodness
gilds and illuminates the poem. All its actors are loving
and tender, and in the modern parts of the poem they display a feminine saintliness. It is nothing but love, friendship, mutual regard, prayers to the gods, veneration to
the Brahmans, the saints and the anchorites. In this last
particular especially, the poem is inexhaustible. This
veneration recurs in it every instant. The whole poem is
tinted with a coloring eminently Brahmanical. Our Hindoo
scholars have been so greatly misled by this appearance
that they at first believed the author or the authors of it
to have certainly been Brahmans, as were those of the
other great Indian epic, the *Mâhâbhârata.* And yet, by
a strange inadvertency, not one of them has discovered
that, in the main, the two poems are in perfect contrast.

Look at this enormous mountain covered with forests.
Do you see nothing in it? Look then at that blue point
on the ocean where the water seems so deep. Do you
see nothing there?

At that very spot, at the depth perhaps of a hundred
thousand fathoms, there is a pearl of such extraordinary
brilliancy that I see it through that depth of water; and
under the enormous mass of that mountain there shines a
strange eye—a certain mysterious thing, which, were it
not for its peculiar glowing, we would take for a diamond in which the lightning flashed. This is the soul
of India, a secret, hidden soul, and in it there is a talis-
man which India herself wishes not to see too much.
If you venture to question her about it you will receive
no other answer than a silent smile.

I must, then, speak for her. But it is necessary first to
prepare my western reader who is so distant from all this.

---

* This is the meaning of the Sanscrit word *Vishnu.*

I could not make myself understood if at the start I did not explain how India recovered at the close of the last century, when her ancient worship and forgotten arts were first made known to Europe, suffered her Sacred Books, which no one had been allowed to read, to be opened to the world—those books which contain her primitive thoughts, simple and naked, and thus throw a profound light on all her developments.

How Ancient India was recovered.

To the last century belongs the glory of recovering the ethical system of Asia, the sacred philosophy of the East, the existence of which had so long been denied and buried in oblivion. For two thousand years Europe had reviled her old mother. One-half of mankind contemptuously spat upon the other half.

In order to bring to light Ancient India, so long buried under error and slander, it was useless to ask the advice of her enemies. It was necessary to go among her own people, and to study her books and her laws.

At the period to which we refer, criticism began to inquire whether indeed the whole wisdom of man was confined to Europe alone, and even dared to attribute a part of it to fruitful and venerable Asia. This questioning was a manifestation of a degree of faith in the general kinship of mankind, in the unity of the soul and reason, which indeed are identical, whatever the diverse disguisements of manners and times.

While Europe was debating, a young man named Anquetil Duperron, eighteen years of age, who was studying Oriental languages at the *Bibliothèque* of Paris, resolved to go to the East and bring from thence the primeval books of Persia and India. He was poor and had not the means to make so long and expensive a journey in an enterprise which so many wealthy Englishmen had undertaken without any result. But he bound himself by an oath to accomplish it, and he did.

An executive officer of the Government, to whom he was recommended, approved of his project and made him fair promises. But that was all. Relying, therefore, upon himself, he enlisted as a soldier in a company of recruits for India. On the seventh of November, 1754, he left Paris, with six or seven others, behind a bad drummer and an old invalid sergeant. It is interesting to read in the first volume of his works the strange *Iliad* which relates all that he encountered, endured, and overcame.

At that time India was divided among thirty Asiatic and European nations. It was by no means the same India that Jacquemont found it at a later day, under the administration of the English. At every step Anquetil met with obstacles. He was four hundred leagues from the city where he hoped to find the books and their interpreters, when the means of advancing failed him. He was told that the whole country was densely wooded, and full of tigers and wild elephants. But he proceeded on his journey ; and even when his guides were alarmed and forsook him, he continued on, the tigers withdrawing, and the elephants respecting him as he passed by. He pressed forward through the forests and reached his place of destination. But though unmolested by the ferocious beasts, this vanquisher of monsters was assailed by the diseases of the climate ; and, what was still more to be dreaded, the women conspired against the daring youth whose heroic soul was concealed beneath a charming countenance. The European creoles, the bayaderes, and the sultanas—all this lustful Asia—endeavored to turn him from his aspirations. They beckoned him from their terraces, but he closed his eyes to their invitations. His bayadere, his sultana, was the undecipherable old book. In order to understand it, he must win over and bribe the Parsees who·sought to deceive him. For ten years he pursued them, pressed them closely, and finally wrested from them what they knew. But their knowledge was defective, and he enlightened them and taught them. And thus the Persian *Zend-Avesta* and an epitome of the Indian *Vedas* were translated.

Everybody knows with what glowing interest the savans of Europe carried on what our hero had conjectured. The whole East is now revealed. Volney and Sacy opened up Syria and Arabia. Champollion, standing by the Sphinx, the mysterious Egypt, construed her inscriptions, and showed that she was a civilized empire sixty centuries before Jesus Christ. Eugene Burnouf established the consanguinity of the two ancestors of Asia—the two branches of the Aryas, the Indo-Persians of Bactriana ; and the Parsee scholars who had been educated in the College of France quoted in the most remote regions of Hindostan this Western Magician against their Anglican disputant.

Then from the depths of the earth was seen ascending a Colossus, five hundred times higher than the Pyramids—monument full of life and vigor—the gigantic flower of India—the divine Rámayana.*

The *Máhábhárata*, the poetical encyclopedia of the Brahmans, the expurgated translations of the books of Zoroaster, and the splendid heroic history of Persia—the Shah-Nameh—came next. It was known that behind Persia, behind the Brahmanic India, there was extant a book of the remotest antiquity, of the first pastoral age—an age which preceded the agricultural. This book, the *Rig-Veda*, a collection of hymns and prayers, enables us to follow the shepherds of that early period in their religious aspirations—the first soarings of the human mind towards heaven and light. In 1833 Rosen published a

---

* It does not become one as ignorant as myself to distribute the glory of this achievement, which belongs respectively to France, England, and Germany, or to indicate the proportion of praise that is due to the founders of Indian lore—to the schools of Paris, Calcutta, and London—to Sir William Jones, Colebrook, Wilson, Müller, Lassen, Schlegel, Chézy—to the three Burnoufs, etc. Some writers have dealt with this subject, and others will yet unfold it better than I can.

specimen of it. It can now be read in the Sanscrit, German, English, and French. In this very year 1863, a profound and able critic, who is also a Burnouf, has expounded its true meaning, and shown its scope.

In consequence of all this research we can now see the perfect agreement between Asia and Europe—the most remote age and the present era. It has taught us that man, in all ages, thought, felt, and loved in the same way ; and therefore there is but one humanity—a single heart only. A great harmony has been established through all space and time. Let the silly irony of sceptics, teachers of doubt, who hold that truth varies according to latitude, be forever silenced. The feeble voice of sophists expires in the immense concert of human brotherhood.

Indian Art.

Whatever the English may do to make it appear that the Indian *Bible* is more modern than the Jewish, it must be admitted that primeval India was the original cradle, the matrix of the world, the principal and dominant source of races, of ideas, and of languages for Greece, Rome, and modern Europe, and that the semitic movement—the Jewish-Arabian influence—though very considerable, is nevertheless secondary.

But if the English were constrained to admit her renowned antiquity, yet they affirmed that India was dead and buried forever in her Elephantina grottos, her *Vedas* and her *Râmayana*, like Egypt in her pyramids. They regarded the country, as large as all Europe, and her population of one hundred and eighty millions of souls, as insignificant, and even contemptuously declared that this numerous people were made up from the refuse of a worn-out nation.

Haughty England, that considered India as a land fit to be cultivated only for the purpose of enriching her rapacious rulers, together with the indignities heaped upon her people by both protestants and catholics, and the indifference of all Europe, made it appear that the Indian soul was really dead. Was not the very race dried up ? What is the feeble Hindoo, with his delicate, feminine hand, compared with the blond European, nourished, surfeited with strong meat and drink, and doubling his force of race, with that half-drunken rage which the devourers of meat and blood always exhibit ?

The English do not hesitate to boast that they have killed India. The wise and humane H. Russell thought so, said so. They have oppressed her with taxes and pro-hibitory tariffs,* and discouraged her arts as far as it was possible. In the more humane markets of Java and Bassora the products of Indian art find a ready sale, and it is solely because of this high estimate of the eastern merchants that her arts exist.

The specimens of Indian art exhibited in England in 1851 surprised and confounded the English people ; and when Mr. Royle, a conscientious Englishman, explained these marvels of enchantment, the jury could not award them a prize, because the prizes were only to be given on "the progress of fifteen years," while these productions of India were the work of an eternal art, alien to every fashion, and more ancient than our arts, which are old at their beginning.

In order to secure a fair specimen of Indian art for the Exhibition, a prize of twelve and a half dollars was offered, and was carried off by Hûbioula, a common weaver of Golconda, who produced a piece of muslin, which threw into the shade all English textile fabrics, and which was so fine that it could be put through a small ring, and so light that three hundred yards of it weighed less than two pounds. It was a genuine gauze, like that with which Bernardin de Saint Pierre clothed his Virginia, like those in

* The production of cotton, which was forced upon India in 1863, will be of no more advantage to her people than was the forced cultivation of opium and indigo, which have been and are the despair of Bengal ; and some of the English governors have loyally tried to remedy this grievance.

which Aureng Zeb wrapped the corpse of his beloved daughter when he laid her in the white marble mausoleum of Aurungabad. But neither the endeavors of Mr. Royle, nor the acknowledgment of the French that they were treated better than the Orientals, could induce England to give her Indian subjects any other reward than these barren words : " For the charm and beauty of the invention, and the distinctness, variety, commingling and happy blending of colors, there is nothing to be compared to it. What a lesson for European manufacturers ! " *

Oriental art is by far the most brilliant and the least costly. The cheapness of labor is excessive ; I had almost said deplorable. The workman lives on a trifle. A handful of rice satisfies him for a day. And then the mildness of the climate, the admirable air and light, the ethereal food which is taken through the eyes, and the singular beauty and harmony of all nature, develop and refine the perceptions and make the senses acute. This is noticeable even in all the animals, and especially in the elephant, who, though huge and shapeless in bulk and rough in exterior, is a voluptuous connoisseur of perfumes, selecting the most fragrant herbs and showing his preference for the orange-tree, which he first smells, and then eats its flowers, its leaves, and its wood. Here man acquires an exquisite fineness of perception and feeling. Nature makes him a colorist and endows him with special privileges as her own child. He lives with her, and all that he does is charming. He combines the most diverse strains, and commingles the dullest hues in such a manner as to produce the sweetest and most exquisite effect.

The sky does everything for the Oriental. A quarter of an hour before sunrise and a quarter of an hour after sunset he enjoys that supreme privilege, the perfect vision

---

* *Report of the Juries*, II., 1858. This has been admirably repeated, over and over again, by our French Juries, Messrs. Delaborde, Charles Dupin, and especially by Mr. Albert de Beaumont. *Revue des Deux Mondes*, October 15, 1861, xxv., 924.

of light, which is then divine with its peculiar transfigurations and inward revealings, with its tenderness and glory in which his soul is swallowed up—lost in the boundless ocean of a mysterious Friendship.*

In the midst of this ineffable mildness the humble, feeble, half-nourished, and wretched-looking being conceives the idea of the wonderful Indian shawl. As the profound poet Valmiki beheld his great poem, the *Rámayana*, gathered, as it were, in the hollow of his hand, so this poetic weaver perceives the whole design that he would execute, and begins his great artistic work which sometimes is continued through a century. His son or his nephew, with the same soul, hereditary and identical, and with the like delicate hand, will follow the same line of thought and carry it on until completed.

In the execution of strange and exquisite jewelry† and in the fanciful ornamentation of furniture and arms, the hand of the workman is unique. Some of the latest Princes of India sent to the Exhibition referred to, arms which had been worn by their ancestors, and therefore so peculiarly dear to them, as well as of such great value, that we can scarcely understand how they consented to entrust them to others. Another of those Rajahs sent a bedstead of ivory, possibly of his own workmanship, as he superscribed his name on it, which was sculptured and carved with infinite ingenuity and delicacy—an exquisite, chaste, or virgin-like piece of furniture, full of love, it seems, and of dreams. Are these objects things? They seem to be almost human, and to be possessed with the ancient soul

---

* In the *Rig-Veda*, the " Friend," Mitra, does not designate the sun, but the effulgence which precedes and follows it.

† The jewelry of India, according to Mr. Delaborde, has not the trifling lightness of the Genoa or Paris filigree ; and her sculptures, so light and airy (as on the Abbas' and other monuments), do not concentrate the attention on one point, nor seek to make an impression by exaggerated reliefs or conspicuous contrasts of light and shade, but entice you to the contemplation of the whole, as if a lace of marble were stretched over it.

of India, as well as with that of the artist who made them, and the Princes who used them.

But these sumptuous productions of rare artists do not indicate the genius of the race so fully as do the inferior arts and the more simple handiwork. Without expense or noise the Hindoos, with apparent ease, produce works that appear to us very difficult. With a little clay for a crucible, and for bellows a couple of the strong, elastic leaves peculiar to the country, a single man in the forest will, in a few hours, turn the crude ore into iron, and again, with the addition of swallow wort, turn the iron into steel, which, when carried by caravans as far as the Euphrates, is called Damascus Steel.

It has been observed by many that the peculiar chemical insight of this people has enabled them not only to extract the most vivid colors, but also the corresponding grade of mordant, which fixes and makes these colors eternal. The Indian spinster,* with her native instinct and no other machine than her spindle and her delicate hands, will obtain a thread of incredible fineness, with which the most intricate and beautiful designs are executed.

Some one has said : " Instead of sending to Cashmere some hideous designs of shawls, which would corrupt the Indian taste, let us send our pattern-drawers to India to contemplate its brilliant nature and to imbibe its pure light." But it would be necessary that these designers should also catch the soul and the profound harmony of India, for between the great calmness of the patient soul of the Hindoo and the subduing mildness of the nature that surrounds him, there is such a complete agreement that the man and the nature can scarcely realize that each is distinct from the other. Nor is this the effect of quietude simply, as some believe, but of that singular faculty, peculiar to the race, of seeing life at the bottom of every thing, and the soul in every living body. The herb is not simply an herb, nor the tree only a tree, but both herb and tree are the vehicles for the circulation of the divine spirit; and the animal is not all animal, but a soul that has been or will be a man. Without this faith they could never have accomplished the first and most necessary of all arts in the earliest times, the art of taming and humanizing the most important and useful servants, without which man could not have long existed. Without the dog and the elephant man would have been at the mercy of the lion and the tiger. The books of Persia and India relate in a grateful manner how the dog was the first preserver of man, and how the men of those days formed friendships and entered into alliances with the very strong and large dogs which could strangle the lion. And, in the *Mâhâbhârata* it is narrated that the hero of that poem declined the reward of heaven unless he could enter paradise with his dog.

In lower India and in hot climates where the dog was lacking in strength, or was easily alarmed and fled from the tiger, men invoked the protection of the elephant; but this was a more difficult alliance, for though the elephant becomes gentle in maturity, it is brutal, irascible, and capricious in youth, and terrible in its gluttony, and in its amusements, and therefore was scarcely less formidable than the tiger. And when we consider that to train a horse, which is so small compared to the elephant, a bit and spurs of steel, and reins and bridles are needed, it must have seemed an almost hopeless undertaking to curb and restrain by force this living mountain, this mighty Colossus.

They succeeded, however, and nothing could have been greater or more beautiful. It was a moral victory. They treated the elephant as if he were a man, a wise man, a Brahman,* and he was influenced by it and behaved accord-

---

* Yudishtra, the Pandu.

ingly. To-day the treatment is similar; the elephant has two servants to look after him, to remind him of his duties and to warn him if he deviates from Brahmanical decorum. The *cornac* sits on his neck, scratches his ears, guides him, and rules him by the voice, teaching him how to behave himself; while the other servant walks beside him and teaches him the same lesson with a firm tone and equal tenderness of manner.

At present some writers speak very lightly about all that. The elephant has not only been disparaged but has greatly degenerated.* He has known servitude and has felt the power of man. But in earlier times he was fierce and indomitable, and to have made him teachable and tractable must have required great boldness, calmness, affection, and sincere faith. Then they religiously believed what they said to him, and fulfilled their treaties with him. They respected the soul of the dead in the body of the living; for, according to the doctrines of their holy sages, the spirit of some departed one lived in this commanding and speechless form.

When they saw him in the morning, at the hour in which the tiger leaves his ambush of night, coming deliberately out of the dense jungle and going majestically to drink of the waters of the Ganges, empurpled by the dawn, they confidently believed that he, too, hailing the opening day, became impregnated by Vishnu, the *All-Pervading*, the good Sun, and while immersing in this great Soul, incarnated in himself a divine ray.

---

* And yet the judicious traveller, Mr. Fouché d'Obsonville, a cool-headed man and free from romantic tendencies, says that he saw in India an elephant, who had been wounded in a battle, go daily to the hospital to have his wound dressed. In that climate there is great danger from wounds festering, and to prevent this they are seared with hot irons. This was the treatment which the elephant voluntarily came daily to receive, and though the pain was so great as to cause him to groan terribly, he never manifested any violence towards the surgeon, but seemed to understand that this severe treatment was for his good, and that his tormentor was his friend.

The Primeval Indian Family.—The First Worship.

We live on light, and our legitimate ancestors are the Aryans, the people of light, who on the one hand have spread over India, and on the other over Persia, Greece, and Rome, and have imparted their ideas, language, arts, and gods along a brilliant track like a long vista of stars. Happy and fruitful genius which nothing has been able to dim, and which still conducts the world in its course by the brightness of its milky-way !

In the origin of civilization no miracles are to be witnessed and but little of the wonderful. A peculiar precocity of good sense and sagacity were the essential elements in the beginning of human history. Those who imagine that at the start man acted absurdly and was governed by wild imaginations, do not realize that the pressing realities of life in those times required the utmost discretion, and that if man had not acted sagaciously he would have perished.

In the venerable Genesis of the Aryans, in the Hymns of the *Rig-Veda*, unquestionably the earliest records of the world,* there is stated that two persons, a man and a woman, join with one accord in an outburst of thanksgiving to the morning light, and sing together a hymn to Agni—(Ignis—the Fire).

" Thanks to the light of the rising day, to the dawn longed for, which puts an end to the anxieties and the terrors of the night.

" Thanks to the hearth, to Agni, the good companion,

---

* Handed down through long generations from mouth to mouth, those Hymns may have undergone some changes in language and form, but not in meaning, and they tell us of the earliest conditions of pastoral life, antedating all other histories. The earliest records of Egypt contain nothing but rituals and inscriptions ; while the *Genesis* of the Jews, compiled from traditions, though partly ancient, has many modern indications, as for example, it alludes to angels (Persans), and coin, and prostitution, and many other ideas which were evidently brought from the captivity.

who makes the winter cheerful and the house smile; Agni the fosterer; Agni the sweet witness of the interior life."

This hymn of gratitude was just; for fire was everything, and without it life would have been uncertain, miserable, and destitute. The light of the fire at night drives away the wild beasts, the wanderers in the dark. Neither hyenas nor jackals like the glimmering of the hearth, and even the lion slinks away growling. But the fires of the morning, and especially the brightness of the dawn, disperse these short-sighted ferocious animals, who dread the Sun.

In our modern cities, well lighted with gas, where the houses are secured and protected, there is no sense of danger; but what traveller, however bold, who has been obliged to spend a night in some lonely spot of a dangerous country, will not confess that he was pleased to see the dawn of day? In those early ages, when men had no arms but the club, and the thick, short sword (such as may be seen on Assyrian monuments), with which to defend themselves against wild animals, and often encountered the lion face to face, there was a feeling of insecurity and dread of beasts of prey. This was the case even in ancient Greece, where were many lions, notwithstanding the cold of its winters; and much more so in Bactriana and Sogdiana where the Aryans lived. There the lion and the tiger were more numerous and much larger than they are at present. It was no uncommon event in those days for the family, men and animals, to be aroused in the night by the faithful watch dog, who heard at a distance the fearful mewing of these monstrous cats (the lion and the tiger). The cow would tremble with fear, and the ass would prick up his ears to catch the approaching or receding sound. According to the *Rig-Veda*, the ass was the first to discover the departure of the lion and to go out into the morning air and salute the dawn; and till it had been seen and consulted none of the family ventured abroad. The large dog, loved and caressed, now led the way and was followed by the men and domestic animals, and next by the women and little children, all happy and gay ; even the plants looked then new and beautiful. The birds drew their heads from under their wings and began to sing on the boughs as though delighted with life, and all the people with grateful hearts united their voices in ascriptions of praise to Light, singing thanks for the enjoyment of another day.

And now we, their remote children, after the lapse of thousands of years, are scarcely less moved in reading of those venerated infancies of mankind—those striking experiences of our ancestors in the simple and ingenuous confessions of their terrors by night and their joys and thanksgivings in the morning.

When at night the wolf springs at the throat of the deer going to drink, man says : " Anxiety has taken possession of me. Come then, come light, and restore to things their forms. Light up the sinister paleness I see yonder," and then adds these words of profound meaning : " The dawn of the morning alone makes us self-reliant." (*Auroræ fecerunt mentes conscias.*)*

That the religion of the Hearth had its origin in the North, and not in the South, is apparent from the language and customs that prevail in the rigid climate of the Asiatic uplands, where the people express the desire to live "a hundred winters," and lavish the most tender caresses upon the fire, the good companion Agni, and where they also speak with great consideration of the sheep of Candahar, on account of its warm and delicate wool. In one of their nuptial hymns the woman choosing her husband is represented as saying, with graceful inno-

---

* This is Rosen's translation, though Wilson is more complete, and I use it more frequently, sometimes comparing him with Langlois. I am persuaded, however, that only Emile Burnouf's recent work recognizes fully the character of the *Rig-Veda*, and yet I could wish that he were more particular in fixing the dates that separate what belongs to Agni from what belongs to Indra, etc.

2

cence : " I come to thee in my weakness. Be considerate
of me, and I will always be *Roma Sâ*, the mild sheep of
Candahar, the silky sheep which comes to warm thee."*

The life of woman among that pastoral people is not
servile, as it is among hunters or warriors. She is so
necessary in all their domestic arts that she is absolutely
the equal of man, and is called, with great propriety, the
DAM—the mistress of the house—a word more ancient
than the Sanskrit of the Brahmans or even of the *Vedas*,
and which comes from an extinct language.† And then
in the last part of the beautiful ritual of their marriage
ceremony there occurs this significant passage, which is
only applicable to the women of the North, who retain
their energies till a late period of life : " May she have
ten children, *and her husband be the eleventh !* " An
admirable sentence, full of beauty and meaning ! An
outburst of joy drawn from the prophetic heart ! The
idea is the same as that I expressed in another book : that
woman, first the child of her husband, later becomes his
sister, and finally his mother.‡

Such is woman in the North ; but centuries afterward
we find her in Lower India, married at eight or ten years
of age—a mere child whom the husband has to form, and
whose place as assistant at the sacrifice is usurped by a
young anchorite, a novice, a disciple. How totally unlike
to the primeval life of Upper Asia, where woman is a person and married at maturity,§ and becomes the *Dam* or
Lady, the mistress of the house, the coadjutor of domestic
worship, and shares equally with man in the pontificate.
There she knows Agni " in his three forms, in his three
languages, and in his three aliments ; " and knows the
male and female fuel which are his father and mother.
She also makes for him the sacred butter and his favo-

---

* EMILE BURNOUF, 136, 240.   † Ibidem, 191.   ‡ *L'Amour.*
§ At present in her fifteenth or sixteenth year. See ELPHINSTON, PERRIN,
etc.

rite spirituous liquor, the Sôma.* The saying prevails in
India to the present day that, "As black coffee is rich in
ideas though poor in love, so Sôma is the friend of joy
and of generation." In the sacred cake, the Sôma, and
in all that makes life cheerful and sanctifies it, there is a
presentiment of what woman will be in the future—the
magician Queen, the bewitching Circes, and the powerful
Medea (without her crimes).

In the hymns of invocation they remind the fire, in
a thousand ways, of his profound relations to woman.
"Everything is ready, dear Agni. We have decked thine
altar as a spouse her beloved. Dear Agni, thou dost repose as the child in her mother's womb."

They had divined that there were male and female
plants, but not knowing how to distinguish between them,
they supposed, in their lively and graceful imagination, that
the female plant was the one which inclined towards or tenderly entwined the other, and willingly lived in its shade.

These plants are the parents of fire. In the mother
they scoop a little hollow, in which they cause the father
to turn briskly.† A patient process. Some of the more

---

* It is said that Soma is the very flesh of the sacrifice; hence its botanical
name: Sarco-Stemma Viminalis, the flesh plant. (Aphylla asclepias acida.
See ROXBURGH, *Flora Indica*.)

Under the name of Sôma, and, in Persia, Hôma, the flesh plant is the Host
of Asia, as the consecrated wafer is the Host in Europe, and to complete
the resemblance it is represented as undergoing suffering. (See STEVENSON,
Sâma-veda, and LANGLOIS, *Academy of Inscriptions*, XIX., 329.) Sôma
fell from the ethereal expanse, a seed of heaven, and grew on a solitary and
quiet hill. It consecrates itself to martyrdom, submitting to grinding, and,
with barley and butter, to fermentation, and then it allies itself to and espouses
the fire, *Aditi*, the ground of the hearth, the womb of the world. Nourishing
victim! rewarding men and gods, then wrapping itself in vapor and soaring
to heaven. All things are renewed. The stars shine brighter. Indra combats the tempests more successfully. The waters flow more freely, and the
earth yields more abundantly.

† AD. KUHN. Origin of Fire, 1859; BAUDRY, *Revue Germanique*, April
15 and 30, and May 15, 1861. A remarkable example of the fruitful aid
which philology affords in ascending the prehistorical ages. Nothing more
luminous or ingenious than the work in which Mr. Baudry has enlarged,

savage tribes depend entirely upon chance for their fire, as when the lightning strikes and fires the forest. The impetuous races of hot countries extract it from pebbles by violence, but many of the sparks that leap from the flint are lost and leave no trace behind except astonishment and obscurity.*

But to return to our subject: By this friction man obtained first a little smoke, and then a scarcely visible flame appeared, which would have vanished at once, had not woman come to its aid. She welcomed the new-born infant, nourished it with leaves, and preserved its life. . . The hymns also testify to the extreme fear which people felt in very ancient times of allowing fires to be extinguished, and thus of not being able to preserve the savior of life. Woman alone is the preserver of this fire. It is to her as a very little child which she loves and nourishes with butter, while it, in grateful acknowledgment, continues to burn.†

---

fathomed, and sometimes corrected, the researches of Mr. Kuhn. It is the foundation of an important book on the capital question of primitive origins. Vico had first divined that the fire of lightning was, at the beginning, an object of religious worship. The solar fire was worshipped afterwards. This worship was natural and by no means absurd, and science in these days acknowledges it. M. Renan, in a remarkable letter to the great chemist Berthelot, says: "You have demonstrated to me, in a manner to silence all my objections, that the life of our planet has its source in the sun—that every force is a transformation of the sun—that the plant, which nourishes our hearths is a storehouse of heat from the sun—that the engine is propelled by the effect of the sun which slumbers in the subterranean recesses of the coal-mines—that the horse derives his strength from the vegetables produced by the sun—and all the rest of the work on our planet may be resolved into the evaporation of water, which is the direct work of the sun. Before religion placed God in the absolute, only one worship was reasonable and scientific— the worship of the sun."—*Revue des Deux Mondes*, t. xlvii., p. 766, Oct. 15, 1863.

* This is strikingly illustrated by the two great races of the world: the Indo-European, patient and methodic, has left its prolific trail of light; the Semitic has darted some brilliant flashes which have troubled the soul, and too frequently have darkened the night.

† The hymn tells us in a most charming manner, and with infinite delicacy, that "the young mother is kind to her frail child, and does not show it, but

As soon as it is strong enough to eat, they feed it with
barley and the sacred cake. To this substantial food they
add the liquid aliment. Man takes from the hand of the
woman the wine of Asia—the Sôma which she has prepared—and throws it into Agni. And now the fire blazes
and sparkles, and as it mounts upward becomes bluish.
The home smiles and rejoices. Divine mystery! The
most obscure parts of the dwelling share in the festival,
and long after are reddened by the fantastical reflections
of the flames.

But at the very instant of the first sparkle and lively
ascension of the flame, a voice ascends from two united
hearts, giving utterance to words full of love and tenderness. Short and artless outburst, followed by deep silence, but what was said can never be abolished. It is a
holy hymn which we may read forever, and which after
six thousand years is as fresh as when first uttered.

At the same moment in which, without prearrange-
ment, with one heart they utter this word which will
never perish, they look upon each other in this divine
glimpse of flame and see themselves to be divine. (He
Deva, and She Devi.)*

In this extreme simplicity, which might be called
childish, appears the true sacrament of harmonious love,
the high idea of marriage. "The mortal has made the
immortal. . . We have generated Agni. The ten
brothers (the ten fingers), entwined in prayer, have inaugurated his birth and have proclaimed him our male
child."

The great characteristic of this race, the foremost in the
world is, that, while it adores, it is conscious that it has
made the gods. In the most enthusiastic hymn the admired phenomenon, which appears under divine features,

---

even hides it from the father. Presently it grows up and stirs. How intelligent it appears, and how lively its movements ! but let us be vigilant, for, of
itself, it aspires to rest."—*Rig-Veda*, Wilson, III., 233; Ibid., 35 ; Ibid., p. 2.

* EM. BURNOUF, 191–2.

is at the same time so well described, followed and
analyzed, that we can easily find its birth and progressive
life. Still more, all these passages in which the names of
the gods appear stand out in a transparent language,
and the names are really nothing but appellations.* (The
Strong, the Brilliant, the Pervading, etc.)

Then, no superstition ! If the god forgot himself, if he
became a tyrant, or would have darkened the imagination
with servile terrors, the mind, armed with such a language
as to remind him of his origin, would have demanded :
'' Who created thee ?   I am thy creator.''

Noble worship, of a high and mighty conception, which
in giving all preserves all. The blessed and beloved gods
do not emancipate themselves from man their creator, but
remain in the circle of general life. If man needs them,
they need him ; they hear him and come at his call. Man's
morning praise evokes and allures the sun. It is a powerful charm, and the sun obeys it. When man kindles Agni
on the brink of the river, on the sacred confluent ; when
the hand of woman has spread around him a carpet of
herbs, the gods come promptly in response to the hymn,
and take their seats in a friendly manner, partake of the
sacred butter and the sparkling Sôma. The gods gave
the fruitful rains which have made the meadows green
again, and man gives them the best he has. The sky
nourishes the earth and the earth the sky.

Is it to be said that on account of this mutual depen-
dence the gods are less revered ? They are really loved
the more. In this benign religion of love without terror,
the gods mingle freely in the actions of human life, elevating them and making them divine. The tender spouse,
while preparing for man the sacred bread which at evening

* MAX MÜLLER, 557. All this is still *fluid in the Vedas. In the
Homeric Greece these adjectives become substantives, and are personal. All is
already petrified.* This judicious reflection of Max Müller ought to have led
him to see more clearly the vast antiquity of a people whose worship is evidently of the first religious period.

restores him, is assisted by Agni, who also acknowledges all her efforts to please him. " Agni is the lover of girls and the husband of women." He sanctifies and makes glorious the happy moment of generation.

Whether Agni burns in man, or shines on the hearth, or darts his beams from the sky, making the *great spouse* fruitful, he is forever the same. Man feels him in the lively warmth of Sôma which elevates his spirits, in the inventive flame from which the winged hymn takes its flight, and in love, as well as in the sun.

Some people will not fail to say : " All this is pure naturalism and without any moral bearing." This is a familiar objection made of old. *The awakening of con-science*, a divine fruit, blossoms from every religion.

In very ancient hymns Agni is recognized as the representative of purity which man must imitate, putting aside every physical and moral taint. If man does not yet know clearly what a moral taint is, he is restless, nevertheless and interrogates Agni as follows : " What is that with which thou dost reproach me ? What is my fault, and why dost thou speak of it to the water (Vârouna), and the light (Mitra) ? " etc. ; and thus his troubled soul enumerates all the forces of nature before which this pure and blameless Agni accuses him.

These tendencies towards purification gave rise to the reformation of Zoroaster. The agricultural tribes, of austere character, held to the heroic dogma of work, which purifies, to the invisible Agni, the organizer of the world.

The shepherd tribes, more imaginative, extended and enlarged the visible Agni to the sky, the sun, the clouds, and to everything visible;* and always celebrated and

---

* In proportion as they observed that heat was in that element or in that form of life, the divine names were multiplied, but not the gods. There is no mistake about this. The hymns express this, and notice in clear terms the monotheistic simplicity which pervades all this variety. " Agni, thou art born Vârouna (water, air), and thou dost become Mitra (the sweet glim-

worshipped him under his primitive name, which also became Indra, the god of the tempests which water and renew the meadows.

This flight of imagination coincides, it would seem, with the changes of abode and climate, and with the migration of the shepherd tribes, who descended towards the East and the South. When a man passes Caboul he is struck with astonishment to see all of a sudden in all its newness and immensity the Indian landscape, and I do not doubt that it was in this place that the transformation of Agni into the powerful Indra took place. It is less the sun in itself than the god, conqueror of the clouds. This country, abounding in large but unequal rivers which sometimes become torrents, is subject to severe drouths followed by great hurricanes. Its climate is one of combats, of contrasts, and of atmospheric war. To wage this war man generously gave to Indra a bow and a chariot and horses. The chariot, as it rolls, mutters. Indra, vanquisher and fertilizer, comes near to the panting earth and makes love to her by the darts of his thunderbolts; and then seeing over the mountain the black dragon of the envious cloud which holds and refuses water, pierces the monster with his arrows, and compels him to discharge the rain from his lacerated sides.

Innocent ornamentation—very translucent, and but slightly charged with either myths or symbols. The faithful preservation of the word, the song, the sacred and holy hymn of their ancestors, was their only art. This people pursued its way for about ten centuries, singing from Bactriana to the Indus, and afterward to the Ganges.

---

mering which precedes and follows the sun). Thou art Indra, the son of strength. Thou art Aryaman in thy relations to girls, for thou dost make husband and wife of one spirit."—*Rig-Veda*, Wilson, III., 237. Thus they had large liberty, but those who used these names did not by any means see in them persons. Religion pursued her way lightly. It helped, but neither curbed, nor entangled the mind with low terrors. It had some of the serenity and nobility of that smile which was subsequently manifested in Greece.

At every step a song, and the totality of all their songs is the *Rig-Veda.*

The boundary was the entrance of Hindostan. These travellers found themselves in the presence of three Infinites, either one of which was sufficient to strongly stir up their mind.

On the south there was the Infinity of the sea—a large river whose shores were unseen, a beautiful mirror every evening burnished by the flaming sun when it plunged in its waters.

On the north a circle of giants, all the peaks of the Himalaya, raised up from thirty mountains, bearing all climates and all vegetables, and crowned with bright snows over a black brow of dark trees. Immense jungles full of tigers and serpents spread themselves at its base. The Ganges, lined with its colossal forests, flows majestically towards the East ; a whole living world drinks of its waters.

At last, and this the most terrible, the burning attraction of the Hindostanic furnace, the caresses and invitation of a nature too charming, and of the yellow race,* mild and defenceless, of from one to two hundred millions of slaves, who so loved and admired the white race that it might have perished in their embraces.

The resistance of the Aryans, this great victory of the soul, is one of the most remarkable moral events which has ever occurred on earth, and was only maintained behind the barrier of castes, which in that climate were readily formed on the very rational basis of psychology and of natural history.

First. There was *the horror of a blood diet*, the idea that meat produces dullness and tends to defilement, renders unclean and offensive, and that the blood-eater seemed to have the odor of a corpse. And meat is unneces-

---

* The yellow race, which easily becomes very black. See Vivien de Saint-Martin's *Geographical Researches*, 1860.

sary in that country, because the fruits of the earth are
there ripened and cooked by the powerful sun, and contain admirable juices, which are both substantial and
nutritious.

Second. There was *the natural terror to be apprehended from the love of an inferior*, the formidable
absorption by the yellow woman (sweet, charming, and
submissive,* as is seen in China) and by the black woman,
the most tender, caressing, and loving. If these Aryans
had not resisted, they would certainly have become extinct.
By·the animal diet they would have become a drove of
gross, sleepy, and excitable beings like the Europeans
who now live there; and by intermarriage with slaves and
inferior women they would have lost the gifts of their race,
especially the inventive power and the brilliant spark that
shines in the *Vedas.*

The yellow woman, with her slanting eyes and the gracefulness of a cat, her inferior and yet artful mind, would
have reduced the Hindoo to the level of the Mongol, degraded the race of profound thinkers to the lower level of
the Chinese workman, and extinguished the genius that
produced the high arts which have changed the whole world.

Even more. In such a climate, with such inter-com-
mingling, the small number of the Aryans would probably
have melted away as a drop of wax in a brazier. India
appears like a dream, in which everything is fleeting—
flows and disappears—is transformed and then reappears
under quite another form. Terrible play of nature, which
jests with life and death! The effort by which the human
genius withstood this was not less terrible. By an immense imaginative power and a harsh legislation, which
may appear tyrannical, the Aryans created a new nature of
invention and force, in order to intimidate, exorcise, and
disarm the other.

---

* Strongly inclined to polygamy. We see this marvelously illustrated in
Yu-Kiao-Li—*Two Female Cousins.* Translated by Stanislas Julien. Chap.
16, vol. 2, p. 195. 1863.

The sober-minded, the thinkers, the haughty guardians of the Indian genius, constituted themselves an isolated people by the absolute abstinence from meat and spirituous liquors. This is the origin of the elevated and meritorious title of Brahman. Even the caste of the warriors, who use meat sparingly, cannot taste fermented liquors without undergoing cruel purifications. At last, by a very beautiful effort, the Brahmanical legislation tried to maintain in love and marriage the high idea of the *Vedas*, the monogamic purity, confining marriage to their own women, who are haughty and disapprove of the life of the harem.

She is free. Marriage is not a traffic (as among many other peoples). The sale of woman is a crime, and an object of horror according to the laws of Manu.

The true formula of marriage, which no society can ever surpass, is found and established :

" Man is not man except as he is triple, that is, man, woman, child.* According to the *Vedas*—the *law* and the *sacred ordinances—and in accordance with the* popular feelings, *the wife is the half of the husband's body,* sharing equally in all his acts, pure and impure." And so much so that every good work of either is of equal advantage to the other. The holy man has the happiness of saving, by his holiness, her whom he loves.†

The equality of the two sexes, difficult and impracticable for this race and in this climate, is nevertheless recognized in heaven and manifested in the temple. It beams from the altar. Everywhere the wives of the gods are seated beside them.

The mother ! In India this sacred name is so strongly imbedded in the heart of man, that it appears to make him lose sight of all religious hierarchy. And although he is the Pontiff of the family, and alone offers the prayers of

---

* MANU, tr. by Loiseleur, IX., 45, p. 322.

† *Digest*, III., 458; MANU, IX., 22, p. 319. The woman, even of an inferior caste, is saved by the virtue of her husband.

the household, he is, notwithstanding, beneath woman :
" the mother is worth more than a thousand fathers ; the
field is worth more than the seed." *

The law seeks to follow out such an ideal in constituting
the woman the companion of her husband. It gives her
the household royalty. "Woman is the home. An
abode in which there is no woman cannot be called a
home." Nor is this an unmeaning saying. The law gives
her the control of the receipts and the expenses. Enormous and decisive concession ! However little energy
woman may possess, if she make use of it, she, by this
alone, becomes the equal of her husband and the mistress
of the house, as much as she was under the *Vedas.*

But does nature permit India, this great prophetess, to
accomplish all that she teaches to mankind ? No. The
tyranny of the climate does not allow the reality to equal
this dream of perfection. Woman is marriageable in her
eighth year. " A man of thirty may marry a girl of
twelve, and a man of twenty-four, a girl of eight."
(MANU). This law will ultimately change everything.
Whatever equality the law may accord to the husband
and wife, this young wife can only be as a little child to
her husband.†

---

* MANU, IX., 52, p. 324, says : that the earth (woman) is worth more than
the seed (man). The *Hindoo-Digest*, III., 504, abounds in such passages as
this : " A mother is worth more than a thousand fathers."

† I will in another part of the present work speak of Polygamy, Polyandry,
the *Mâhâbhârata*, etc. It will be enough to say here that Polygamy is the
result of certain social causes, and not of the climate. It appears that in
India monogamy is satisfactory. The wedding is a frigid affair. In the ceremony, and on the very evening of marriage, the husband feigns to start as a
pilgrim and return to a life of asceticism and penance. His friends prevail on
him to return to his wife, and compel him to be happy. This husband is no
longer a young man, for, in this peculiar climate, the man marries late in life,
as he is prevented, especially if a Brahman, by a long series of examinations,
trials, and penances, and above all, by religious dreams. The husband is
therefore infinitely far from the child that is given to him, and the child, not
understanding him, looks upon him inquiringly. (*Digest*, II., 1, 35.) She
is to him as much a pupil as a wife, and the law authorizes him to chastise

I am not writing the history of India, and therefore I will not relate how the Brahmanic law, which was at first her safety, became, little by little, her scourge. This is not peculiar to India or her laws, but is the common history of all religions. We find it in Persia and Egypt.

Religion, at first springing from a vital cause, and almost always indicating the sincere longings of the heart, formulates itself in laws, and establishes a priesthood. This law gradually becomes overcharged with harsh prescriptions, and the priesthood becomes tyrannical and sterile. It is like those greenish islets in the seas of the south, which by degrees become encumbered with corals and shells, then disappear under their growth, and finally become nothing but calcareous masses, on which nothing can germinate.

In India no historical work, but two very solemn legends explain to us the struggle between the Brahmans and the warriors. The former conquered at first, and if we can credit them, they owed their victory to a valiant Brahman —Parasu Râma—*Râma with the hatchet* (one of the incarnations of Vishnu), who made a terrible slaughter of the warriors. These latter, while they submitted to the spirit-

---

her when necessary, "as a little pupil." (MANU, VIII., 199, p. 296.) This, however, does not prevent the law from saying, with charming contradiction (the law doubtless having in mind the adult woman), "Do not strike your wife, with even a flower, though she has committed a hundred faults." (*Digest,* II., 209.) These laws are embarrassing. On one side there is sympathy for the wife, and on the other there is fear of her, for the little silent girl, who demands nothing, does not appear less formidable in the eye of the law. The law feels that the woman has an infinite absorption of threatening power, conspiring unconsciously with that of the climate. The law is evidently troubled for the conservation of the helpless man, and so provides that he is to live a portion of the time isolated from his wife, and not to love her more than twice a month, if he aims at perfection. It would exempt him from taking a second wife, but the first wife soon ceases to be a woman, and the mortality of children is terrible, so that it becomes necessary to take another wife. But there is no cause for fear, for as soon as the perpetuity of the family is assured, the indulgent law permits him to leave everything and to become an anchorite among the roots of some Indian fig-tree.

ual authority of their conquerors, were no less powerful, and continued to be the Kings and Rajahs of the country. Their bards or court poets (such as may yet 'be found among the Siks and other tribes) opposed to the Brahmans a rival legend, stating that one or two thousand years after the Brahminical Râma, Vishnu incarnated himself in a warrior who was also called Râma, and who was the son of a King. This Rama, belonging to the warrior caste, but of a mild and peaceful disposition, is the complete idea of India—the hero of the *Râmayana.**

The Profound Liberties of India.

That which makes the *Râmayana* a wonder, in spite of its innumerable additions, is its interior soul, equipoised between two souls, its sweet contradiction, the charm of a free mind partly obscured. It is the timid Liberty adoringly veiled in Grace. It shows itself. It hides itself. It asks pardon for existence.

Under the powerful law of Manu, during the Brahmanic reign, when the domineering Caste had laid hold of the whole life in infinite detail, and filled the earth with thirty thousand gods, nature still existed. Nature protests in a low voice, and exhibits herself in love, in pity, and in boundless tenderness towards the weak and the humble; not by palpable appearances nor by strong flashes of light, but by ineffable glimmerings. It is a delicious lamp which shines through alabaster. It is the

---

* We can never praise sufficiently the beautiful Italian translation of M. Gorresio, who, under the supervision of Burnouf, has likewise edited the original text. But why do not people praise the excellent French translation of M. Fauche? He is, of all Orientalists, the man who has made the greatest sacrifice to science. Poor and in the depths of solitude, finding no publisher, he has *printed with his own hands, and published at his own expense,* the nine volumes of this great poem. He is now engaged in translating the Mâhâbhârata—a still greater undertaking. But what of it? He lives out of our times—is more active, and no less a Hindoo than if he were a Brahman or a Rishi.

divine, the chaste charm of the pearl at the bottom of the sea.

It was not always thus. The live opposition of the Castes began, on the contrary, as soon as they came into existence in the remotest antiquity. Witness that peculiar song (was it the first satire of the world?) in which the people daringly parodied the teachings of the Brahmans.* Witness the traditions according to which ancient Indra, the conqueror and the scoffer, the mirthful god of nature, who sends the rain and fine weather, overtakes and rails outrageously at the difficult chastity of the holy ancho- rites. Witness, above all, the legend of the Rajah Viçvâ- mitra—a boastful history which from age to age has pursued and threatened the Brahminical authority. This king, celebrated as a writer of Hymns of the Vedas, re- nowned for his hundred sons, and for his generous adop- tion of the inferior tribes, took a fancy to become a Brahman, but was rejected and underwent the most se- vere mortifications and self-tortures for a thousand years, acquiring by this means such merits and such formidable power that he could annihilate the whole world, earth and heaven, men and gods, by a single frown. The gods, affrighted, came down to his hermitage, and, surrounding him, besought him to spare the world, and secured his promise that it should exist. It is to be noticed that this terrible saint never dies. He is always dangerous. He lived at the time of the *Vedas*. Some thousands of years afterward he reappears in the *Râmayana*. He is the most profound and intimate embodiment of the Indian soul. This soul makes and can destroy, creates and can annihilate. It reminds all the gods that it created them, and can with a frown blot them out. It has the power but will not exercise it. Entirely free, it has a most tender regard for the gods and would be horrified if they were injured. It loves them especially, because,

---

* It is the song of the frogs, who preach and teach. MAX MÜLLER, page 494.

through their cloudy and sublime existence, it has a glimpse of itself.

It is the enormous privilege and the unique royalty of this Indo-Grecian race to see where the other races do not see, to penetrate worlds of ideas and dogmas, and the deep strata of gods, piled upon each other. And all this without effort, without criticism, and without malignity; by the simple exercise of a wonderful vision, by the simple force of a look, by no means ironical, but terribly clear, as through a hundred lenses placed one over the other.

This transparency is the peculiar grace of the *Râmayana*. From the beginning the author prostrates himself and remains on his knees out of regard to Brahmanism, but sees perfectly through it. In his first songs he ascribes all that can be imagined of veneration and tenderness (and is evidently sincere) to the high and sacred Caste. But at the same time he unfolds a new revelation, a new ideal of holiness : the *god-warrior*, incarnated, not in the *Brahmanic* Caste, but in a Chatrya* (a warrior).

And that which he says, and which I have already quoted in the second page of this volume, is no less strong : that the *Râmayana* addresses itself not only to the Brahman and the warrior, but also to the *merchant* (Vêsya), which is a very numerous Caste, and which, according to the etymology of the word, originally meant the *people*. He does not dare to speak of the Sudrâs, but what he adds is stronger than if he had mentioned them. He leaves them out, but he says : " If a slave hears this poem sung, he is ennobled." Now the slave is far beneath the Sudrâ, who is of the fourth Caste. The slave is out of all Castes, out of the Indian world ; and if this outcast may be ennobled and share in the benediction of the *Râmayana*, no one is beyond the reach of divine mercy. All

---

* This is something analogous to the revolution which St. Louis introduced among Christians; when people saw a layman, a warrior, a king—the most powerful King of Europe—becoming the ideal of holiness, they exclaimed : " O holy layman, whose works the priests ought to imitate ! "

may be saved. The salvation is extended to all. After the ancient Râma of the Brahmans (the Râma with the Hatchet) and of the severe law, came the Râma of the warriors, clement and merciful, the universal Savior, the Râma of Grace.

The groundwork of the poem is very simple. It is the story of the old King Daçaratha and of his admirable, accomplished, and adorable son Râma. Being worn out, the king is on the point of consecrating his son and abdicating the throne. But a favorite woman, a mother-in-law, prevailed upon the aged man to grant her whatever gift she should demand, and asked the exile of Râma and the crowning of her own son. This son declined the crown, but Râma, out of respect to his father's promise, insists on his accepting, and then goes into exile. Accompanied by his wife and a younger brother, Râma started for the solitudes. Admirable occasion for the poet ! Love and friendship in the desert ! A sublime and delicious hermitage in this Indian paradise !

" From the first moment that I saw the marvels of this magnificent mountain—the holy mount Tchitrakoûta—I care not for my exile, my lost crown, or this solitary life. Let my years be spent here with thee, my dear Sitâ, and with my young brother, Laksmana, and I am satisfied.

" Behold those sublime crests of the mountain which reach up into the sky and dazzle with brightness ! Some in masses of silver, some in purple and opal, others in emerald green, and this one like a diamond sparkling with light.

" The great forests are peopled with thousands of birds, apes, and leopards. Cedars, sandalwood, ebony, lotus, and banana trees, make shades embalmed with flowers and opulent with fruits. Everywhere springs, brooks, and murmuring cascades. The whole mountain seems to be a gigantic elephant intoxicated with love.

" Child with the candid smile, look yonder at the sweet Mandakiri—the river of limpid waters, with its cranes and

3

its swans—shaded by the red lotus, the blue nenuphar, by
its children of flower trees and fruit trees, and studded
with beautiful islands. O how delightful the sight of that
flock of gazelles, coming one after another to the bank of
the river to slake their thirst !

"Look at these trees at the base of the mountain,
which under the wind so modestly bend, and pour down
a shower of flowers. Some of these flowers perfuming
the ground, and others here and there floating on the
waters. Look at the red goose mounting in happiness to
the sky, and with a cheerful song saluting the morning.

" It is the hour in which the pious Rishis plunge beneath the sacred waves. Come then thou with me. This
is the holiest of rivers. Tell me, my dear, are not this
river and this mountain worth the empire and the opulent
cities, and all that we have renounced ? Thou and my
beloved brother, ye are my delight ! "

All that Râma says here about this beautiful landscape
is characteristic of the entire poem. In its incomparable
richness the poem is worthy of that India which it surrounds, and magnificently adorns. The process seems to
be that of the charming art of the country, the sovereign
art of the Cashmere, the persevering industry of the continued web in which successive ages have put their work
and their love.

At first it is an exquisite sacred shawl, or scarf for
Vichnou, in which the marvellous birth of Râma, his city,
his marriage, and his beautiful Sîtâ, form the warp of the
poem.

Around this warp all nature, mountains, forests, rivers,
Indian landscapes, the seasons of the year, all the good
friends of man, animals, and vegetables, are woven as if
into a charming carpet.

This carpet, however grand, enlarges itself and compre-
hends arts, trades, palaces, towns, kiosks, bazars, and
harems. It then becomes like a tent, a marvellous pavilion,
in which the whole world may be sheltered.

Suspended from the immense forests and the peaks of
the Himalaya, it shades the whole of India, from the
Indus to Bengal, and from Benares to Ceylon, without
obscuring the sky, for that very tent is the sky of India.
But let us rest here. This book is not a literary history.
It pursues only the great moral results.

In Râma are reunited the twofold ideals of the two great
Castes. On one side he attains the highest point of
Brahmanic virtue, and on the other he adds to it the
highest devotion of the warrior, who, for the sake of
others, hazards not only himself, but sometimes those
whom he loves more than himself. In the defence of the
frail, of solitary anchorites, who are troubled by wicked
spirits, he sacrifices more than his life—his love, his charming, faithful, and devoted wife, Sîtâ. The complete man,
this Brahman warrior, is then still nearer to God than is
the Brahman who simply prays, but does not make any
personal sacrifice.

Râma follows the exact ideal of the Khatrya, the high
ideal of the chivalry, *to win and to pardon—to wait until
the wounded enemy recovers—to give and never to receive.*

In reading this poem we are almost persuaded that
we are reading the *Shah Nameh* or our Celto-Germanic
poems. This peaceful warrior is the very opposite to the
irritable character which the poet attributes to even the
holiest of the Brahmans, who, for slight causes or involuntary offences, hurl the terrible anathema, which dooms a
man to be bound, bewitched, and sometimes to be transformed into a monster. Referring to the remark " *not to
receive anything whatever,*" the poem with its uniform
sweetness, but with a winning art, makes, through Râma,
an indirect satire on the Brahmans, who always received
and frequently exacted. From this we perceive that in
the future will appear the mendicant Brahman, the glutton,
and the buffoon of the court, who will become the subject
of satire in the Indian drama. (See *Sakuntalâ*.)

The *Râmayana* was evidently composed to be sung

at the tables and in the courts of the Rajahs, where the Brahmans had only a secondary rank, and hence the recitals of innumerable combats, monstrously exaggerated, which are the great blemish of this poem. But in compensation we find in it a generous grandeur, outbursts of a frank nature, and heroic imprudences, of which a priestly book would never be guilty.

In a maternal transport, the mother of Râma, indignant because of the exile of her son, says to the King : " Remember, O mighty King, this celebrated and powerful couplet : ' Brahma one day declared that he had weighed in his scale truth against a thousand sacrifices, and that truth outweighed the sacrifices.' " Sîtâ also, led away by her grief and her desire to follow Râma, pronounced this potent sentence, which overthrows the very foundations of the Brahmanic edifice : " A father, a mother, or a son, in this world and in the next, eats only the fruits of his own works ; a father is neither rewarded nor punished for his son ; neither is the son for his father. Each one by his own actions brings on himself the good or the evil," etc.

Who is this little girl, this bold-spirited child ? Let us try to comprehend her.

The great King Viçvâmitra, one of the ancestors of Râma, and author of many sublime hymns, notwithstanding his great piety, seems to have paid but little heed to the barrier of Castes. Fifty of his hundred sons were born of Dasyas, captives, and yellow women, on whom he had bestowed his favors. Hence it would appear that this high type of Priest-King embraced in his immense heart all Castes and all conditions.

The *Râmayana* does not state with sufficient clearness whence comes the wife of Râma, the lovely Sîtâ. Now she is the daughter of a king, and now she is born of the *furrow* (which is the meaning of Sîtâ). It may be that Râma took her from among the natives—a woman who was the daughter of a king and a captive maiden—after the example of his illustrious ancestor ; or possibly she may have belonged to the gentle Chinese race, so much esteemed in the harem, whose winning grace and lustrous drooping eye troubles the saints, and even the demons, with whom, perhaps, the Chinese women have some relationship.

But beyond the human Castes, there is still another Caste—a prodigious Caste—very humble, and very numerous. This is the poor animal world, which is to be saved and elevated. This is the triumph of India, of Râma and of the *Râmayana.*

The Redemption of Nature.

One is never saved alone. Man does not deserve his salvation but by the salvation of all. The animal has also its rights before God. " The animal ! Mysterious ! Immense world of dreams and silent griefs ! Without language, too many visible signs express these griefs. All nature protests against the barbarity of man who disowns, degrades, and tortures his inferior brother."

This sentence which I wrote in 1848 has frequently recurred to me. In the month of October of the year 1863, near a lonely sea, in the last hours of night, while the winds and the waves were silent, I heard the humble voice of our domestic animals. These voices of captivity in faint and plaintive tones, came to me from the lowest parts of the house, from the depths of obscurity, and filled me with melancholy. Impression, serious and positive and not of vague sensibility. The more advanced we become in life, the more we appreciate the full significance of its realities, the more clearly do we understand the serious and simple things, which in the ardor of life we overlook.

Life, death, the daily destruction involved in animal food, are hard and bitter problems which rise up before me. Miserable contradiction ! The feeble nature of the North, with her poverty of vegetation, could not restore our energies, and fit us for labor, which is our first duty, without animal food! death! forgetfulness of mercy! Let us hope that in another world we will be spared from the degrading and cruel fatalities of this.

In India piety has produced the effects of wisdom. It has made the conservation and salvation of all beings a religious duty, and has been rewarded. It has secured to her an eternal youth. Notwithstanding all her disasters, the respected, cherished, multiplied, and superabundant animal life, has given to India the renewals of an inexhaustible fertility.

No one can evade death either for himself or for others. But mercy demands at least that none of these short-lived creatures should die without having lived, and loved, and transmitted through love its little soul, and performed that sweet duty which the tenderness of God imposes, " to have had the divine moment."

Hence the beautiful and really pious beginning of the *Râmayana* is this exquisite outburst of Valmiki upon the death of a poor heron, in which utterance he weeps : "O, hunter, may thy soul never be glorified in all the lives to come, for thou hast stricken that bird in the sacred moment of love !"

His moanings are measured by the ebb and flow of his heart ; and this is poetry. The wonderful poem begins. This immense river of harmony, of light, and of divine joy, the largest that ever flowed, has its origin in this little source—a sigh and a tear.

True benediction of genius. While in the West the most dry and sterile minds are proud in the presence of inferior nature, the Indian genius, the richest and most prolific, knows neither the little nor the great, but generously embraces the whole as a universal brotherhood, as if all possessed but one soul.

You may cry " superstition !—that this excessive goodness towards animals comes from the dogma of the transmigration of souls." It is just the contrary. It is because this race, of acute sensibility and penetrating, feels and loves the soul even in the forms of the inferior, in the feeble and simple, that it has created the doctrine of trans-migration. It is not faith that makes the heart, but the heart that makes faith.*

Whatever may be its heart or faith, India cannot alto-gether escape from this contradiction of the world.

The vegetarian Brahman remains feeble and needs a warrior to protect him. The warrior has not the strength, but in partaking of a little animal food acquires it, to-gether with the passions which it engenders. Hence the *fall* and *evil*. Hence the catastrophe which makes the plot of the *Râmayana*. This poem had its origin in mercy and its drama in the oblivion of mercy. Woman, the most tender-hearted of beings, is tempted and drawn away from her natural goodness by, I know not what bad dream, earnest wish, or fondling desire. It is not greedi-ness. The Indian EVE does not molest the fruit on any of the trees of Paradise. Her paradise is love, and she covets nothing else. She is nothing but sweetness and timid innocence.† Nevertheless, by an utmost unaccount-

---

* A new criticism, stronger and more serious, is now offered. Religions, so profoundly studied at present, have been subordinated to the *genius* that made them, to the soul which created them, and to the moral condition of which they are the fruit. We must first locate the race with its proper apti-tudes, its surroundings, and its natural inclinations; then we may study it in the fabrication of its gods, who in their turn influence the race. This is the natural course. These gods are *effects* and *causes*. But it is essential to first prove that they are effects, the offspring of the human soul; if on the other hand we admit that they came down from heaven and suffer them to domineer over us, they oppress, absorb, and darken history. Such is the modern method, most clearly and decidedly. It has recently given its princi-ples and its examples.

† When Râma began the war in the forests against the Spirits that troubled the anchorites, she humbly gave him this peaceful advice: "Râma, I have been informed that in former times an holy anchorite received in gift a sword. Walking with it, the sword suddenly changed his inclinations and gave him a taste for blood. From this time he began to kill incessantly." Râma, in the name of duty, put aside this excess of prudence. He was not in the least intoxicated with the sword, nor excited for blood.

able change, she becomes bewildered and for a moment is cruel. Seeing a brilliant and lovely gazelle passing with hair shining like gold, she exclaimed, " I will have it, I will have it."

What is the matter with her ? What caprice ? It is not a taste for blood. Can it be the splendor of this soft savage fur with which she desires to make her sweet countenance still more charming ? No, for in such a climate an adornment like this would be oppressive. She thinks of something else, and half says it : " I wish I could sit on it. I feel that it would not be right. But I desire it. It is one of those desires which will be gratified at any cost." She covets the gazelle for the purpose of making of its skin in the wild cave, her bed, her couch of love.

She is, however, too pure and too simple not to feel and confess the reproach which her heart bestows upon her. She confesses and afterwards overcomes it, and then wishes to deceive herself. She says : " If it would only allow itself to be captured, it would serve for our amusement." She says this, but does not believe it. We may readily imagine that the animal would flee, and only under the fatal dart would yield, with its life, to be the object of this sensual desire.

The worst is that this desire is shared. Râma is troubled, and for the first time in this immense poem he suffers an angry word to escape him, and says to his brother, who wishes to prevent him from killing the animal : " Kings can kill with their darts the inhabitants of the woods, for the sake of their flesh or for amusement. Everything in the forest belongs to the king."

He hides under this harshness his condescension to his beloved, and starts, leaving her to the care of his brother, who is commanded not to forsake her.

For a long time the gazelle eluded him, and caused him to wander to a great distance. Sîtâ, thinking that she heard his voice, crying for help, exclaimed : " Great God !

my husband is in danger ; " and compelled the young brother to leave her and go to his rescue. Another sin, and yet still of love. Alas ! its punishment is too great. She is alone, and feels insecure and weak on account of her twofold sin and her fatal delusion. The roebuck was the demon, the formidable Râvana, the king of evil spirits, and the voice heard was his. He came to her under the semblance of a Brahman—a holy anchorite. He flattered her and tried to entice her, and finally carried her to an inaccessible island guarded by the ocean.

The despair of Râma was unbounded. The brightness of his wisdom was obscured. He could no longer see clearly. He experienced all the griefs of man, and was overwhelmed with the bitter doubts which come in such moments. " Alas," he says, " of what avail is it that I have always done my duty ! " He had no knowledge whatever of his divine parentage, and did not in his extremity exclaim : " My Father, why hast thou forsaken me ? " The passion of this young god would have been deprived of its merit, had he been conscious that he was divine or of divine origin. In the poem great pains are taken to conceal from him this too consoling mystery. It leaves him a man, ignorant of his destiny, uncertain of the fate of his Sîtâ, and unable to decide what to do in the dark horror of this shipwreck, without one glimmering beam in the horizon.

The season of deluging rains had begun, and the range of wild mountains among which Râma has taken refuge are overspread with dense clouds. The earth and the sky weep. The torrents come down with vehemence. The winds moan. All the elements sympathize with the grief of Râma. In their mournful compassion he feels still more deserted. Where are the parents, the court, and the subjects of this son of a king ? His brother has gone in quest of assistance ; but the more lonely and desolate his situation, the more sympathetic and compassionate is nature towards him. All our friends, the animals, that anciently were less disdained, are his friends and approach him without diffidence, and hasten to offer him their services. A holy insurrection of all living creatures is begun in behalf of him who was so good. Great and sublime alliance ! It is one of those elements of faith which man found in his heart in the first ages of life.*

Râma cheerfully accords to these worthy auxiliaries the glory of fighting for him ; although, armed with divine powers, he could doubtless alone have vanquished all his enemies. But it gave them delight to manifest for him their zeal, and under him to wage this holy war. It was so glorious a boon to be the soldiers of Râma in this holy crusade, that they felt themselves by it both honored and elevated.

No Brahman nor holy Rishi in the lonely depths of the forest, by prayer or mortification, or by the deep absorption, which makes them equal to the very gods, could have secured the merits which these simple animals deserved by their zeal for Râma, and for the cause of goodness, mercy, and justice. Accordingly in the *Râmayana* the army is open to all. All creatures are enlisted, the most fierce and savage, the enormous bears and the gigantic apes. All can speak, and they display great intelligence. All are transformed in heart, love, and faith, and rush towards the south. Faith removes mountains, and subdues and defies the seas. When all this wild multitude, at the extremity of Hindustan, sees the threatening waves which separate it from Ceylon, it indignantly uproots the rocks and the forests and hurls them in heaps into the sea, making an enormous bridge, over which the great army

---

* India and Persia believe in it. The *Shah Nameh*, which in modern form gives so many ancient traditions, exhibits to us exactly the same picture as the Râmayana. In the terrible contest in which its hero is going to engage against the evil spirits, all the animals are on his side, and without fighting or diminishing the splendor of his victory, they paralyze the enemy by their terrific cries, hisses, and roars. The enemy feels himself vanquished beforehand by this solemn unanimity of nature, and by her high maledictions, anathemas, and condemnations.

passes with barbarous pomp; while from below the as-
tounded and vanquished Indian Ocean looks on. All this
is history in a dramatic form. We are now sure that
Ceylon was once connected with the Continent.

This battle of the good animals fighting for man is likewise historical. It is what really took place and what is
constantly occurring. In that country, especially, man
could not have existed without them.

And now let it be observed that the most creditable
position is given to the *cow*, the good nurse of man,
beloved and honored, which furnished the most wholesome nourishment, intermediate between the insufficient
vegetables and the horrifying animal food—the milk and
butter, which for a long period was the holy host, and
which alone, in the great journey from Bactriana to India,
sustained that primitive people. In the midst of so many
ruins and desolations, man has lived and will continue to live
by means of this prolific nurse, which incessantly restores
to him the earth.

But many other animals, less beloved and less familiar,
have served man and still serve him in the twenty different
wars, which are continually waging in the forests of Hindustan. Those gigantic forests are peopled at every stage
of their enormous heights with combatants. At their
roots the rubbish, which accumulates and ferments, pro-
creates two most terrible and murderous scourges in the
form of putrid emanation and vindictive insects. Here no
life could have been possible without two benefactors
which are to-day too lightly esteemed. The serpent, a
hunter of insects, pursues them and catches these vermin
where the bird cannot reach them; and the purifying vulture, the great wrestler with death, forbids death to show
himself, and unceasingly transforms death, and makes life
from death. It is an indefatigable agent of the divine
circulation. A little higher than the roots, among the
inferior trees and wild vines which adorn this floral cathedral, death is everywhere. The lion and the tiger are

ambushed. It was man's good fortune that in the higher regions of these vegetable products he found another auxiliary to aid him. The orang-outang, inoffensive and frugivorous, but of incalculable strength, who playfully twists a piece of iron in his fingers, wages against these animals an incessant warfare. He arms himself with a branch of a tree made into a club, and associates himself with others. In groups of three or four they attack and kill the elephant (stronger than the lion or the tiger), which would deprive them of the fruits of the trees and the sugar-cane. The orang-outang is really the Hercules that can fight and defeat monsters. Endowed with great agility, alternating from air to earth, balancing from the boughs of the trees, and flying by daring jumps, he has great advantage over all the beasts below. When the tiger with an immense bound springs upon the man or dog, the enormous ape, watching it from above, leaps like lightning on its head and crushes it. This formidable being, when not provoked, has nothing hostile in him. In the first songs of the *Râmayana*, we see the orang-outangs passing in troops (as apes do to-day) under the leadership of their chief or king. At the sight of them, Sîtâ is alarmed, but Râma beckons to the chief, and they turn away peacefully on the other side. We must not judge of the orang-outang from what we see of him to-day. No being more than the ape has been scared and perverted by the harshness of man. At present we are horrified by his convulsions and his nervousness. He looks as if half mad and epileptic. But in the remote times, when man lived with him on terms of familiarity, this imitative being was calm and grave, after the style of the Hindoos, and became a sedate and docile servant. Woman especially exercised much power over him, and she could make him the most submissive of slaves, if she began to domesticate him while he was yet young.

One thing which charms us in the *Râmayana* is that even what is fictitious is at the same time true to nature.

The apes that fight for Râma are no less true to their characteristics, because he is so holy a chief.* They are genuine quadrumane, gluttons, trifling, capricious, inconstant, libertines, and not over respectful to the limitations of Brahmanic interdictions, or the degrees of consanguinity. They are easily annoyed and tranquillized, and pass from excessive dejection to high elevation of spirits, and are comical, charming, amiable, and without malignity.

Hanuman, the favorite, the ape-hero of the *Râmayana*, most admired on account of his broad shoulders, in his devotion for Râma, carries off great mountains on his back. Born of the air, conceived of the wind, and somewhat vain, he desired and dared the impossible ; and he is reminded by his strong lower jaw, which is defaced, that he had the madness, while still young, to attempt to mount to the sun, but having fallen, he and all his race have been marked with this deformity. Thus in this poem a slight but loving and sympathetic smile is everywhere interwoven with the great, the holy, and the divine.

We are not to imagine that in this country of light, the King of the Demons, Ravâna, had the slightest trace of the grotesque and vile Devil with tail and horns, the ugly creation of the Middle Ages. He is much more the Demon by virtue of his noble and royal beauty, by his genius, by his science, and by his grandeur. He reads the *Vedas*. Lanka, his colossal and delightful city, far surpasses the Babylons and the Ninevehs. He has a wonderful harem, unenclosed and unguarded. All voluptuousness abounds in it. It is his immense attractions, and his numerous votaries and friends, which make him so dangerous. He is ardently worshipped. He blazes in the refulgence of art and the splendors of nature. Beyond

---

* We do not find in this poem, as in the awkward legends of the middle ages, false animals converted, devoted crows, and penitent lions which beseech for a benediction.

all this, he possesses the formidable power of creating by magic an adverse and deceptive nature, and also ethereal and charming beings, endowed with mischievous faculties, which they can exercise at will.

Râma brings against all this marvellous power only simple creatures, rude, wild beings ; nothing but strength of heart, goodness, and right. And this will give him the victory, and will protect his unfortunate Sîtâ, even in the Palace of Râvana. By her calm courage and heroic resistance she elevates herself to the level of the primitive Indian woman, the noble spouse of the era of the *Vedas*, who has been lost to the world for the last one or two thousand years.

Through all these tragical events, Hanuman, the ape-hero, is both amusing and interesting. His great heart, and his mild virtues, mixed with a little of the ludicrous, excite at once to laughter and weeping. It is he who is the real Achilles and the Ulysses of this war. He ventured alone into that terrible Lanka, and the dreaded harem, and into the presence of Sîtâ, whom he comforted by his tender respect. He did more than any one else towards her liberation. After this achievement, Râma honored and crowned him. An important event which is destined to change nature now occurs.

In the presence of the two armies ; in the presence of men and gods, Râma and Hanuman embrace each other ! Let no man again speak of Castes. Indeed, the poem henceforth carefully avoids their mention, but in reality the barrier is removed and will never more exist. The Caste of *Beasts* is suppressed. How then could any human Caste exist ? The most debased of men can now say : " Hanuman has made me free." Thus is exploded the narrow heaven of the Brahmanic religion.* All social

* If additions have been made to the *Râmayana* since the reformation of Buddhism, the general outlines, and especially the groundwork of the poem, most certainly antedate that reformation ; and I have not the slightest doubt

distinctions are at an end. The whole world embraces amid great rejoicings. In this great day of Grace, can there exist any wicked or any damned? No. The sinner was a negative being, an absurdity, a misconception. He has made expiation; he has been pardoned. The monster was nothing but a covering under which a poor soul was imprisoned by a fatal enchantment. This stricken soul is delivered and instantly mounts upward; is happy, and, in amazement, renders thanksgiving.

---

that this poem contributed largely to the abolition of Castes, emancipating four hundred millions of men, and founding the largest church on earth.

CHAPTER II.

PERSIA.

The Earth and the Tree of Life.

THERE are no Castes among the Persians. In respect to religion all are equal.* All are considered and called *pure.* Each is the pontiff of his house and prays for his family. They have no temples, no ceremonies, no worship, except prayer and exhortation. They have no mythology, no imaginative poetry. All is literal, positive, grave, and strong. It is energy in holiness.

Notice a precocious vigor of wisdom and good sense. The fire is no more a god, but a symbol, the benevolent spirit of the hearth. The animal is not glorified, but beloved and well and magnanimously treated, according to its rank in the house and the nature of its soul.

The law, simple and thoroughly human (above all the laws), which Persia has left, which has never been surpassed, which will live forever, and which will always be the path to the future, is : *heroic husbandry, the courageous struggle of Good against Evil, the life of pure light in labor and in justice.* Hence a code for man and toiler—not for

---

* This refers to primitive Persia. Although the *texts* are confused, we are enabled to distinguish three ages—the *patriarchal;* that in which the *priest* appears; and lastly, that in which the Medo-Chaldean *Magianism* was engrafted over Persia. The Magians were not properly a Caste but a tribe. Magianism was not completely organized until after the conquest of Babylon. The Greeks did not know Persia until this late and very confused period. I take the *Avesta* solely in that which is most ancient. I adhere very closely to the opinion of Burnouf in his *Yacna,* and in his *Researches* which correct Anquetil. His pregnant conversations have confirmed me. I do not think that I have anywhere varied from his opinions.

The recent German works of Messrs. Haug, Spiegel, etc., have been admirably summed up by Michel Nicolas. *Revue Germanique,* vols. VII. and VIII.

the idler, Brahman or Monk—not abstinence and revery, but active energy, all comprised in this : " *Be pure to be strong." " Be strong to be creative."*

At midnight, the fire growing dim becomes anxious, and awaking the head of the family, says : " Arise, put on your clothes, wash your hands, bring the wood to make me bright, or the evil spirits will glide in and extinguish me."

He arises, puts on his vestments, and revives the fire with its nourishment. The house is made resplendent. The prowlers, spirits of darkness, wandering in the disguise of jackals and adders, will do well to depart. The bright spirit of the hearthstone is vigilant, and its host, close beside it, is already anticipating the dawn of day, and meditating on the work of the morning. The pure, the *irreproachable* fire guards him, his house, and his soul, so that he may indulge only in wise, vigorous, and generous thoughts. What are these thoughts ? They are briefly :

" Render to all their rights."

" Give to the fire and the earth their natural nourishment."

" Deal justly with the tree, the bull, and the horse."

" Be not ungrateful to the dog, and take care that the cow does not low against thee."

The earth has a right to the seed. Neglected, it curses ; fertilized, it thanks. It says to the man who cultivates it thoroughly : " May thy fields yield all that is good to eat ; may thy numerous villages abound in all good." To the man who neglects it, it says : " May the pure food be far from thee, and the demon torment thee. May thy fields for nourishment give thee great terrors."

" All honor and homage to the earth ! the earth, the holy female which supports the man ! It exacts good works. Homage to the springs of Ardvi-sura which make the pure females conceive and bring forth ! " *

---

* *Yaçna,* lxiv.

4

The first of good works is to quench the thirst of the earth, to come to its aid, to cause it to bring forth life and freshness unceasingly. This is a kind of creation. Persia is not, like Egypt, a gift of the Nile.* Its torrents pass away rapidly and leave it dry. The earth dries and cracks open. It is necessary to search for water with diligence and earnestness. It must be evoked from the most obscure depths of the mountain and brought to light. This is the absorbing thought of man, and the paradise of his dreams: to behold the water gushing from the rocks and rising from the sterile sand, and see it fresh and limpid, coursing and warbling and murmuring.

And now he says: " I pray and invoke all the waters. Come forth ye bubbling springs from the depths of the earth! Ye beautiful nourishing canals! Ye soft and limpid waters, sweetly flowing, which renew the tree and purify the desire. Be good and flow gently for us!"

The day has dawned. Man arises, and with the iron (the short sword, or rather strong dagger, such as may be seen on Persian monuments), before the rising of the friendly sun, opens and rakes the earth, and makes in it the wholesome wound. In this deep furrow he scatters the seed.

All *the pure* are on the side of man. The eagle and the hawk greet him with their first cry at the break of day. The dog follows and escorts him. The horse neighs with joy. The strong bull with willing heart draws the plough. The earth smokes from moisture; its animating breath is the pledge of its fruitfulness. All are in accord. All are conscious that man is just and that he labors for their good.

Man is the common conscience. He feels that he is engaged in elevated work which invigorates the body, and,

---

* Rains are neither heavy nor frequent. There are but few navigable rivers. Deserts of salt. A few trees, or rather bushes. Malcolm, Hist. of the Persians, vol. I., p. 45.

by the co-operation of the forces of nature, nourishes his soul. He says most positively, and not without grandeur, in the language of good sense, strong and rugged, which goes to the point: "He who eats listens better to the sacred word. He who does not eat has no strength for pure works. He who is famished cannot have robust children nor can he be a valiant laborer. Such as it is, this world exists by nourishment."

Elevated by his effective, persevering work, his courage increases in the presence of the rising sun, and he says to himself: "Dress and sow! *He who sows with purity fulfills all the law!* He who gives to the earth vigorous seed is as much ennobled as if he had made ten thousand sacrifices."

The earth responds: "Yes!" but in its own language. Its answer is in the golden grain of the year. Be patient and give it time, and it will respond more and more with new, rich, and hardy plants, continually increasing. Already as high as man, next season they will be taller. Look at that tree in the midst of the field. Rich, abundant, and grateful, it tenders to man its branches and its foliage, it offers him a delightful and longed-for shade at noon-day, a tutelary protection from the scorching sky, shelter and subsistence without fear. But the sun begins to descend; and man, before renewing his toil, turns to his benefactor and says: "Hail, tree of life! You came from the earth; but whence came I? From my father. But whence the first father?" This is a profound question, which engages his thoughts as he follows the plough in the afternoon, and which he answers by the two forces with which he is acquainted—the force of youth in the tree which is daily renewed, and the force of action, the toil of his companion, the ox. Why may not the vigorous man come from the ox or the tree? Inasmuch as the tree lives so long, why may it not be the life of former times, and the life that is to come? The tree is IMMORTALITY.

Its sacred name is Hôma. Not the fleeting Sôma of India, the plant fallen from the firmament, which sparkles in the fire, mounts joyously to the sky, and nourishes the gods. Hôma, the robust, solid, firmly-rooted in the earth, is the immortal Tree of Life, the strong. In order that man may also be strong, he must eat its apples of gold. Or, grinding them, he expresses the powerful juice, "the liquid which places the soul in the good path." Do not imagine that this is mere allegory. It is repeatedly said in the law that Hôma is eaten, desires to be eaten, and inclines his branches that men may partake of his golden fruit.*

The heroes of Persia were the first who ground Hôma with their glorious hands and made it ferment. After this, it foamed, was restless, became audible, spoke, and would have made the stones speak. It is the Word itself.

Supreme miracle among a grave and silent people, whose Cyclopean language, unformed, and spare of words, is, if we dare say it, an idiom of the dumb.† The workman, who all day long toils in the field after the oxen, is weary and has need of rest at evening, and requires but few words. The Hindoo, in his fluent language has polished the Sanskrit, but the silent Persian, out of respect, has preserved the old Zend. If this dumb speaks, it is Hôma that speaks in him.

Word and *light* are two identical words in the primitive sacred language.‡ This is not without reason. Light is, so to speak, the voice of nature, and the word, in its turn, is the light of the mind. The universe hears and answers. An eternal dialogue is kept up between nature and the soul. If the soul did not translate and make luminous the voice of nature, nature would re-

---

* EUGENE BURNOUF : *Researches*, page 231. (8vo, 1850.)

† This language, the Zend, singularly harsh, seems to sound like flint, and its written characters look like daggers, heads of arrows, wedges and nails. Hence the name—Cuneiform.

‡ BURNOUF : *Yaçna*, 214.

.

main in obscurity, uncomprehended, and as if it did not exist.

Hôma, the *word-light*, is the supporter of existence. It unceasingly invokes it. It names, one after another, all the beings, to assure them of life. Each name is a charm to awake and arouse that which would fall asleep and return to nothing.

Such faith is very elevating to man. When the chief of a family, arising in the depth of night, while his wife and children are sleeping, pronounces before the fire the words which vivify the world, this is truly great. What will be the importance, the holiness of the man, who feels himself so necessary to universal existence! In the silence of midnight, and all alone, he feels himself in harmony with all the families of the pure, who at this hour also pronounce the same word of life.

There were no castes, no magians, no kings, then in Persia. The father of each house was the Mage and King. He was still more, the conservator of beings, the Savior of all life. The extraordinary power which India accords to a Rishi, to the great King Viçvamitra, in Persia resides in all, even in the lowest laborer. He who in the morning, with his hand on the plough, makes the earth productive, at night, through the Word, still creates, begets the world, the uncertain life of which is suspended on his prayer.

The Combat of Good and Evil.—The Final Restoration to Holiness.

The husbandman is an anxious being, a mind without rest, a soul in pain. The shepherd has time for singing to the clouds the fantastical victories of Indra. He has time to observe in the skies of Chaldea the long journeys of the stars. But the Persian agriculturist must, night and day, watch, work, and fight. Battle against the earth. It is hard and obstinate, and does not yield at one stroke. It sells to labor that which we think it gives. Battle

against the waters.   The delightful waters, so much
desired, frequently come down violently, laying waste and
carrying everything away.   Sometimes they are suddenly
exhausted ;   drunk up by the sun.   It is necessary in
this climate to protect these daughters of night, (evoked
from the earth,) from the light, and shelter them in hidden
canals. A subterranean circulation of infinite work, which
makes the laborer a miner and a constructor.

When all this is done, nothing is accomplished.   The
feeble wheat of tender green, the delicate child shoots up.
It escapes from the protecting womb, betrays itself, and
sees itself in the midst of enemies.   A hundred robust
and evil plants are there, and will choke it, unless the
paternal hand comes to wage war against them.   A
hundred devouring beasts come, monsters which man cannot repel.   What are these ?   They are neither lions nor
tigers, but peaceable flocks.

It is the shepherd, especially, who is an abomination to
the laborers.   It is against him that the field is guarded.
The gloomy laborer, with his poniard marks out the
protective boundary.   He excavates a ditch, and planting
its borders, there grows up a hedge.   He fixes the boundary, and puts down stakes and stones.   But this is the
least that he does.   He encloses his field with his word
and his malediction.   Woe to him who trespasses !

Eternal war ! we find it everywhere.   It is this which
constituted the divorce between the Hindoo of the *Vedas*
and the Persian, the shepherd and the agricultural Aryân.
The shepherd thinks the appropriation of land odious and
unjust.   He laughs at landmarks and ditches.   His animals
shrewdly make it their sport to leap over them.   The
goats injure the hedge.   The cow thoughtlessly passes
through it.   The gentle sheep, in looking innocently for
its little food, nibbles the sprouting wheat to its roots ; this
sacred wheat—this dear hope in which the soul of the
husbandman is absorbed.   It is necessary to protect this
wheat.   Day by day the agriculturist becomes more and

more dreamy and gloomy; and in these mischievous animals, that destroy more than they eat, he thinks he sees and denounces the agents of evil spirits, the army of wickedness, "of nonsensical caprice," the perverse games of magic.*

The Hindoos departed towards the East. But from the North quite a different neighbor appeared, the frightful Tartar shepherd, an unorganized chaos of Mongols, Centaur Demons, whose little horses of diabolical instinct, make of every field a pasture. It is the accursed empire of Turan, eternal enemy of Iran (Persia). These black sorcerers (see the *Shah Nameh*) go and come like the bat, or the night-insect which spoils and disappears. On the other hand there comes again and again from the mud of the Euphrates, to sleep on Iran the impure Assyrian dragon, steady and stupid, the monstrous reptile, which Babylon adored,† and which the Persians say lived on human flesh only.

These cruel strifes, which continued through long centuries, for thousands of years, gave to this people great positiveness and a peculiar poetic character.

They elevated themselves to their sovereign conception, the constant contest between the two worlds. On the

---

* The movable Indra of the shepherds, who plays on high with the storms, the warrior-god whose smile is the lightning, who, in order to give freshness to the meadows, hurls down the waters which crush the ripening wheat, seems to the agriculturist a cruel magician. He makes of him the demon Andra [Andra-inanyas], for whom he does not hesitate to create a hell. The Daevas, whom the Hindoos revere as gods, likewise become demons. The Persians call themselves *Vi-Daevas* (enemies of the Daevas). To the illusions of these Daevas, who are scoffing spirits, this derisive response is given (which appears to be a popular song): "When the field produces, the Daevas hiss (*and feign to laugh*). When the plants bud, they cough. When the straw is tall, they weep. When the harvests are gathered, they take to flight. . . . In the houses filled with the sheaves, the Daevas are severely scourged." (*Under the scourge* which beats out the wheat?)

† *Daniel* (apocryphal): "There was a great dragon which they of Babylon worshipped." The *Avesta* records this ascendancy as the dominion of Bobak, or rather "the serpent Dahoka, in the reign of Bawri," or Babylon.—ED.

one hand, the holy reign of Iran, the world of Good, the garden of the tree of life, the Paradise (garden); and on the other, the vague, barbarian world of Evil and of unjust caprice. Everything appeared peopled with contrary spirits. Between the rough plains of the North, in which the demons hiss, and the desert of sand in the South, in which the demons breathe forth fire, Persia, with good reason, decided that she was the blessed land of works, of order, and of Justice. Nor is this justice an idle word, a mere play of the fancy. It was a firm purpose, a determination to be *just.* Men sometimes have such moments. A celebrated writer (Montesquieu) says that there once came to him a quick outburst of conscience, a strong and decided desire "to be an honest man." It is precisely such a moment that Persia represents in human nature: *the determination to be just.*

Just to himself in the first place, in opposition to the vice peculiar to the laborer, the sordid economy; just in the house towards the humblest and most defenceless servant, the animal, for example. " *The three pure* complain of the unjust man who takes no care of them. The plant denounces him: ' Be without children, thou who givest me not the thing which delights me' (water). The horse says: ' Do not expect that I will love thee and be thy friend when thou dost mount me, thou who dost not give me the nourishment and the vigor to appear with honor in the assembly of the tribe!' The cow says: ' Be thou accursed who dost not render me happy, who dost not wish me to be fat except for thy wife and thy children.' "[*]

But these three servants belong to his own house. How much more difficult to be just away from home! To be just in his own vicinity, with wrangling neighbors, about land-marks, etc. Consider that the life of Persia depended upon invisible boundaries of waters that ran under the earth. How numerous the interests to be respected! All

---

[*] ANQUETIL, *Avesta*, Vol. I., part 2, with corrections of EUGENE BUR-NOUF. *Researches*, p. 106. (8vo, 1850.)

are miserly and solicitous of water that is so rare. It is easy to divert the water, and the temptation to do so is strong. The regular distribution of the water is a proof of great honesty. We are struck with admiration when we learn from Herodotus that at that time there was an immense system, comprising forty thousand canals, running in all directions under the ground. Marvellous and venerable performance of toil, meritorious life, morality, and justice.

How good is justice, and how rich is its nature ! It overflows in humanity like a superabundant spring. Grace is begotten of Law. In this Persia, which appears so exclusive, in which the ties of consanguinity, the purity of blood, and the pride of family and of tribe seem to be so strong,* the foreigner was not regarded with hostility as was the case in Rome. The erring girl, though unknown, who is brought back, is protected and guaranteed. " Thou shalt seek for her origin, her father, and if he cannot be found, thou must report to the chief of the Canton. You nourish and regard as sacred the bitch which watches the house, and will you not nourish this girl, who is surrendered to you ? "†

Yes, this was unquestionably the·garden of justice, in which flourished the Tree of Life. Men heartily unite in the defence of this sacred world, in the great combat of Good, which protected this paradise.

The army of Good, formed in the image of Persia, divided into tribes, marched under the leadership of seven Spirits, seven chiefs, the luminous Amshapands, whose names are those of seven virtues : Science, or the wise teacher (Ormuzd),‡ Goodness, Purity, Valor, liberal Gen-

---

* So strong was this feeling that consanguinity was most desired in marriage. The Persians married not only sisters, but daughters and even mothers—ED.

† ANQUETIL : *Avesta*, II., 394.

‡ According to Eugene Burnouf, Ormuzd, Ahura Mazda, does not mean the *wise king*, as Anquetil believed ; nor the wise Living, as Mr. Bopp believes,

tleness, and the Geniuses of Life—producers and vivi-
fiers.

The izeds or yazatas, inferior geniuses, the ferouers or
fravastus (winged souls, guardian spirits) of the just,
even of the good and pure animals, form the immense
army of Good.   Opposed is the world of serpents,
wolves, jackals, and scorpions.

Let us look at the battle in the grand and faithful picture which Edgar Quinet, following the text itself, gives
of it.*

All beings take part in it.   At the extremity of the
universe, the sacred dog which watches the multitude of
worlds, terrifies with his fearful bark the detested jackal ;
the hawk, with his piercing eye, the sentinel of the morning, has uttered his cry and fluttered his wings.   He
sharpens his beak for the fierce battle.   The horse erects
himself and paws the Impure with his feet.

The stars in the sky are divided into two hostile bands.
But the bird with feet of gold spreads his wings over the
holy kingdom of Iran.   In the desert of Cobi the monstrous serpents with two feet, griffins, centaurs, which
dart the devouring simoom, snort and hiss in vain.

The struggle goes on in the very depth of all beings.
Each has its spirit, its angel.   A luminous soul sparkles
in the diamond.   The flower has its guardian angel.
Everything, even to the dagger, has its ruling spirit—the
blade lives.   All fight, pursue, strike, drive off, and
wound each other with anathemas and magical incantations.   In the heights above, the Deva, with bodies of
brass, and the Darwands, with the folds of serpents, fight
the white Ferouers, the Amshapands, with wings of gold.

---

but the wise teacher.   No one can pass grammatically from the Sanskrit
Asura (*living*) to the Zend *Ahura*.   *Yaçna*, 77, 81.   An important remark,
which entirely changes the idea which had been formed of the first of the seven
spirits.

    * QUINET : *Genius of Religions*.   This luminous volume formulates in
burning sentences the profound intimacy between religion and nature.

The shock of their armor resounds and re-echoes. Wonderful spectacle, but by no means confused. It steadily becomes more and more clear and orderly. The army of Good becomes more cautious and united.

The first of the seven Amshapands, from moment to moment becomes more and more conspicuous, dazzling, and refulgent. All light centres in him. Night, vanquished and constantly diminishing, and more and more hotly pressed, flies with Ahriman. Happy religion of Hope! Not of inactivity, not of idle expectation, nor of sleepy asceticism, but the heroic faith of valiant hope which creates that which it expects and wills, and which, through labor and virtue, daily diminishes Ahriman, enlarges Ormuzd, conquers and merits *the unity of God.*

To achieve a divine victory, to make God a conqueror, a unique achievement! Oh! beautiful deed! The highest of which the soul ever dreamed, and the most efficacious to make man grow in holiness. To say to every furrow: "I unite myself to the great Workman! I extend the field of Good. I circumscribe the field of Death, of Evil, of Sterility." To say to the tree planted: " Be thou in a hundred years the glory of Ormuzd and the shelter of unknown men!" To say to the springs of the mountain, evoked or directed: "Go! may you carry life from my fields to yonder tribes, who, not knowing whence they come, will say: ' This is the stream of Paradise!'" Behold something grand and divine, a high society with God, a beautiful alliance, a noble conquest. . . . The *other* retreats, vanquished, disconcerted. Ahriman is soon nothing but a black cloud, empty smoke, a wretched fog, nay, less, a mere gray speck in the horizon.

Worth prize of Work! In the idle Middle Ages, Satan constantly grows. A dwarf at first, so small at the introduction of the Gospel that he hid himself in the swine; in the year 1000 he becomes great, and in the thirteenth and fourteenth centuries he was so large that he wrapped the world in darkness, and held it under his black shadow.

Neither fire nor the sword has been able to subdue him.
As to the friends of Zoroaster it is precisely the contrary.
The Gheber, the Parsees, resigned laborers, have, through
all their evils, believed more and more, that Ahriman,
tottering, would soon fade and vanish, absorbed in
Ormuzd.

From the first, Ormuzd indicated that he was the true
king of the world, the future conqueror, the only God.
How ? By his great goodness. He began the war with
the intention of saving the enemy. He prayed Ahriman
to be good and to love the good, and to have pity on
himself. Afterward his indefatigable Grace summoned
him every moment to reform himself, to convert himself,
to work out his salvation, to attend to his happiness.

Jean Reynaud, a man certainly indulgent toward the
Church, frankly confesses that from Persia to the Church
of the Middle Ages there has been a strange and terrible
progress, but it has been in the inverse order. The idea
of an endless Hell ! Of a God whose vengeance is never
gratified ! Of a God who imprudently selected for his
executioner the very person who would most abuse his
office, the foul spirit,. the Perverse one, who gloats in
tortures, and finds in them execrable amusement ! Astounding conception, suited to make man cruel, exces-
sively fond of crime, and which we may call the teaching
of crime.

When we reflect how much man is an imitative being, we
should carefully consider the Divine prototype, which we
offer to him, and which he will certainly follow. A good
and merciful God makes men gentle and magnanimous.
If they fight, they know that it is for the good of their
enemy. This *wicked*, who will soon be wicked no longer, is
less hated from this day ; and will be the good of to-morrow. That the war continues is only a secondary consideration ; the great, the essential, is the suppression of
hatred and the subduing of hearts.

Many great spirits of our day have felt this, and, without

delay, have rallied to this faith, which is evidently the true, and is immutable and will endure. " I maintain," says Quinet, " that there is not at present an idea more living." Every manly heart will rally to it. All at morning and evening, without hesitating, will repeat the most ancient hymns of the *Yaçna* (30, 31, 47), on the conversion of Ahriman, and of the ultimate unity.

" Ormuzd, grant me the grace, the joy of seeing him, who makes the evil, be brought to comprehend the purity of the heart. Grant that I may see the great chief of the Darwands, loving nothing but holiness, and forever speaking the Word among the converted demons ! "

The Winged Soul.

" I offer prayer, honor, homage, to pure Law ! Homage to the Mount of Ormuzd ! (from which descend the waters over the earth). Homage to the good spirits, and to the souls of my family ! *Homage to my own soul !* "

Who thinks to pay homage to his own soul, to adorn it, to embellish it, in himself, and for himself, in the interior tribunal ? Who thinks of making it such that it will be the image of law, so at one with law that it can do no wrong, nothing except what the law authorizes ? This great, austere idea constitutes the foundation of the whole social structure of Persia.

No pride. It is the natural relation of Liberty and of Justice.

Persia pursues it through twenty different paths. She draws from it her entire system of morals. Let us quote a few sentences at random.

Zoroaster, in his sublime familiarity with Ormuzd, asks him : " When does the empire of the demons flourish ? When do they prosper and grow great ? " " It is when thou doest evil."

Evil is not only the criminal act, but everything that mars the original integrity of the soul : indecency or license (even in justifiable pleasures), violent and angry

words, etc. Profound idea! Among the grievous sins
which man always confesses with shame, there is the *sin
of chagrin.* To be sad beyond a certain measure, to permit the soul to fall from its position of firmness and dignity,
is to injure the state of sovereign beauty in which it must
at last soar aloft, a virgin with wings of gold. (*Fravashi.*)*

The more elevated this idea of the soul, the greater
our wonder, anger, almost indignation, that this heroic
virgin, which we carry in ourselves, should become weak,
depressed, and abandoned to sickness and death. Since
the personality appears so forcible, hence the gloomy
storm of questions arises which trouble the heart. Death ?
—What is it ? What signifies this departure which a man
makes in spite of himself? Is it a journey ? Is it a fault,
a sin, a punishment ? If a punishment, what ? What
must a man suffer ? Will the poor soul in the underworld
find that which it had here ? What will its nourishment
and its dress be ? The cold especially troubles it. Over
the high plateaus of Persia, there are heavy frosts in the
month of August.† The trouble is profound ; the compassion, the affliction profound. In the festivals of the
dead, which occur at the end of the year, during ten
nights the dead are heard speaking among themselves,
and asking for food and clothing, and to be remembered
by the living.

India, in the time of the *Vedas,* was less embarrassed.
What was the wish of the dead, who, from the leisure of
shepherd-life, passed into the leisure of the Eternal? It was
to make an immense, free, and uncumbered journey into
heaven and over the earth ; he would know the mountains and " the variety of plants ; " he would know the
depth of the great waves, measure the clouds, and take a
trip round the Sun. It is the same Sun (Sûrya), father of

---

* Feminine word which we awkwardly translate, in the masculine,
Ferouer.

† " The 17th of August," says Malcolm, "there was an inch of ice in my
tent."

life, who also *produces* the *measure of life*, Yâma, or
death—in fact, no death at all—Yâma is *the law of existence.* Nothing of gloom in this. This traveller may be
evoked by his relatives, from the great empire of Yâma,
and occasionally return to see his home.

In Persia it is entirely different. Death is a positive
evil. It is by no means a journey voluntarily undertaken.
It is a defeat, a route, a cruel victory of Ahriman. The
dead person is one vanquished by a stroke of the wicked
one, who seeks to consign his victim to night and darkness, away beyond the kingdom of light.

This perfidious being, who hates life and labor, is the
inventor of idleness, sleep, winter, and death. But man
will not yield to him. He does not think himself defeated.
On the contrary, the human soul, under the gnawing of
grief, becomes grander, creates and expands itself into a
kingdom of glorious light beyond the grave, duplicating
the empire of Ormuzd. Behold thy victory, O execrable
One!

What word is most frequently uttered by the dying man
near his last gasp? "Light! more light!"

This eager desire is realized, obeyed. How hard, how
cruel against nature, if the answer to this utterance were
to consign him to the dungeon of the sepulchre and the
black horror of night! It is that that was feared. Death,
in its utmost, is regarded as less severe than is the exclu-
sion from light.

It is not necessary that the living should here hypocriti-
cally say, "It is for his honor that we bury him, that we
hide him in darkness." No, no; those who truly love are
not so impatient as to tear themselves thus cruelly from
their beloved. Love cannot believe in death: it ever
doubts, even after the lapse of time, and says: "If it
were *false?*" The ancient Persians did not hide the body
of the beloved one, nor banish him from the day. The
living did not abandon the dead, but the dead left the
living. However much altered and changed the form, the

family fearlessly accepted the most disagreeable consequences, providing they could but still see their beloved.

The dead person was placed before the sun, on an elevated stone, beyond the reach of the beasts.   His dog,*
his inseparable guardian, which while living always followed him, remained beside the body to watch it.   There
this soldier of Ormuzd, this man of light, who always lived
on light, continued in its presence at his post, with his
face uncovered, assured and confiding.

During two or three days, his relatives, in tears, surrounded him, to observe and watch.   All things go on
according to the ritual of nature.   The sun adopts the
dead.   With his powerful rays redoubled in the mirror
of the marble, he draws and attracts him up to himself.   A process that leaves less than a useless cover, a
shadow so light, that the children, the widow, the most
wounded hearts, are quite confident that he is no longer
there.

Where then is he ?   Above.   The sun has drunk the
body.   The bird of the sky has taken the soul.   The bird
was his friend.   Through all his labors on earth the bird
followed him, clearing the furrow.   It followed his flock,
warned him of the weather, and predicted the storm.   It
is the augur, the prophet, the counsellor of man.

In the long, monotonous work, it pleases him with its
airy movements.   Around the laborer, steady at work, it
is as a light spirit, another self, more free, who comes,
goes, flies, and chatters.   It would not be astonishing if,
on the day of the funeral, it came near the dead.   And if
at that moment a luminous ray gilded the bird as it was
remounting, and transfigured it in the sky, his friends
exclaimed : " The soul has gone ! "

Do you know what death is ?   To the survivors, it is an
education, a positive initiation.   Man receives from it the

---

* The only sacred animal, which, at its death, was honored with funeral
ceremonies, as it were a man.

sovereign charge, the solemn impression which he preserves through all his life. At this moment the heart is
broken, without strength, without nerve, without consistence, like passive metal, softened by the fire, on which an
impression is to be made. Death, the heavy coining instrument, falls and strikes. This wretched heart is stamped
forever.

Great and terrible difference, whether it is the death of
bravery which is stamped upon him and gives him its
noble image—or the death of terrors, the death of servile
fears, fear of night, fear of evil demons, and fear of being
buried alive. Alas! how pale and debilitated the man
returns from such a funeral! Made fit only to die like a
coward and to live like a slave! Fit subject for a tyrant!
The vampires which know how to absorb the soul at
the moment of its passage when disarmed, are superior
teachers of cowardice, able practitioners at delivering to
tyrants the men from whom all heart has been robbed.
The travelling soul of the Hindoo started with buoyancy
and without terror, and left no sorrow behind, and more
than one person would have accompanied it merely
out of curiosity. The courageous Persian, who recoiled
not, who still braved Ahriman, and was calm before
the sun, confided in the light (having always lived the
worshipper of light), did not, on his departure, leave to
his relatives and friends, the pitiable legacy of apprehension and servility.

They knew what takes place after death. During three
days the unsettled soul, guarded by good spirits, and protected from the assaults of the bad, hovers around the
body. After the third night it makes a pilgrimage.
Encouraged by the brightness of the sun, led by spirits to
the summit of the mountain Albordj, it sees before it the
great crossing, the pointed bridge of Tchinevat. The formidable dog which watches the flocks of heaven does
not oppose its passage. A charming, smiling figure, a
beautiful girl of light, " vigorous as a youth of fifteen,

5

tall, excellent, winged, pure as the purest thing on earth," guards the bridge.*

"Who art thou? Beautiful! Never have I beheld such splendor." "Why, friend, I am thy very life, thy pure thought, thy pure converse, thy pure and holy activity. I was beautiful. Thou madest me very beautiful. Behold me, therefore, radiant, glorified before Ormuzd."

The soul admires, is agitated and hesitates, but she throws her arms around her neck and tenderly carries her away and places her on a golden throne. They are already as one. The soul is reunited with itself. It has found its true self, its true soul—not fleeting, not in misery and illusion—but beautiful, steadfast, and true—above all, free, winged, and floating in the beams of light, soaring with the flight of the eagle, or penetrating the three worlds or paradises with the lightning-like flight of the hawk.

To be just to Persia we must notice the sublime austerity with which this great conception of the winged soul, of the angel is maintained. This angel has nothing of the weakness, of the fantastical arbitrariness, which the bastard ages have more recently mixed with it. It is not the

---

* *Khordah-Avesta*, Fragment 22, Spiegel's: "In that wind comes to meet him his own law [the *nous* of Plato], in the figure of a maiden, one beautiful, shining, with shining arms; one powerful, well-grown, slender, with large breasts, praiseworthy body ; one noble, with brilliant face, one of fifteen years, as fair in her growth as the fairest creatures.

"Then to her speaks this soul of the pure man, asking, ' What maiden art thou whom I have seen here, O fairest of maidens in body ? '

"Then replies to him his own law : ' I am, O youth, thy good thoughts, words, and works, thy good law, the own law of thine own body ; which would be in reference to thee like in greatness, goodness, and beauty, sweet smelling, victorious, harmless, as thou appearest to me. Thou art like me, O, well-speaking, well-thinking, well-acting youth, devoted to the good law, so in greatness, goodness, and beauty, as I appear to thee. Thou hast made the pleasant yet more pleasant to me, the fair yet fairer, the desirable yet more desirable, the one sitting in a high place to be sitting in a yet higher place in these paradises."—ED.

blonde son of Grace, a Gabriel, a deserved confidant, with whom we make bargains, whom we may hope to soften, and whose peculiar indulgence can dispense with your justice. The winged virgin, which is the angel of Persia, is justice itself, is the law which *thou hast made to thyself*, the exact expression of thy works.

Great poetry! but of profound reason! The more it is severe and wise, the more is it also probable.* It is for this life on earth the noblest emancipation. In its presence man finds himself highly elated and lifted up. He feels as if wings were growing out of him. All the lower world appears as a beginning. Innumerable worlds, and a far-reaching view opens before him into the infinite of heaven. Man occasionally gets such a glimpse, but it is so bright that it causes his eyelids to close. Obscurity is made by the vividness of the light. Man remains dumb. Is he rejoicing or sad?

The Eagle and the Serpent.

If anything in any country attracts the attention of the laborer over his furrow, and arrests his plough, it is the sublime and fantastic spectacle in the heavens which outlines the strife of the bird and the serpent; a savage conflict in which both are frequently wounded. It is not without experiencing the tooth and venom that the eagle, crane, or stork, captures the dangerous reptile. Man mentally takes part with them in the combat. The struggle is uncertain. Sometimes the bird appears to falter at the vigorous blows of its convulsed antagonist. The sharp, pointed, violent zig-zags which the lightning traces in the clouds describe the contortions of the black serpent in the sky. But the bird does not let go its hold of its captive. They mount into the air. They are scarcely

---

* The strong, touching, penetrating book on this subject is the *Immortality*, by Dumesnil, the product of a situation full of death, full of life. Life overflows in it. It is more than a book, for he wrote it for his own comfort, *pro remedio animæ.*

distinguishable. The eagle carries away its prey into the profound depths of heaven and disappears in the light.

The bird most appropriately appertains to Persia. It hails the return of the day. It looks and longs for it as much as the serpent avoids it. Persia venerates the bird, and aspires to its free and elevated life. In the eagle, she recognizes herself; while in the serpent she personifies and denounces her foes, both of Turan and of Assyria.*

Although the myth† is often a spontaneous product of the soul, quite independent of history, we are disposed to believe that, among the Persians, who were far less imaginative than the Greek or the Hindoo, there was for it a basis in history. The Persians say that there came to them from the West, probably from Assyria, a scourge, the invasion of the monster Zohak, having on his shoulders serpents famishing for human flesh. This haughty Persia, this eagle, became the slave of the serpent, and endured a servitude more cruel than that of Judea. The Assyrians, according to Daniel, worshipped the living dragon, concealed in the lowest part of the temple.

By the Euphrates, the Ganges, the Nile, and still more in Guinea, boiling with humid heat, in the countries which insects at times make uninhabitable, the serpent is the friend of man. These insects are so terrible that the chamois and the elephant flee before them from one extremity of Africa to the other. The hunter of insects is blessed. It brings peace and fertility. It is subtle, prudent, and wise. But to understand what it says, the fine, delicate ear of woman is necessary. The negroes of Guinea, who have not changed any more than Africa her-

---

* In the *Khordah-Avesta*, the Assyrian power is personified as " the snake Dahaka, with three jaws or heads, in the region of Bawri," or Babylonia. The Medes and Armenians also commemorate it under the names of Dahaka or Deiokes, and of As-dahaka or Astyages. Turan or Tartary appears to have been signified by " the great Serpent," which devastated Aryana-vaeja. *Avesta*, Fargard i.—Ed.

† The Aryan migrations, indicated in the first Fargard of the *Avesta.*

self for the last ten thousand years, or longer, annually commemorate the marriage of the woman and the serpent. The maiden given or consecrated to the serpent becomes extravagantly attached to it and utters oracles. Thus came a whole world of fables in Greece, in Judea, and everywhere, about the seductions of the serpent, its amours, which occasionally afforded a view of the future, and opened its mysteries, sometimes resulting in the begetting of a divine son.* The conception is altogether different in dry, elevated countries, such as the high plains of Persia, where insects are less numerous. Here the serpent is the adversary, and excites dread and horror, even when it cowers down in winter in a corner of the stable, utterly defenceless. Its wave-like motions, its spiral coilings, its strange changes of skin, its cold scales, everything is repulsive. Among the animals it is the treacherous one ; to-day torpid, to-morrow hissing and furious. It frightens beyond its real power of hurting. Its form is imagined in everything which causes terror. In the cloud —the serpent of fire—which, hurled from on high, dashes to pieces and kills. In the torrent—the foaming dragon— which, unexpected, launched by the storm, rushes from the mountain and devastates with incredible swiftness the fields, the gardens, and the flocks.

We can form some idea of the horror which Persia had for the crawling god, and her mortal disgust for the obscene fables of the Æthiopian † world, the impurities of Assyria under the corrupting power and the fascinations of the serpent. The abhorrence was rendered complete by the exaction of a tribute of children for the insatiable Babylonish monster to devour. Among this simple, agricultural people, the strong man who delivered them was a

---

* V. *Collected Texts*, by Schwartz. *Ursprung der Mythologie.*

† Æthiopia anciently embraced the whole country occupied by the Hamitic race. India, Beluchistan, Caramania, Susiana, Arabia, Syria, Asia Minor, as well as Northern Africa, were comprised in its boundaries; everywhere, the serpent was worshipped.—ED.

smith. His coarse leather apron became the glorious banner of emancipation. The dragon crushed on the anvil by the powerful iron hammer writhed and writhed again ; its sharp tail, its hideous head, its scattered joints were never re-united.*

Assyria is divided ; she has two heads, Nineveh and Babylon ; while Persia, on the contrary, becomes more firmly bound together. The tribes of Persia are a people of fire, a conflagration in march, who wish to purify everything, and to subdue everything to the light. We feel this new spirit in a prayer to Hôma, a very blast of trumpets, which sounds a religious conquest, a purifying, puritan, iconoclastic propaganda, in which all the people are soon involved.

" Golden Hôma, give me energy and victory. Grant that I may go courageously ; that I may march over the countries, triumphing over the hateful, and *striking down the cruel.* Grant that I may conquer the fury of all, of men, of devas, of deaf demons, of murderous animals, of wolves with four legs, and of the army of terrible troops which run and fly." †

The world is changed. Persia is strong. She is going to overflow. The peaceful, the pure, have taken the sword for the defence. They have identified themselves with war. The first Amshaspand has become Ormuzd, the King of Heaven, against Ahriman, the King of Darkness. The peaceful have elected a King of the Earth, who rallies the tribes ; and seems the great Ferouer of Persia, her brilliant soul. This winged soul flies to war ; is about to

---

* Persia for three or four thousand years commemorated her smith in songs. She made work honorable, and was not ashamed of it. In her great poem of national tradition, Gustasp, her hero, who is going to see the Empire of Rome, finds himself without resources. In this Babylon of the West, what would Roland have done ? What would Achilles and Ajax have done ? Gustasp is not embarrassed. He offers himself to a smith. But his strength is too great. With his first stroke he splits the anvil in twain.

† EUG. BURNOUF: *Asiatic Journal,* August, 1845. Vol. 4, 148 ; *Researches,* 241.

march over the countries and purify Asia with the sword
of fire.

The impious Babylon, with her dragon-god, cannot
stop her. She hastens towards Egypt, and falls plump
upon the blacks of Africa, sworn enemies of light. She
menaces the pale West. To arrest her furious career will
require no less than Salamis.

" History," says Quinet, " has put itself in march."
We feel it on the bas-reliefs of Persepolis, in which the
Persian conquerors appear in long files. We hear the
noise of their tread. But this review is speechless. They
pass, and have uttered nothing. The history of this people
of light remains obscure to us.

Their monument, the *Avesta*, a simple collection of
prayers, and a ritual, is as a heap of the remains of a great
shipwreck.

Suppose that a book like the *breviary, mass,* and *ves-
pers,* inverted, survived the extinction of Christianity, with
the confused mixture (Jewish, Greek, Roman, Christian)
of religions, of different societies which offer such compila-
tions,—it would not be a bad resemblance of the *Avesta.*
The magianism of the Medes and Chaldeans confuses
utterly at every instant the true spirit of the primitive
Iran.

The *Avesta,* however, still contains the principal
stream. The remainder is accessory. The Jews, disciples
of Persia, the Greeks, her enemies, offer us but subsidiary
information. The Greeks see in Persia only a confused
Chaldean mixture, frequently attributing to her either the
glory or the shame, the science, or the corruption, of
Babylon, her adversary.

Had Babylon swallowed Persia? Was she drowned,
lost in the immensity of that conquest? Conquered in
her turn, humiliated by the strong Greek genius, and by
Alexander the Great, had she abjured and abandoned
herself? We might have believed this, were it not that
under the Sassanides she was found again immovable in

her faith, more Zoroastic than ever. The fall of the Sassanides and the successive conquests made no change in her
belief, and could not. She maintained under each empire
the holy Soul and the identity of Asia ; preserving herself
not only in her ascendancy over her sons, the poor and
honest Ghebers or Parsees, but especially, and still more
in her indirect ascendancy over the Mussulmans, her conquerors, and over the innumerable tribes, the Sultans and
the Dynasties of every race which passed over her. During their short stay, however, the barbarians had abundant
time to render homage to this superior soul, to know its
tradition, to become imbued with it, and to embody it.
The Turkomans from the North, the Arabians from the
South, left their recitals and their legends on the threshold
of Persia, as the reverential pilgrim deposits his shoes at
the entrance of the mosque. They enter, take the great
antique soul, its songs, and its poems. They sing nothing
but the *Shah Nameh.*

The Shah Nameh.—The Strong Woman.

The holy soul of Persia, under all the floods of barbarians, had preserved itself in the earth as living water, which
flows fresh and pure in the obscure depths of forgotten
canals. Towards the year one thousand (after Christ)
there made his appearance one who was imbued with the
ancient spirit and worship of the sacred fountains. All
were reopened to him, rich as ever, murmuring, eloquent
of antique things which had been considered lost.

It is not from caprice nor by accident that I have drawn
this comparison of the waters. It is really because these
very waters, which made the country, made the poet also.
They were the first inspiration of Firdusi.

The waters which hide and show themselves, lose and
find themselves, which, sometimes obscure and nocturnal,
come again to light, and say in murmurs : " Here we are "—
are certainly not persons, but they have the appearance of
souls—souls which were or will be, which await organiza-

tion and prepare it. A country entirely engrossed by them, in their evokation, in their distribution, in their departures, in their returns, was by this alone led to dream of the soul, of its births and re-births, and to hope in immortality.

Firdusi was born a Mussulman. His father owned a field near a stream and a dry canal. The child went daily alone to meditate by the old canal. This ruin of ancient Persia was eloquent in its silence. The old canal was formerly the life of the country. The water, abandoned to its caprices, now exhausted and now overflowing, was often the scourge of the country. The ancient *Paradise* of Asia, the garden of the tree of life, whence flowed the rivers of heaven, health, freshness, fertility ; this Persia, what had she become ? The contrast was very great. In a very small canton there remained twelve thousand aqueducts,* abandoned and dilapidated, to glorify the ancient period and condemn the present. Sluggishness and pride made the conquerors despise the sacred arts of the Zoroastrian times. Everything was becoming desert, salt, sands, pestiferous marshes. As is the earth, such is man. The condition of the family is that of the country. It was languishing, desolated, and sterile in the miserable harems of the Mussulmans.

The *genius of the place* spoke ; the soul of the country awakened in the child. In the true spirit of a Gheber, a feeling altogether Zoroastrian, he said to the canal : " When I shall be a man, I will make a dam in the river, and a dyke, and then thou wilt no longer be thirsty."

More and more attached to Persia, he listened, collected, and wrote out its ancient traditions without being intimidated by the execrations which Mohammed had hurled against Fire-Worship. From his sixteenth year he began to sing them, scan them, and consecrate them in poetic measures. Out of peculiar respect, which poets so rarely

---

* MALCOLM, p. 6.

feel, he continued faithful to the old narrations, which
came to him out of the depths of centuries. The translator, Mr. Molh, in his beautiful introduction to the *Shah
Nameh*, remarks that Firdusi by no means floated in the
hazard of the fancy. " Even his faults," he says, " prove
that he followed a marked path, from which he would
not deviate." This was of advantage to the poem. His
persons are not simply transparent shadows. They have
a character singularly real. Whoever has read his *Gustasp*
and his *Rustam*, for instance, has seen them face to face,
and can draw their pictures.

Who could have believed that this immense and powerful
work would come down through so many misfortunes, from
the waves of barbarisms, active and violent, which have
passed over the ancient world ? How on a bed so troubled
will roll this renewed river of ancient days ? Can it be
other than corrupted, surcharged with varied elements
either coarse or subtle ? (Another mark of barbarism.)
No matter ! How noble this river ! How high its source,
and how impetuous ! How grandly it flows, and with
what a sublime purpose !

There is a mystery underlying this, which has not been
explained. How this Mussulman, this member of the
conquering race, found at the hearth of· the Parsees such
astounding confidence that they gave to him their heart,
and disclosed the tradition of their country ? It must have
been the powerful attraction of the heart of the poet, the
child-man, to whom they could refuse nothing. Imbued
with the spirit of ancient Persia, for sixty years he glorified her soul, and this soul, thus enchanted, came to him.

It happened, by singular good fortune, that everywhere
under the conquerors, the chiefs of the native families had
held, with the patriarchal life, the precious deposit of the
ancient past. Even a special name, as a historical priesthood, was assigned to them. They were called *history
cultivators*. At the hearth in the evening, with closed
doors, Persia came back, the ancient shadows, the naïve

but sublime dialogues of Ormuzd and Zoroaster, the exploits of Yima or Jemshid, of Gustasp and of Isfendiar, the apron of the smith who was of old the savior of the country. The mothers especially perpetuated the traditions. Woman is tradition itself.* More learned in Persia than elsewhere, she exercised very great influence in the land. At the hearth she was the queen and mistress, and to her son she was as the living God. The son was never permitted to sit in the presence of his mother. The queen-mothers, Amestres, Parisatis, appear to have reigned under their sons. In the *Avesta*, as we have seen, the Angel of the Law is a woman. The soul of the just is expressed by the feminine word *Fravaschi*. The ideal of purity is not only the infant girl, and the virgin, but the chaste and faithful spouse.†

---

* In Western Asia and Europe the Great Mother was worshipped at the Thesmophonia as the institutor of civil society.—ED.

† This is in antagonism to the doctrine of the Jew and the Mussulman. Woman, among the Jews, was the cause of the apostasy, and does not recover from it. The Arabian woman (see BURKHARDT, etc.), adventurous and romantic, descended from bad to worse, each husband being permitted to divorce her by the gift of a camel. The Persian maid and wife, on the contrary, are the objects of religious respect. "I pray to, I honor the holy soul of the girls who are marriageable; of the girl of prudence, of the girl of desire (pure desire), of the holy girl who does good, of the girl of light." The betrothed maiden, that at least who is no longer regarded as a child, must be consulted and consent to the marriage. If after marriage she remains sterile, she can authorize and introduce another wife.[1] The spouse must be gentle; every morning she must offer herself to her husband, and repeat nine times, "What dost thou wish?" (Anquetil, *Avesta*, II., 561.) The husband must not neglect her, and every nine days, at least, must render to her his duties.[2] The Persian contracts marriage without hesitation, and respects its obligations. He believes that if marriage is holy, all that relates to it is holy. The chaste and faithful spouse is devoted to him, and ardently renders

[1] This explains the story in the Hebrew scriptures, of Sarai, in the book of *Genesis*, who having no children gave Hagar, the Egyptian, her maid, to Abram to be his wife; of Rachel, who gave her maid Bilhah to Jacob; and doubtless of Elkanah, the father of Samuel, who had two wives, "Peninnah who had children, and Anna who had no children." Much of the bigamy that is now practised in the East is for a like motive—to rear children by the prolific spouse, to overcome the reproach of the barrenness of the other. The Hebrew story was doubtless inspired by the Persian custom.—ED.

[2] The laws of Solon contained the same provision.—ED.

Firdusi does not even allude to the Moslem women who are bought, sold, and made captives. He pictures only the Persian women. The heroines in his book, faithful to the true traditions, have an antique dignity and grandeur. If they sin, it is not through weakness. They are very austere and valiant, bold in initiative, and of heroic fidelity. One of them, instead of being carried away, carries off her sleeping lover. They fight by the side of their husbands, and brave every peril. We already see among them the Brünhilda of the *Niebelungen*, the ideal of the strong virgin who subdues man, and who, on the night of marriage, binds and enchains her husband. But all this is lofty and pure. There is no corrupt ambiguity, no ridiculous, obscene plot, as that which the *Minnesingers* have put in their famous *Night*. But that which is far more beautiful than this rude ideal of strength is the conjugal heroism, of which Firdusi delighted to multiply the models. He greatly admired the daughter of the Emperor of Roum, who was persecuted by her father, because she had married the hero Gustasp, whose sufferings and glorious poverty she shared. He also admired the daughter of Afrasiah, King of Turan, the great enemy of

---

her duty, and, thus doing, preserves her supreme virginity of soul. "A magician, arriving with seventy thousand men, said he would destroy the town if no one could answer his questions. A Persian presented himself.

"Tell me what a woman loves."

"That which delights her—the love of her marriage duty."

"Thou liest! that which she loves most is to be the mistress of the house and to have beautiful clothing."

"I do not lie. If you doubt, ask your wife."

The infidel, who had married a Persian woman, presumed that she would not dare speak the truth. He commanded her to be conducted to him, and interrogated her. She remained silent; but finally, constrained to speak, fearing that the town would be destroyed, and that she would go to hell, she asked for a veil, covered herself, and spoke thus:

"It is true that a woman loves dress, and to be the mistress of the house, but without the union of love with her husband, all this good is nothing but evil."

The magician, indignant at her courageous freedom, slew her. Her soul ascends to heaven, saying—"I am pure, most pure!"

Persia, who having taken for her husband a young Persian
hero, defended him, nourished him, saved him. When
the cruel Afrasiah, in order to prolong his sufferings,
sealed him, alive, under a stone, she begged food for his
support. Noble image of devotion, which no history, no
poetry, has ever surpassed ! He was at length released.
His glorious spouse accompanied him to Persia. She
triumphs, is worshipped, carried in the heart of the
people.

A political accident favored Firdusi. An intelligent
chief, Mahmoud the Gaznevide, having become the ruler of
Persia, thought that, in order to enfranchise himself from
the Calif of Bagdad, it was necessary to make an appeal
to local patriotism. He made a strange *coup d'état.*
Although a Mahommedan, he proscribed the dialect of
Mahommed, forbad the use of the Arabic language, and
adopted the beautiful Persian, mingled with so many ancient words. He founded a new empire on the idea of
this renaissance, expecting that through this language the
people would revive their remembrances of their heroes.
But in order to give to this language its rhythm and the
popular charm, an inspired poet was necessary. At this
juncture Firdusi was found. The monarch's enthusiasm
for the poet knew no bounds. He named him "the poet
of Paradise." * He wished to load him with gold. Firdusi
refused, not wishing to be paid till he had completed the
poem ; so that he could erect the dike, retire to his canal,
and, having become old, could see his native fields fertilized anew with fresh waters.

Mahmoud lodged him in his own palace, and caused a
kiosk to be erected for him in his gardens, into which no
one could enter except Aïyar, the favorite of the Sultan.
On the walls of this pavilion were painted the battles and
the heroes which the poet was to render immortal. Firdusi in his solitude had not only the nightingales, but also

---

* This is the meaning of Firdusi.

a young musician, a literary friend, whose graces as well
as his lute, awakened his genius.

In the course of this long labor things changed strangely.
Mahmoud, having nothing now to fear from the West,
invaded India and despoiled the pagodas of their treas-
ures.   Rapacious and fanatical, he broke open statues
of idols filled with diamonds.   On account of his re-
actionary movement the envious took advantage of him.
A thousand slanders were circulated.   One day he was
described as a schismatic, another day as a Gheber, and
finally as an atheist.   Although master of the palace, his
subjects were forgetting his rank, and even neglecting to
supply his commonest wants.

Firdusi, now upward of sixty years of age, had lost his
son of thirty-seven, to whom he had looked for support.
His work and life pressed him heavily. His poem was
far from completion. He had almost reached the trying
and delicate part of his poem, the epoch in which the
hero Gustasp received from Zoroaster the ancient worship,
adopted it, and imposed it on the whole earth. What
could the poet do? Would he confess his respect for this
worship? Would he stand by Gustasp and Ancient Persia
at the moment when his master, the dreadful Mahmoud,
was becoming again a zealous Mussulman? Severe moral
struggle! He felt his restraint. His kiosk, his beautiful
gardens, what were they but the iron cage of the poor
dog in the vicinity of the lion? Hear his story: "The
gloom was black as jet. The night was without stars, in
an air which seemed to be of rust. I felt on every side
Ahriman. At every sigh he heaved, I saw him as a frightful negro, blowing over blackened coals. Black was the
garden; the brook, the sky, were immovable. Not a
bird, not a beast. No word either good or bad. Neither
height, nor depth, nothing distinct. My heart, little by
little, was closing. I arose and descended into the garden, where my friend came and found me. I asked him
for a lamp. He brought it, with wax-candles, oranges, and

pomegranates, wine and the shining goblet. He drank
and played the lute. An angel charmed me, soothed me,
and made the night into day.

"He said, ' Drink! I will read an history.'

" ' Yes,' I replied. ' My dear friend, slim as the cypress!
and sweet-looking as the moon! Relate to me the good
and the evil which fills heaven with contradictions.'

" 'Hear, then! This history, which thou wilt put in
lines, is taken from the old Pehlvi book.'"

Wine, the liquor hated by the Arabian apostle, but
blessed by the Persians, now reinvigorates his heart. I
think this song is the best in the *Shah Nameh.* He assures
us in vain that he has taken it from the old Gheber poet
Dakiki, his predecessor. He vainly maintains that this
song is not worth a farthing. No one believes him. He,
himself, having finished it, lets drop this sentence of profound joy:

" Behold the world and its revolutions. The empire is
without a representative. It wavers ; he who holds it is
weary of it. . . . Do not sow evil ; as much as possible
avoid it. Pray to the Lord, the only God, to permit thee
to live on earth long enough to finish this book in thy
beautiful language. After its completion, let thy mortal
body return to dust, and let the eloquent soul go to the
holy Paradise!"

The bigoted Mussulmans rejected Firdusi. The Parsees
boldly took him for one of themselves. Mahmoud,
indisposed, devout through avarice, allowed himself to be
advised to perfidy, and sought to pay in silver pieces
what he had agreed to pay in gold. Firdusi, when in the
bath, saw the favorite Aïyar approaching with sixty thousand pieces of silver. Without complaining he gave a
third part to the messenger, another third to the bath
tender, and the remainder to the slave who brought him
drink. At this Mahmoud was so enraged that he wished
to crush him by the elephants. Firdusi mollified his
anger, but resolved to fly. Poor, after so many years of

profitless labor, with the staff of a traveller, the garb of a
Dervish, he set out alone. No one accompanied him, or
came to bid him farewell. He left to Aïyar a sealed
paper, to be opened after twenty days, by which time
Firdusi expected to be beyond the territory of the Gaz-
uevide monarch. The paper was found to contain a daring satire, in which the poet said to Mahmoud :

" Son of a slave, hast thou forgotten that I also have
a sword which pierces, which can wound and shed blood ?
These lines which I leave to thee will be thy portion in
all coming centuries, while I will give shelter and safety
to a hundred men more worthy than thyself."

Nevertheless, it was a serious affair to have such an
enemy, who pursued him, claimed him, and demanded
that he be delivered to him. Under this terror the unfortunate man wandered in disguise. He was eighty-three
years old when Mahmoud, near death and the judgment,
desired to atone and make reparation. He sent to
Firdusi the promised gold. Its bearer entered through
one gate into the town in which Firdusi had just died,
while his funeral cortège was passing out of another. It
was proffered to his daughter, who nobly refused it. His
sister accepted it, but only to fulfil the vow of his infancy,
to execute his will, build the dike which he had promised
to the old canal, and which was to bestow upon the canton
new life and fertility.

Is this a digression ? A thoughtless reader would be
tempted to say so. But it is quite the contrary ; it is the
basis of the subject ; it is its soul. This soul of Persia,
primarily evoked by the mystery of the waters which
created the country, returns obstinately three thousand
years after Zoroaster, and contrary to all expectation, the
soul revives the Mussulman's spirit and floods it with its
abounding goodness and its rich inspiration.

The torrent of legends in the heroic *Sagas* had always
flowed through the popular voice, but was covered and
darkened by magianism. Ceremonies and purifications

were held in higher estimation than the history of heroes. The conquest and obliteration of magianism were necessary in order that the Mussulmans themselves, in their sterility, should search under the ruins for the hundred thousand disappeared canals of the heroic life, and that a genius should reunite them in this immense river of poetry which carries them into eternity.

6

CHAPTER III.

GREECE.

The Intimate Relation between India, Persia, and Greece.

THE three Hearths of light, India, Persia, Greece, shone separately, without reciprocal reflection, without commingling, almost without knowing each other. This was necessary, in order that each should freely accomplish its mission, and impart what it contained.

The beautiful mystery of their intimate relation, opened by the *Vedas* in the mystery of dogma, is simple. Here it is formulated for the first time in all that is essential. The *Veda* of the *Vedas*, the Indian secret, is this . " Man is the oldest of gods. The hymn originated everything. The word created the world."

" The word supports it," says Persia. " Man watches, and his word continually evokes and perpetuates the flame of life."

" Fire carried off from Heaven itself, and in spite of Zeus," adds the bold Greece. " This torch of life which we in running pass to each other, was lighted by a genius and given to man in order that he might produce art ; make himself a creator, a hero, a god. Hard work ! No matter. Though in Prometheus a prisoner bound, in Hercules he mounts to Heaven." Behold the real identity of the three brothers, their common soul, veiled in the former two, and blazing in the third.

Whatever was the interior unity, it was essential to the freedom of mankind that it should not be perceived till a later period, so that Asia, already old (500 B.C.), should not stifle Greece, and that Persia, transmuted by the Chaldean intermixture, should not impose on Greece her confusion. It had come to her in the impure cortège of Babylon, of the Phœnician Moloch, of the foul Anaïtis, whose infamous altar Artaxerxes everywhere erected near the Altar of Fire.

The great event in this world, incomparably, is the victory of Salamis, the eternal victory of Europe over Asia. This was an event of immense consequence, before which everything disappears. We read of it over and over again without satiety. Platea, Marathon, Salamis, always delight and draw out the same outburst of joy; not without cause. It is our birth.

" Our minds become exalted," as says the Cid. It is the epoch of the birth of the European mind, or rather of the human mind in its sovereign liberty, and in its strength of invention and criticism. Spiritual savior of the world : its victory over Asia assured the light by which Asia herself was illuminated.

Greece, so small, has done more than all the empires. With her immortal works, she has given the art which makes them, especially the art of creation, of education, which makes men.

She is *the Instructress of Peoples.* This is her great name.

Such was the strength of life in her that, two thousand years after the long age of lead, a light shadow, a distant reflex of Greece, was enough to produce the *renaissance.* What was left ? A mere nothing. This trifle threw into the shade, subordinated, and eclipsed everything.

This little was necessary. Some scattered fragments, some worm-eaten sheets, some trunks of statues are excavated from the earth. Humanity shudders. With both hands humanity embraces the marble torso. Humanity has again found herself. This is more than any work ; it is the heart, the strength, the power which comes back ; it is the boldness and the liberty, the free inventive energy.

The true genius of Greece is *transformation, education.*

It is the magician, the great master of metamorphoses.
Mankind surrounds and laughs. " It is a sport," say the
people ; "an enchantment. It is an amusement of the
eyes." Afterwards, they gradually perceive that this
cycle of varied forms, in which men and gods appear, is a
profound education.

Nothing is hidden. All is luminous. Nothing takes
place behind the scenes, in the gloomy crypt. Everything is done in the open air, before the sun, in the broad
light of the palestra. This beautiful genius is neither avaricious nor jealous. The doors are wide open. Approach
and contemplate. Humanity will perceive how humanity
forms itself.

How came about the generation and the education of
the gods in the thousand years of poetry which are con-
densed in Homer ? It is the heroic work of Ionia. We
can see through its transparent progress.

How, through the long centuries of the Dorian gymnastics, have the games and the festivals made living gods,
types of strength and beauty, the races of Hercules and
Apollo ? We see it, we know it, we assist at it.

How the immense effort of statuary creation, the delicate
art of immortalizing the beautiful, wrestled with time and
envious death ? We can study it notwithstanding the
greatness of our losses.

How, finally, from the double analysis of the drama
and of philosophy, the struggles of the moral man were
illuminated, till that sublime moment in which, freed from
the dogma, came forth the flower of the world and its
true fruit, the *justice* from which Rome takes its point of
departure ? It is the most luminous history which human
genius has left behind.

Terra-Mater—De-Meter or Ceres.

Homer is so brilliant that he interrupts the view of the
long past behind him. He enshrouds it in darkness by
the intense brightness of his light, as a dazzling portico of

Parian marble, glittering under the sun, prevents the sight of the immense temple, the ancient sanctuary, of which it conceals the entrance.

If we start with Homer, as the primitive Greece, Greece would remain an inexplicable miracle. It would, like Pallas, Athenè, come out in entire panoply, sword in hand. It would be full-grown and matured at birth, prepared to fight, with an adventurous spirit. Things never begin in this way. Æschylus, the profound Æschylus, very justly calls the Homeric divinities the "young gods." One of these young gods, the god with the arrows of gold, who spreads death in the Grecian camp, the Dorian god Apollo, makes all the plot of the *Iliad*.

Birth requires a soft cradle. Nothing comes from war. Peace and culture, the agricultural family, these are fruitful. Everything is born of earth, of woman. Thus Greece was born at the breast of Ceres, or Demeter, Ancient Deity, who rarely appears in the poet, but very frequently in tradition, and is the real life of the people.

She was originally nothing but the earth, *Terra-Mater*, De-Meter,* the good mother, and nurse, so naturally worshipped by grateful humanity. The Pelasgi, first inhabitants of Greece, honored De-Meter in grottos before temples were erected. This rude and primitive worship was maintained in ancient Arcadia, which believed itself to be even older than the moon (*Pro-Seleni*),† and which, enclosed by mountains and forests, remained the wild sanctuary of the ancient religions. Centuries passed in vain;

---

* Some writers are fond of deriving the name De-meter, from *Ge*, the Earth, and *meter*, or mother. It is possible, however, that this is not a correct etymology. The letter *g* is hardly transmutable into *d*, in any language. De-meter, also written Deo, is more probably from the Pelasgian, and akin to the Sanskrit *Deva-matr*, or Goddess-Mother, a title of Maha Lakshmi, or the Great Mother of gods and created beings.—ED.

† This is probably another false etymology. It is more likely that the Proseleni were the older race, who occupied Greece, as well as India, before the Seleni or Lunar tribes, the Ionians, who worshipped the younger and female deities.—ED.

the Homers and the Pheidias made everything radiant with art ; but Arcadia held to its primitive gods up to the end of Greece. Pausanias tells us that many frequently journeyed to visit a shapeless image in which barbaric genius had boldly undertaken for the first time to express the complex personality of the earth. It was black, like the prolific soil, and supported all kinds of wild animals. In each hand it held the symbols of water and air, in the form of a dove and dolphin. The whole was crowned with the head of the horse,* the most noble animal produced on earth. Discordant and coarse image which gave only the exterior. The genius of Greece was not satisfied with it, and, wishing to express the interior of the earth, its mystery, its maternity, gave to it a daughter. This daughter is, itself, the earth, seen under a different aspect ; it is the earth in its gloomy and fruitful depths, filled with springs and volcanoes. Silent abyss in which descends all life, fatal kingdom to which all must go. It is the true black Ceres, the Sovereign, the imperious, the Despoina (lady, or our lady), Persephone or Proserpina.†

She appears as aged as her mother. In this same Arcadia there was a sacred enclosure, where temples were erected at a later day, which contained an image of Despoina, and near it, a Titan (son of Ouranos and Gaia), one of those geniuses of the earth who represent its unknown forces. Was he the father of Despoina? Very probably. Long after, when imperial Zeus or Jupiter was born, and when Despoina was made his daughter, this Titan became subordinated, and was simply the nurse and protector of the goddess.

Ceres and Proserpina, the ruler of the earth above and

---

* The mare, or *hippa*, whose head surmounted the statue at Phigalea, was a symbol suggested by the fact that the name was a pun on that of Hippa, the ancient goddess, mother of all, identical with Ceres and Ghilo. —ED.

† The *Despoina* was the offspring of Ceres by Poseidon, the god of the Hamitic or Ethiopian world. If she is to be regarded as identical with Proserpina, the myth must be a variant of the Grecian one, which makes the latter the daughter of Zeus.—ED.

goddess of the earth below, were very generally revered. Without the first, it would be impossible for men to exist, and sooner or later all are received by the latter into her gloomy kingdom. War and invasion, which respect nothing, paused before their altars. They were the guardians of peace. They had sanctuaries everywhere in Pelasgian Dodona, in mysterious Samothracea, where they took for their coadjutor the geniuses of fire, in volcanic Sicily, and especially in the narrow pass of Thermopylæ, where the gate to Greece could be opened and closed. From Eleusis, they ruled over Attica. The Arcadian gave to Proserpina the name of Soteira, *Virgin of Salvation.*

Affecting worship, and of very singular conception! It is marvellous to comprehend what Greece found in it. No poem, no statue, no monument, is so creditable to Greece as her wonderful perseverance in searching out and fathoming this holy mystery of the *Spirit of the Earth*, penetrating it from myth to myth by a progressive creation of deities or geniuses, and by a series of fables, all of them very wise and profoundly true. The charming Ionian genius united to it the solemnity of the more ancient race, the Pelasgians, who were also the parents of ancient Italy. Hence was evolved a religion full of peace and humanity, allied alike to Estia, Vesta, the pure genius of the hearth, and to the wise Themis, who, indeed, seems to be no other than Ceres herself. Both at Thebes and Athens Ceres brought men together, and made the laws. No culture can exist without order. Justice is born from the furrow.

The little we know of this primitive Greece indicates gentle manners, more nearly allied to the original Hindoos, to the humane genius of the *Vedas*, than to the warrior age depicted in the *Iliad*. The most ancient traditions which remain of Greece relate to the profound horror inspired by the effusion of blood, especially in human sacrifices, which were detested as a peculiarity of barbarians, and severely punished. Lykaon was changed into a wolf* because he had immolated men. Tantalus was tormented in the underworld with intense thirst that nothing quenched.

That which is Hindoo-like, and even appears Brahminical, is their scruples against the killing of animals. Their very ancient ceremonies are a perpetual witness of the struggle which troubled the simple souls, who, having a horror for blood, were nevertheless condemned by their climate and work to nourish themselves with animal food. In order to immolate a victim they tried to persuade themselves that the animal was guilty. A bull, for example, ate a sacred cake on the altar; this sacrilege drew down the vengeance of heaven; it was necessary to punish the animal. No one would otherwise have had the heart to kill this ancient servant, this companion of husbandry. They called a stranger, who struck and fled. A solemn inquest was made over the animal, the blood of which had been shed. All who had taken the least part in the slaughter were cited to judgment; the man who had offered the weapon to the sacrificer, the man who had whetted it, the women who had brought water for its sharpening, all were called to account. They accused one another, and endeavored to place the blame on each other. At last all the guilt was imputed to the knife, which, not being able to defend itself, was condemned and thrown into the sea. They then made to the bull all the amends in their power. They raised it, stuffed it with straw, and put it before the plough, where it seemed to live again and take once more the honor of the work of agriculture.

This peaceful people was incessantly exposed to enemies from the sea and the islands. The pirates of Asia and Phœnicia made frequent invasions for the purpose of kidnapping children and women. Cruel kidnapping! These poor creatures, unexpectedly carried off and sold in Asia, were never found again. From the remotest

---

* Another symbol suggested by a pun. *Lykos* is the Greek term for wolf; but Lykaon was a name of Zeus, as Pythias was of Apollo.—ED.

period up to the times of modern barbarism, the same misfortunes, the same griefs, the same cries, have existed. The poets and historians of all ages speak of this carrying off. It is the abduction of Io, of Europa, of Hesione, of Helen. Still more cruel was the terrible tribute of children paid to the Minotaur. Homer has described the silent grief of the father who, having lost his daughter, mournfully follows the shore, where the bitter and outrageous waves bound and laugh at his sorrow. What can be said of the despair of a mother when the fatal boat carries off her treasure, when the daughter in tears vainly spreads her arms, flies, and disappears over the waves?

These tragedies, and especially the uneasiness under the expectations of such great misfortunes, contributed more than anything else to sharpen the faculties of this people, to give them so early that powerful sensitiveness whence broke forth their great religious creation, the legend of Ceres and Proserpina, the pathetic history of the *Maternal Passion.* There was no need of fiction for the design, or embellishment. All was nature and truth, and this is what made it so enduring, so strong, so long-continuing. Humanity still retains the impression, and will preserve it forever.

The heart is impressed with the analogy which occasions grief, at the annual sight of the flower which separates and flies away from the plant, and is forever lost to its mother. What will happen to this flower, this grain, which has fled? Where will the little one go? The wind blows and rudely carries it off. The passing bird picks it up and departs. More frequently it seems as if it must die; swallowed up, it falls in the black and obscure soil in which it is ignored, as if in the forgetfulness of the sepulchre; and often man, for his own use, tortures it in every way, drowns it, grinds it, pounds it, and inflicts upon it a hundred tortures. Every people sings of this. Every tribe of mankind, from India to Ireland, has related in ballads the adventures and the miseries of this young creature. These narratives are frequently playful. Greece alone, which is regarded as so trifling, never laughed, but wept instead.

The drama was formed before. That which truly belonged to genius was the creation of Ceres, the idea of a mother worthy of adoration, whose infinite goodness makes still more sensible the cruel adventure. Afterward came the conception of the divine heart of woman, expanded by grief, who became the universal nurse and took all men for her children; the whole of humanity is her Proserpina.

Conception infinitely pure, and the purest that ever was! The senses have nothing to do with it. The tender Isis, who weeps for her Osiris, makes no mystery of her ardent African love, of her poignant desire; she weeps, she searches, she calls her husband. As to Ceres, the object worshipped and wept for was a daughter; therefore her legend will never undergo the ambiguity of those more recent religions in which the mother weeps for a son, and in which she, restored to youth by the arts, and becoming younger than he, is frequently less mother than spouse.

Ceres is the earnest thought of all agricultural people. Work makes serious. There is but little of delicate or mystic refinement among a people who bear the burdens of life. Nothing subtle, nothing false. Truth in her most affecting aspect, the profound agreement of things which sophistical and unspiritual ages have separated, the heart and nature at one, the beauty of the infinite goodness, is what simple men conceived and even expressed in the first endeavor of the Grecian art. Long before the marbles of Ægina, ominous image of combats, the worshipped head of peaceful Ceres adorned the admirable medals of Sicily.*

---

* See those in the cabinet of medals (Paris), and also *Trésor de numismatique et de glyptique*, the Medals published by M. De Luynes. The Collection Campana (Rome) had a very beautiful Ceres, which is supposed to be of the time of Phidias. Alas, she has been carried off to Russia! In Russia

Noble equipoise of simple rural, royal beauty. The rich hair of her head mingled its gold with that of the grain in the ear.

Amidst joy, tears, the alternatives of good, of evil, of sun, of storm, she has one thing immovable—goodness. She loves the plants, as well as the innocent flocks, the gentle sheep, and especially children (malo-trophos, kou-ro-trophos). She is to all mother and nurse. Her swelling breast is constantly eager to be suckled, even when she is in tears. She is the love, honey, and milk of nature.

Hard contrast of destiny ! This genius of peace, Ceres, was born in the midst of two contending powers. She flourishes in places in which the action of elements is more terrific, in the volcanic islands, in Sicily. However chaste and pure she may be, she is the object of two serious attractions. Goddess of fertility, she cannot accomplish her work, except in receiving the dew of heaven, and on the other hand the obscure influences of subterranean heats, of powerful breaths which are exhaled from the earth. Zeus, as well as Pluto, assails her. She is a woman ; the dark depths affright her. How can she, being all love and life, decide to become the spouse of the king of death ? She hesitates, but, in the meantime, she cannot prevent the outpouring of the heaven in her bosom. All that this poor innocent knows about it is that she will have a little Ceres, who will bloom out of her, as the flourishing plant has a daughter which is itself.

Her history is well known.* The young girl, in spring, not far from the sea, was gathering flowers in the meadow with her nymph companions. The first narcissus was in

---

this daughter of Greece and of Sicily, this mother of the arts, and of humanity !

* This history is the legend which was everywhere represented in sacred dramas. It is of superior antiquity, and perfectly distinct from that of the *Hymn to Ceres*, attributed to Homer ; as well as of the Mysteries of Eleusis, in which the poor Ceres, encroached upon by the worship of Bacchus, undergoes such sad alterations.

bloom. She earnestly desired this flower of the legends, which, as is well known, was a child. She attempted with both hands to tear it up and to carry it off, but the earth opened. The black Pluto suddenly appeared with his chariot and fiery steeds. She was carried away, the little unfortunate one, in spite of her tears and cries. She was so childish that she desired to retain her flowers. In vain. The flowers overspread the earth, which became verdant and flourishing.

In her forced flight everything seems to disappear before her — earth, sea, and sky. In this we are reminded of Sîta (the daughter of the furrow), who was carried away by the evil spirit Râvana; but how superior and how much more touching is the incident in Greece! Sîta had no mother to weep for her.

Poor Ceres! All the gods work against her. They agreed among themselves to rend her heart. Jupiter consented to it. No one dared tell her what had become of her daughter. She prayed, she addressed herself to all nature. No augur; even the birds were silent.

In despair, she tore off her head-band and released her long tresses. She adopted the dress of mourning, the blue mantle. She partook of no nourishment. She did not wash her beautiful body. Distracted, carrying the funeral torch, she rushed over the earth for nine days and nights. She was finally exhausted, sick. Hekatè and the Sun finally took compassion and revealed all to her. Irreparable misfortune! She will never again return to that unjust heaven. She will forever wander in misery over this lower earth.

Bowed down by grief, she tottered like an old woman. She seated herself at noon under an olive tree, not far from a well. The women and girls who came to draw water spoke to her with compassion. Four beautiful maidens, daughters of the King, conducted her to their mother.

"Who are you?"

"I am the *seeker*. Pirates carried me away. I fled.
Give me a child to nourish and bring up."

At this moment she darted out rays of such resplendent
benignity that the Queen was agitated, dazzled, moved to
tenderness, and placed her child in her arms, her cherished
and last child, the child of her old age, who came to her
twenty years after her daughters.

In the meantime the heart of the goddess had been so
oppressed by the gods that she could neither speak nor eat.
No prayer, no tenderness could prevail on her. A surprise
was necessary. A rural girl—bold, young, joyful, and lame
—caused the goddess by her playfulness for a moment to
forget her grief, and surprised her into a smile. She
accepted nourishment, neither wine nor meat, but flour
perfumed with mint, the future host of the mysteries.
Sweet communion of the benign goddess with humanity.
For ambrosia and nectar she took bread and water. Even
more, she adopted the child, who thus from this time had
two mothers, and became the son of earth and heaven.

We may presume that, favored by her divine breath,
he throve at her breast. Pervaded by her affluence, his
nature became changed. She desired to make him immortal. Fire and trial by fire alone can deify. In later
times Hercules arose to heaven from the pyre. Ceres,
who made the delicate plants germinate by heat, knew
well how to impart the heat to her child without pain or
peril. Every night she placed him on the hearth. Unfor-
tunately the curious mother came to observe, was alarmed,
and cried out. "Alas, all is over ! Man will not be immortal. He must endure the evils and miseries of humanity."

Thus Ceres, who had lost her daughter, lost also her
adopted son. More desperate than ever, she again com-
menced her wanderings with dishevelled hair. She appeared to be devoured with grief. Heaven oppressed her
heavily, and the earth was odious to her. The soil dried
up and became unproductive ; when its goddess suffers
can the earth be any other than a dreary desert ? Ceres

had renounced her useless divinity; she wandered in the dusty roads, and as a mendicant sat by the road-side. All our necessities besieged her; she sank under fatigue and hunger. An old woman compassionately gave her a little broth, which she swallowed greedily. To crown her calamities, she was scoffed at. An unworthy boy jeered and pointed the finger of derision at her, and mimicked her greediness. Cruel ingratitude! that man could laugh at the kind nurse that alone supports human life. But malice punishes itself. The boy dried up in his wickedness; became a reptile, the slim, tapering lizzard, the dry occupant of heaps of stones. A good lesson to make us charitable. Child, never laugh at a supplicant. Who knows that he is not a god?

The earth suffered so much that heaven is touched and alarmed. No harvests, no animals. The gods, without sacrifices, are also famishing. They send down Iris, Mercury, and all the messengers of heaven.

"No; give me back my daughter."

It is necessary that Pluto should yield, at least for a brief period. Her beloved daughter escaped from the world of the dead, arrived in a chariot of fire, and embraced her mother. Ceres was almost overcome from joy. But how changed the daughter! More beautiful than ever, but so gloomy! Injured beauty! Frail beauty! Death and flowers! Winter and Spring! Behold the double Proserpina, charming and formidable, who almost imposes even on her mother.

"Ah, my daughter! art thou mine? Dost thou not still belong to the under world? Hast thou partaken of anything there below, in the world of the dead?"

Indeed, Pluto had not allowed her to depart until she had taken a kernel of the mysterious fruit of fecundity, the pomegranate, with its numerous grains.* In other words,

---

* The pomegranate, or *rhoia*, is a sexual symbol, suggested by the pun upon the name of Rhea, the Great Mother, and also by the female *eidolon* upon

she brought back the dark fecundation of the black empire, to which she must return ; and thus, year after year, in the autumn, she is again separated from her mother. She falls into the depth of her night ; but Ceres, in the spring, has the joy of again finding her, mingled with the sadness of the expectation of her departure.

Behold life and its alternatives. Ceres bears all the burden. Who will console her? Work, the good which she does to man. She has not been able to make of man a god, as she desired, but she has made him a worker, a Triptolemus, grinder of the soil with the plough, and of the grain with the mill-stone—the just Triptolemus, the child of husbandry, peaceful, economical, full of respect for the work of others, and wise friend of order and law.

Beautiful history ! And so true ! Mingled with joy and sadness, and particularly with wisdom and admirable good sense! It was interpreted in two popular festivals, very simple, quite natural, and, at the time, without mystery or refinement.

In spring the *Anthesphoria*, the festival of flowers. The beautiful Proserpina then returns to cover the earth with vegetation ; she brings back the enchantments of life. She does not bring everything; she leaves our beloved dead behind. Our joy is not without tears, since they do not return. We weave wreaths for them and for their tombs. Smiling, but tenderly, woman crowns with flowers her aged father, her little child. It is good that there are births, since there are deaths. Grief commands love. This floral festival was that of the human flower, the great day of the women and of the serious joys of marriage. The very chaste Ceres thus wished and ordained.

In the autumn, the *Thesmophoria*, festival of women,

---

the fruit. The goddess Nova, eating one, is said to have become pregnant of Atys ; and at the Thesmophoria, where women were required to observe the strictest continence, the pomegranate was interdicted. It was sacred to Proserpina, because all who are begotten are denizens of the region of mortality; Venus-Urania and Queen Korè are substantially the same.—ED.

festival of laws. It was to women that the goddess had entrusted her laws of order and humanity. Not without reason. Who is so much interested in society as mothers, who have so much at stake, the child? Who so much as they are stricken by anarchy and war?

Autumn has a double character. For man, refreshed and rested, who has but little more to do than to sow and taste the new wine, it is gay and sometimes too joyous. But women remembered that autumn is for Ceres the sad moment, in which she sees her daughter descending into the earth, and for this reason they rejected the attentions of their husbands and abandoned them for several days. Smiling at their own affected austerity, and at the complaints which this separation elicited, they went either to the sea, to the gloomy promontory where the goddess was worshipped, or to the celebrated temple of Eleusis, after it was built. They conveyed in solemn procession the laws of Ceres, laws of peace, which, on their return, they easily made their eager husbands promise under oath to obey from regard to the welfare of the child, whose advent they so earnestly desired.

What are those powerful laws which have bound society so firmly together? Very simple, if we judge them by those which have been preserved. They prescribed the *love of family, the horror of blood*, and nothing more. But this was of prodigious influence. In the spirit of Ceres the family, enlarged, became the neighborhood, the tribes, which, united, became the village; the united villages became the commonwealth. No bloodshed of men or animals. No offerings to the gods but fruits. If the animal was spared, how much more man! No war, eternal peace. At least, a spirit of peace even in necessary war. From this I can see the *altar of compassion* erected in Athens. I see *peace* deified at the great festivals of Olympia and Delphos, which united the States and made them one people.

This respect for human life, considered precious to the

gods, sacred and divine, certainly contributed more than
anything else to produce the conviction of immortality.
If the flower only dies to be born again, why should not
the human soul, this flower of the world, live again ?
Wheat, in its birth and in its eternal re-births, taught the
resurrection far better than any dogma. St. Paul, in his
epistles, many centuries afterward, makes use of no other
illustration than the lesson of Ceres.*

In this and in everything else Ceres was the great teacher.
Her worship, popular, enriched and dramatized in an imposing manner, culminated in later days in the mysteries,
which, although attacked by Christians, were imitated by
them.

Her benefactions have been immense. She gave a basis
of ardent love to the light, Ionian temper, which was very
fickle and changeable. She created the Athenian commonwealth, and drew the outlines of the social system
which were peculiarly *humane.*

It is not the variable fancy, the imagination which could
engender life. To make a world it is absolutely necessary
that there be great love, great truth. The maternity of
Ceres, her pure love, which overflows with goodness, was
the cradle of Greece. Long before the Olympus of Homer
there were vast, silent centuries, which were incubating
the future. Powerful, fruitful hearth ! From this legend
of a mother, Greece received the flame which quickened
her as a mother also. In order to understand the ages in
which she enlightened the world, it is necessary to consider

First Epistle to the Corinthians, xv., 36–45 : "Fool, that which thou
sowest is not quickened except it die : and that which thou sowest, thou sowest
not that body that shall be, but bare grain ; it may chance of wheat, or of some
other grain : but God giveth it a body as it hath pleased him, and to every seed
its own body. . . . So also is the *anastasis,* or future life of the dead. - It is
sown in the corruptible, and is raised in the incorruptible; it is sown in the
unhonored, and is raised in glory ; it is sown in weakness, and is raised in
power ; it is sown a physical body, and is raised a spiritual body "—*i. e.,* sown
under the physical and moral influences of earth-life, and lives again invested
with the divine qualities of the heavenly world.—ED.

5

her, first as a child adopted by Ceres ; second, when she took the torch from the hand of Ceres, or when, under the care of Ceres, she gathered the flowers of Eleusis or Enna.*

The Vanity of the Ionic Gods.—The Strength of the Human Family.

Science marches and light advances.   The new faith is confirmed in finding under the earth its substantial roots in the remote antiquity.   The memorable conflict which I witnessed while still young, between liberty and theocracy, the true and false erudition on the Greek origins, is finally ended.   Chief, living question, of eternal interest !   Was this most brilliant people its own Prometheus, or was it taught and moulded by a priesthood ? †   Was it the work of a sacerdotal caste, or the spontaneous fruit of the human mind ?

Thirty years of work have decided the question and severed the knot forever.   The results are so clear and decided, that the enemy dare no longer breathe.   From below, in all details, from point to point the enemy is beaten.   From on high a great flash of sunlight, the youthful philology, overwhelms him still more, bringing out into full daylight the fact that in those ancient origins there is no artifice of a sacerdotal caste, no complicated symbolism, but the free action of good sense and of nature.

---

* Enna was denominated the amphalos of Sicily, as Delphi was of Greece. Its importance as the seat of this myth is evidence that it pertained to Asia and Phœnicia, rather than to Greece.—ED.

† Mr. Guignaut, a truly learned man, who has devoted his life in the immense work of translating, completing, and connecting Kreuzer's *Symbolique*, has been among us, in this century, the true founder of the study of religions.

This beloved teacher was the guide of us all.   The Renans, Maurys, and all the eminent critics of this age have sprung from him.   He opened the way even to those who, like myself, incline toward the *anti-symbolique*, toward Strauss, Lobeck, and believe with the latter that if Ceres is very ancient, the Mysteries of Eleusis, and the Orgian myths are of recent origin.   See LOBECK, *Aglaophamus*, 1829, Koenigsberg.

The venerable worship of the soul of the earth, of Ceres and of Proserpina, affecting, but not without terror, which showed in twenty different places the abyss closed, the door of Pluto, would have created anywhere else than in Greece a powerful sacerdotal order. It was twice attempted and failed. In the most ancient times this worship was subordinated to the joyous elasticity of the Ionian transformations, the fancy of strolling singers, who varied the fables and the gods. Later, when the mysteries, aided by the arts and by an ingenious system of worship, could have taken strong hold of the people, the commonwealth existed, incredulous and mirthful. Æschylus was banished, Socrates was put to death, but sacerdotal rule could not be established, and fell under the popular scorn.

The latest results of modern criticism are as follows:

First, Greece has received nothing, or almost nothing, from a *foreign priesthood*. What she believed to be Phœnician, Egyptian, is profoundly Grecian. In her ages of strength and genius she delighted only in herself, and scorned all triviality. This preserved her youth, the perfect harmony which produced her fertility. When, at length, the gloomy gods of Asia stealthily crept into her bosom, she had accomplished her work, and was beginning her decadence.

*Second, at no period has Greece had a real and organized sacerdotal order.** The vain supposition that she had such a caste *before her historical period* is without proof or probability. She has not been guided. It is for this reason that she has marched forward erect, and with wonderful equilibrium.

One of the most serious effects of priestcraft is to absorb everything, and crystallize it into some form, to engross

* The book of Benj. Constant, frequently superficial, is strong on this point, and deserves great attention. Its principal assertions are confirmed in the learned work in which Mr. Alfred Maury has compiled all the recent labors of Germany, arranging them in an excellent and new order, which throws great light on them. *History of the Greek Religions*, 3 vols. (1857.)

all life in one organ, one sense only. This is of infinite advantage to the part. It gives you, for example, a monstrous hand, while the arm is dry, the body consumptive. This is what appeared so forcibly in Egypt, and still more in Europe, during the middle ages, which had some exquisite sense, or some gigantic organ, while the whole was feeble, poor, sterile. In Greece, left to her free genius, all the faculties of man—body and soul, instinct and work, poetry, criticism, and philosophy— everything grew up and flourished together.

Third, Greece, *mother of fables*, as she is very pleasantly called, had two gifts at once—to make fables and to give but little credit to them. Imaginative without, internally reflective, she was but slightly the dupe of her own imagination. No people exaggerated less. She could incessantly invent and relate marvels. Such things did not disturb her mind. The miracle had but little hold on her. A heaven, made and remade by the poets and the strolling singers, her only theologians, did not inspire her with sufficient confidence to induce her to fold her arms over her breast, and wait for what was to come to her from on high. She started from the idea that man is the brother of the gods, born, as they were, of the Titans. Work, art, and struggle, eternal gymnastics of soul and body, constitute the true life of man, which, in spite of the very gods, and even despite their jealousy, make him a hero and almost a god.

How, then, could this Olympus, made by accident, as it seems, improvised by the blind, the singers of cross-roads, of temples or of banquets, the Phemius, the Demodocus ; how could it acquire any unity ? For different audiences the muse was different. The fables, which were sung about the temples at sacred solemnities, became warlike, and possibly playful, in the palaces of the kings, as are some of the songs of the *Odyssey*. Will not utter confusion result from all this ?

By no means. Everything becomes gradually arranged.

These singers are, at the bottom, of the same soul as the people, and their life, manners, surroundings, differ but little from theirs. Their art is the same, their process the same. They speak to the same person, to Nature, whose voice answers.

We see to-day, by the true etymologies, that these mythological creations in Greece, as in the India of the *Vedas*, are at first simply elementary forces, Earth, Water, Air, Fire. In the Grecian world, which alone personifies and defines objects, the evocation of the poet brings forth everywhere spirits, lively and active, like that of the poet himself. It calls into action a number of beings, which were believed to be things. The oaks were compelled to open themselves, to set free the nymphs, which they had long enclosed. And even the stone, erected on the road-side, suggested the enigma of the Sphinx.

Innumerable voices, but not discordant. The great concert is divided in parties, in groups, in harmonious scales. We have seen that of the earth. From Ceres, the venerated, formidable, chaste goddess, the people knew how to draw out an immense world of amiable gods. Friend of heat, parent of Fire (or Estia), she aspired to descend into the Earth. To spare her this subterranean voyage, they created for her a daughter, another Ceres. To spare her the severe labor of tillage, an inferior genius was born, a rustic, male Ceres, the *grinding* Triptolemus. To defend her kingdom, the field, the harvest, the boundaries, laws and penalties were necessary. But would the good Ceres punish? This charge was given to Themis, the cold Ceres of the law, whose sword was Theseus, legislator of Athens, the valiant Ionian Hercules.

The *gamut of Fire* is no less rich—beginning with the deformed Cabiri, proceeding to the Cyclops, thence to the workman Vulcan, and culminating in Prometheus the artist—while from night (Latona) radiated the splendors of Phœbus, and from the charged, gloomy brow of Jupiter springs forth the ether, the sublime brightness of Minerva, of wisdom.

But all these gods astoundingly differ, if I dare say it, in stability. A book could be written on their different tempers: the Physiology of Olympus. Let us admit that many will remain in the fog or even something less, being merely adjectives, like the synonymes of Agni, from which India made the names of God. Others, a little more firm, as Max Müller well says, are already *coagulated*, of some consistence, but still remain transparent, diaphanous; we see through them. Their father, the Ionic genius, does not allow them even occasionally to act as *persons*, except on the condition that they remain *elements*, which, as such, are always subject to metamorphosis. In this condition he can always dispose of them, vary them, enrich them with new adventures, marry them, and draw heroes from them.

This mythological manipulation is very easy to follow in the *gamut of the gods of the Air*, who were naturally fluctuating, and furnished easy facilities for transformations.

The superior Air, the heaven, the father Zeus, Jupiter, has necessarily the highest place, the throne of nature. He causes rain, he produces everything. Successor of the old gods, of the Titans, he engenders the family of the Hellenic gods. He rules, he has the thunder, and terrifies the world. He rolls it with great noise, performing the functions, which Indra discharges in the *Vedas*. As to the winds, he delegates his power to Æolus, a little Jupiter, who keeps them confined in leathern bags in obscure caverns.

If Jupiter is the great fertilizer below, it is because he is also a celestial fecundity above. In Asia he would have been a double-sexed god. In Greece they divide him in two, and give him a consort, who is but the Air, the female Air, Here or Juno. Air, troubled, agitated, angry. This is not sufficient. In the sublime heights, above the clouds, in the pure ether, we see quite another thing. Jupiter becomes triple. They create for him a daughter, Pallas-Athenè, who is produced out of him alone, and not of his Juno. Afterward came the Dorians, who compelled him to share his rule of the storm with the young god Apollo, who was furnished with arrows, like the Indra of the *Vedas*, to pierce the dragon of the clouds. Thus from Zeus, or the Father Heaven, is made a whole series of gods, not fortuitous nor in disorder, but well-linked, progressive, harmonious, a beautiful gamut of poetry. Zeus, doubled, tripled, quadrupled, nevertheless maintains his supreme rank, and his noble representativeness.* He is the father of all the young Olympians, and, as toward the end all will recognize themselves in him, will see that they are nothing but him alone, his superiority prepares for philosophers their future conception, the unity of God.

Greece, in a peculiar instinct of moral progress, does not allow her gods to rest and fall asleep. She fashions them incessantly, from legend to legend, humanizes them, educates them. We can follow her process from age to age. The *gods-natural* in vain personify themselves; they grew pale. The *gods-human* started up, the *gods-moral* increased. The gods-judicial, heroic redressers of wrongs, whose triumph closes divine history, throw away their robes at last, show the true hero, the *wise man.* Of Hercules there is left the Stoical, that scholastic philosophers very appropriately call the *second Hercules.* It is the living stone, the firm rock of Right, on which Rome soon enthroned her jurisprudence.

---

* The Grecians always speak grandiloquently of him, with an emphatic grandeur, which is not by any means expressive of real respect. He is a god of pomp and decoration. They pay him with ceremonies. As to the seriousness, the reality, he is by no means on a plane with many gods, who appear to be inferior. He is easily deceived. This King of Olympus, jocosely caught by his wife, who lulled him to sleep on the Ida (*Iliad*), duped by Prometheus (Hesiod), who, for his part of the victim, made him take the skin and the bones, recalls something of the Charlemagne of the *Four Sons Aymon*, who falls asleep on the throne and is scoffed at in his sleep.

This is the supreme and distant aim toward which we walk blindly, but very surely : *it is necessary to make the Hero.*

To say that the gods come down and incarnate themselves, as they do in India, would avail but to lull human activity to sleep.   The important thing is to establish a succession of gradations, a ladder on which we can ascend and descend, and on which the man of strength and labor, having developed that which God put in him, would mount as on wings, and himself become divine.   Neither the language nor the Greek spirit allowed the poets to express divine births except by divine loves.   The more ethereal among the gods, the aërial Jupiter, had the part of a great lover.   The popular minstrels did not spare him.   While they gave him the imposing figure and the dark eyebrows, the threatening beard of the Father of the gods, they launched him into a thousand youthful adventures.   All this playfully, and in a light, loquacious manner.   Not even one impassioned trait.

There was nothing more transparent than this in the language.   There is scarcely any possibility of being mistaken.   The physical meaning is always clear.   The translation only is obscure.   It exaggerates the personality of these elementary beings.   "*Zeus rained in the Force (literally the name of Alcmenè), and begot the Strong (Alcides)*."   *Zeus rained through the storm in the Earth (Semelè),* which, thunderstruck, *conceived* Bacchus, or the ardent wine.   What more clear to those primitive tribes, who led only an agricultural life ?*   These fables of the loves and of the divine generations appeared truly scandalous when Euhemerus, and those like him explained

---

* In a small book, admirable for strength and good sense, Mr. Louis Minard says very appropriately of this agricultural age, still very near to nature, which had just made these symbols and which saw perfectly through them : "No one took more offence at the thousand marriages of Zeus and Aphrodite than one thinks to-day that the oxygen is debauched because it is united with all bodies."   L. MINARD's *Morals before Philosophers* (1860), p. 104.

them in the pretended history of the kings of time past, when Ovid and other story tellers enlivened them with witticisms of libertine freedom, when at last the enfeebled minds of the decadence, a Plutarch for example, entirely disregarded the primitive signification. In vain the Stoics, by a just interpretation, which philology now confirms, showed in these fables the mixture of the physical elements. The Christians carefully avoided the consideration of their merits; they simply laid hold of these legends to attack and denounce them.

In the times of Byzantium, when all elevated meaning became dull, no one was keen enough to perceive the double character of these antique fables, the clare-obscure in which they floated between the dogma and the tale. Dully and authoritatively they interrogate Greece: "Dost thou believe? Dost thou not believe?" It seems to us that they are like a schoolmaster scolding a child of genius who has, as we have at that age, the gift of imagining and half believing all he fancies. These old blockheads do not know that man begins thus. They overlook the fact that between belief and unbelief there are infinite gradations, innumerable intermediates.

With this inventive people, of a fluent and thoughtless speech, so long as the gods had their true lives, their ready mythological vegetation, the gods were too changeable to weigh heavily on their minds. In the places where tradition located their divine adventures, in the vicinity of an oracle or a temple, there was doubtless more credulity. The popular minstrels eloquently related the marvels of the temple to the enraptured traveller, who learned them in verses in order the better to remember them, but not without adding some poetical variations. These tales were constantly transmitted with changes, each new minstrel feeling the same right over the muse and the inspiration.

I have said elsewhere how much of liberty the interior soul of India preserved against her dogmas, notwithstanding the appearances of a very strong sacerdotal yoke. But
5*

how much more this liberty existed in Greece, which had no such yoke, and which made and remade herself incessantly. She had no need whatever of severe criticism nor of harsh irony in order to defend the moral significance of the light eccentricities of the religious fable. It was enough for her to have that which best preserves from divine tyrants, the smile.

Greece had not that severe attitude, that solemnity, which are the characteristic of some nations. But the genius of motion, the inventive power, which was indefatigable in her, a certain light vivacity, always wafted her above vulgar and low things. A very pure air, not in the least enervating; the sublime ether of a blue sky, freely circulates, and keeps life buoyant. That which domineers there is not properly the scruple of conscience, the fear of sin, the intention of flying from this or that. Her own nature, a sap severely fresh for action, art or combat, the innate flame of Pallas, keeps her in the heroic state.

This is wonderfully expressed in her beautiful traditions. When Agamemnon set out for a long absence to conduct the war against Troy, whom does he place near Clytemnestra? Whom do we see sitting near her at meals, and in the hours of relaxation? A priest? No. A singer, whose noble measures will sustain her heart. Respectful guardian, this minister of the chaste muses will battle against the reveries, the effeminate languors in the woman. He will talk to her of the sublime history of the past— Antigone sacrificing her love and life to sisterly affection; Alcestes dying for her husband; Orpheus following his Eurydice down to the under world. As long as he sings, the spouse is entirely absorbed in the remembrance of the absent Agamemnon, so that the perfidious Ægystus could not succeed in leading her astray, till he had forcibly carried off the lyrist. He expelled him to a desert island. The queen, abandoned by the muses, was also abandoned by virtue.

That which astonishes is, that certain things, in a south-

ern climate, remind us of the cold purity of the north.
The youngest daughter of Nestor bathes Telemachus.
Laertes, father of Ulysses, caused his daughter to be
brought up with his young slave Eumeus. The daughter
of the wise Centaur Cheiron, who yields in nothing to her
father, educates a young god and teaches him all the
mysteries of nature. We think that we are in Scandi-
navia; that we are reading the *Nialsaga* in which the
noble maiden has a warrior for her preceptor.

Greece exhibits the exact opposite of the middle ages.
In the latter, all literature, or nearly all, glorifies adultery;
poems, fables, Christmas carols, everything celebrates
cuckolding. Of the two great Grecian poems, one punishes adultery by the overthrow of Troy ; the other is the
heroic return of the husband, and the triumph of fidelity.
In vain the suitors besiege Penelope. In vain the Calypsos,
the Circes, gave themselves to Ulysses, and desired that
he should, with love, drink immortality. He preferred
his Ithaca, preferred Penelope and dying.

Horrible thing, which makes a father of the church
shudder : " Saturn devoured his children ! What an
example for the family !" Be assured, good man. He
swallows stones instead of children.

In reality the Greek family relation is very strong, and
no less pure. The history of Œdipus and others shows
plainly how much horror the Greek had of such unions as
they regarded suitable only to *barbarians.*

Before the Dorian invasion, those cruel wars, which
transformed the archaic world of Greece, the family was
altogether the holy association, which is seen in the *Vedas*
and in the *Avesta.* It had its normal and legitimate harmony. When Philosophy, the sweet Socratic wisdom of
Xenophon,* logically investigates what is the true *rôle* of

* With great regret I deny myself the pleasure of citing the admirable chapter of Xenophon's *Economy.* We perfectly perceive that if war, public life,
constant danger, separated the Greek from his wife, and tore the family asunder, the ideal of marriage was always the same. The heart was still the heart.

woman, it has nothing to do but simply to come back to what the *Odyssey* describes.

In Homer the mistress of the house has half the government, all the interior cares, even those of hospitality. She sits opposite to her husband, and is his equal at the hearth. It is to her that the supplicant must first apply. The amiable Nausicaa, who received the shipwrecked Ulysses on the shore, recommended him to speak first to her mother. This mother, the wise Arete, appears to all a kind providence, and even to Alcinoüs, her husband, who has long had an easy time of it, and, to use his daughter's words, "drinks like an immortal." Arete supplied his place ; by her prudence and peaceful disposition she settled disputes, prevented litigation, and was the umpire of the people.

The wife was much esteemed by both husband and son. Laertes, says Homer, would have loved his beautiful and wise slave, Eurycleè, very much, but did not, "from fear of the wrath of his wife." This wife, mother of Ulysses, was tenderly loved on this account. There is nothing so artlessly pathetic as the interview of this hero with the spirit of his mother. He tearfully asked her the cause of her death. Was it destiny ? Was it the arrows of Diana, who by disease carries us off from life ? " No, my son, it was not Diana, it was not destiny—it was the remembrance of thee, it was thy goodness which killed me. It was the regret for a son who was so good to me."

It changes less than is supposed. There is nothing more charming than to read in Xenophon the wise household royalty of the young mistress of the house, who not only governs her male and female servants, but also knows how to make them love her, and takes care of them in sickness (chap. vii.). The husband does not hesitate to say to her : "The sweetest charm will be when thou, having become more perfect than myself, wilt make me thy servant. Time does not affect it. Beauty increases by virtue." In order to deceive us in this, and make us believe that woman (even in the Homeric times) was dependent upon her son, the words of Telemachus to Penelope are quoted ; but at this particular moment Telemachus is inspired by a god to speak with such unusual authority. He needed to overawe the suitors with those stern words, etc. Benj. Constant has explained this delicately and very judiciously.

The Invention of the Municipality.

The first work was Olympus, the second was the City.

The latter, wonderful work of Grecian genius, new then, unheard of, without example and without precedence. All the effort of man, heretofore, had made only towns, a bringing together of tribes, aggregating villages, uniting them for their security. Entire nations have collected themselves in the enormous towns of Asia. Those prodigies, Babylon, Nineveh, Thebes with its hundred gates, notwithstanding their splendor, their riches, are nevertheless monstrous. To Greece alone belongs the creation of the City, supreme harmony of Art which is all the more natural for it, a pure, regular beauty never excelled, subsisting by the side of formulas of reasoning and of geometrical figures, which Greece has also traced.

Has the City of the Olympus prepared that of the earth? Yes, Olympus already inclined to the republic. The gods are somewhat free ; they deliberate, they plead, they have their Agora. Pluto, Neptune, in their subordinate kingdoms, were independent. Nevertheless the monarchical element predominates in Jupiter, the Agamemnon of the gods. The Commonwealth beneath is quite different. It bears but a light resemblance to the irregular government of heaven. The republic on high is a childish work compared to the human republic. From this poor ideal there is an immense stride before we arrive at last to the real miracle, Athens ; to the all-powerful cosmos, living organism, the most fertile that ever existed.

The work was neither altogether human, nor of spontaneous calculation. Terrible necessities acted, helped, compelled. Danger redoubled genius. Through the violent crisis which, elsewhere, would have extinguished it, this genius made, and fashioned itself, was its own *Vulcan*, its industrious *Prometheus*, briefly *Pallas-Athené*, Athens.

It is a long history, which I do but indicate.

I have said that all the Greek world, in its beautiful equipoise of fancy and criticism, was born from a smile. On one hand the gracious genius which made the gods of Greece ; on the other hand the light irony, altogether instinctive and scarcely conscious, which however kept the soul wonderfully serene, free from the fear of both gods and destiny.

This smile appears on the marble of Ægina, where people kill each other amidst bursts of laughter. " Is it accidental ? " some one may ask. " Is it the impotency of an awkward art ? " The same expression is noticeable in twenty places in the *Iliad*. The blood flows in swelling waves, but the heroes stop willingly to converse. There is great wrath, no hatred. Achilles explains obligingly to Lycaon, who asks for his life, why he will kill him. He had before made him prisoner, but he had escaped, and he had found him again. " Patroclus," he said, " is dead, and I also, must I not die young ? " Then die, friend ! *

Here is a very primitive characteristic. Among many modern, superadded things, the *Iliad* in general preserves its character of rugged youth. It is not the dawn of Greece, but the morning. The air is keen. A strong vigor is felt throughout. The earth is green and the sky blue. A vernal breeze ruffles the hair of the heroes. They struggle, they die, they kill. They have no hatred. They scarcely weep. This is the lofty serenity of a haughty era which hovers over death and life.

But do they know what death is ? We may question it. It appears brilliant and almost triumphant. To ascend the pyre with the purple and the armor of gold, to vanish in glory, to leave the sun for the delightful light of the Elysian Fields, where we can sport with heroes, is not a great misfortune. Death, either given or received, does not materially change the soul. While Judaism

---

* *Iliad*, xxi., 'Αλλὰ φίλος θάνε χαι σύ.

promises long life to the children of God, Greece says: "They, whom the gods love, die young." She who is youth itself, wishes no other life than youth. She has compassion only on Tithonus, old husband of Aurora, old without remedy, who cannot die.

The Greeks continually quarrelled and came to blows among themselves. But their combats were trifling. With much good sense they respected the seasons of labor and of sowing. They appeared in their struggles, in their surprises, in their ambushes, to aim, above everything else, to make light of the enemy, and at the glory of dexterity. Their most excellent achievement was to carry off their enemy and ransom him. But they did not care to make slaves; they did not know what to do with them. Their great simplicity of life, their husbandry so little complicated, often confined to olive trees and a little pasture, scarcely needed slaves. The household slave, employed in the personal cares, appeared intolerable. It would have been a punishment to them to have forever in their homes the enemy, a gloomy and silent figure, a permanent malediction. They made their own children serve them.

The Locrians and the Phocians never had slaves. If a Greek on the shores chanced to buy a child from pirates, it became one of the family. Eumæus, in the *Odyssey*, sold to the king Laertes, is brought up by him with his daughter. He is like a brother to Ulysses. He waits for his return for twenty years; he weeps for him, and cannot be consoled for his absence.

A most singular thing—which, however, is established by the most positive testimony, that is, by the language itself, and by a proverbial phrase—war created friendships. The prisoner—led to the home of his conqueror, admitted at his hearth, eating and drinking with him, his wife, and children—was one of the household. He became what was called his *Doryxenos*, the guest whom he had made with his spear. Having paid his ransom and returned to his own home, he entertained his former host, lodged and fed him without exciting distrust, when his conqueror visited the market towns or the national festivals of his country.

"The slave is an ugly man," says Aristotle. Slavery is the ugliest of things. Such a monstrosity was for a long time unknown in Greece, the country of beauty. It was in perfect contrast with the fundamental principle of such society, with its manners and its beliefs. How, in fact, could slavery, "which is a form of death," as the juris-prudents well say, agree with a religion of life, which sees in all force a divine life? This joyous Hellenic religion, which even in things inert feels a soul and a god, has justly for its foundation the liberty of all beings.* Slavery, which *kills the soul* while the body yet lives, is the opposite of such a dogma, its contrary and its negation. Greece, by her mythology, emancipated the elements and enfranchised even the stones. Was this to change man into a stone? She humanized the animal. Jupiter, in Homer, has compassion on the horses of Achilles, and consoles them. Solon made a law, based on the ancient religious prohibition, which forbade the killing of the ox that plough-ed the earth. Athens erected a monument to the faithful dog that died with his master. The Athenian slave was almost a freeman, "and did not yield the walk to him," says Xenophon. The comical writers bear witness to this, that the slave often mocked the freeman.

Greece would have remained, perhaps, in a certain state of effeminacy if the Dorian invasions had not introduced a decided contradiction. Sparta did not inflict even misery on the vanquished, as the Thessalonians did the Pen-estes. She did not apportion them by lottery to each indi-vidual, like the *Clerotes* of Crete. She kept them *en masse,*

---

* "Slavery is the negation of polytheism, which has for its basis the Auto-nomy of all beings." New, just, and profound observation of L. Ménard, *Polytheism of Greece,* p. 205.

one body of people, but constantly degraded.* A thing horribly dangerous, which held the conquerors themselves in a strange condition of effort and tension, of war in time of peace, under the necessity of watching under arms, attentive to everything, and thus becoming terrible and almost inhuman.

Laconia was a great manufactory, a people of industrious serfs who sold cloth, shoes, and furniture to all Greece. It was a great farm of agricultural serfs, who were contemptuously called Helotes or Heilotes, from the name of a wretched little town which was destroyed. They paid light taxes, so that, though workmen and laborers, they were quite easy, and throve under the outrage and ridicule of the others, who, through a special education, remained a distinct race. The Helote did as he pleased: he appeared almost like a freeman—free under the suspended sword—free—less the soul. The hardest thing for these unfortunates was that they were so much despised that the Spartans did not fear even to arm them. Each Spartan at Platea brought with him five Helotes. Even the children treated them disdainfully. Every year, at vacation, they hunted them, watched them, and outraged or killed those whom they met isolated.

Sparta, in this, as in all things, warred against nature. Her Lycurgus was the great danger. Her famous institutions, so little understood by the Greeks, show, save a little elegance, only the manners of the savage heroes of North America, the morals of so many other barbarians. From a distance this atrocious heroism of Sparta deceives. She appears a sublime monster.

What shocks us the most is, that with a life so strained and of rude appearance, she had neverthelss a heavy

* Pliny says: "The Lacedæmonians invented slavery." He means to say a servitude, till then unheard of among Greeks. This word, besides, was taken from the ancient Greek historian, Theopompus, whose words Atheneus quotes, adding: "The gods punished the Chians, who first imitated this example of buying men to make them servants, when others served themselves."

8

Macchiavellianism, like an art of terror and of fatal torpor to weaken the Grecian cities. This art, very simple at the bottom, consisted in supporting in each city the aristocratic party. The *best* (*Aristoi*), the *honest people*, proud of the name of friends of Sparta, gradually stifled the free local spirit. This contest existed more or less secretly in each town. The people, driven to the wall, elected a *tyrant*, against whom the wealthy invoked the favor and the assistance of Lacedæmon, that magnanimously interfered and *established liberty*. This is how she gained one place after another. Scarcely possessing two-fifths of Peloponnesus, she controlled it, and by degrees the whole Hellenic world.

Now that Greece has accomplished her destiny, we can judge of all this much better than she could herself. The title of Sparta, that which was admired in her, was that she was able to keep free from the arts. She expended all her art to have no art. She declared that she knew how to fight, not to speak. She scarcely condescended to let drop a few rare oracles. She everywhere gave the ascendency to inefficient, idle men—to the dumb and indolent party, made up of the ancient families, and of the rich. She crushed the active crowd, the true Grecian people, clamorous, unsteady, restless, if you will, unbearable, but prodigiously inventive and productive.

Let us sum up. The contest was between war and art.

Two things go to make us believe that the art, the Greek genius, would be fatally stifled. On one hand the disheartening, the fatigue of the public spirit, when rolled from crisis to crisis, between the factions, without being able to advance. On the other hand, the terror of those new forms of war, of those unheard of servitudes, the destiny of Messena and of Hela, the absorption of so many other towns.

This was a heavy blow to the gods. The *Moria*, the hard destiny which divides men, as, after the pillage of a town, people share the captives, was the great deity. Under other names, the Parcæ and Nemesis were indignant at the happiness of men. They appeared to have spread a heaven of brass—the hard snare in which the most just, wise, and skilful are caught. Any moment man may be ruined. The free and happy citizen may to-morrow, with all his possessions, women and children, bound under the spear, be exposed in the markets of Sicily or of Asia. A terrible belief prevailed, that the gods, far from being a providence to man, were his *jealous* enemies, and watched to surprise and crush him.* Hence an unexpected thing, not quite natural to Greece, very strange, melancholy. It is rare, exceptional. Nevertheless it may be seen in Theognis, and in Hesiod. They have but little hope. They fear much. Their wisdom is timid. Even in housekeeping and domestic economy, Hesiod followed the counsel of extreme caution.

There is much earnestness in the *Odyssey*. Centuries separate it from the young smile of the *Iliad*. Through the trials of Ulysses, his dangers, his wrecks, the unjust hatred of Neptune, we always see the noble and helpful Minerva hovering near, ready to assist the shipwrecked. Minerva has disappeared in Hesiod, who expressly says that the gods are jealous of man, intent on undervaluing him, on punishing him for the least advantage he acquires, on re-covering from him all that through labor, through art, he has been able to conquer.

In this poet, honest, of medium capacity, who aims in all things to be moderate, we are surprised, almost afraid, to find related the terrible legend of the great trial against the gods, *the legend of Prometheus*.

The savior Prometheus was the municipality. The more man is abandoned by Jupiter, the more he should be to himself a vigorous providence. His Caucasus, not

---

* See all the reunited texts in *Nægelsbach*, and the important *Theses* of Mr. Tournier, *Nemesis and the Jealousy of the Gods*. (1863.)

of servitude, but of free energy, was the Acropolis of
Athens, where all the world on the sea-coast, and the
Ionian race, and the old tribes of Acheia, gradually
rallied.

Athens, more threatened than any other city, having the enemy before her very port, on an island, made
wisdom apparent, smiling, but strong and terrible when
necessary, harmonizing all genius, peace, war—liberty
and law; weaving, like Pallas, all the arts of peace, while
the heroic flash darted from her powerful glance. The
city, leading the city, was her law to herself. All doing
everything; each in turn magistrate, judge, soldier, pontiff, and mariner, for they manned their own galleys.
"Then, was there no special forces?" Do not believe
this. The soldiers were Æschylus, Socrates, Xenophon,
Thucydides, and I know not how many geniuses.

"But," says Rousseau, "this was painful; the slavery
of some made the liberty of others." Of Greece, Rousseau
had read scarcely anything more that Plutarch, the Walter
Scott of antiquity. He had no idea of the vigor of Athens,
of her burning intensity of life. He imagined that the
masters did nothing, but lived like our creoles. It is quite
the contrary. At Athens, the citizen reserved for himself
what required strength—the heavy armor, the violent
exercises; and what is more astonishing, as we learn
from Thucydides, the very rough trade of oarsman! The
Athenian rarely decided, and only in extreme cases, to
entrust to slaves the vessels of the Republic and the dangerous honor of rowing against the enemy.

This was the safety of Greece. Athens, by her vessels,
striking everywhere unexpectedly, tired out the heavy
Dorians. Pallas-Athené, from the summit of the Acropolis,
watched the fury of Mars, and, as in the *Iliad*, knew
well how to paralyze it. Athens had some allies very near
Sparta—Arcadians, Achaians, the small town of Argolides,
which formed, under Athens, a league, an amphictionary,
on a neighboring island. Here was erected an altar to

Neptune for the Greeks of the islands, of whom Athens gradually became the chief, for the common safety.

This saved Sparta herself. What would she have done, flooded by Asia, without Themistocles and Salamis?

Education.—The Child.—Hermes.

The human genius of Greece, and her charming facility, the magnanimity of Athens, shone forth especially in two things—the favor with which she welcomed the Dorian gods, and her admiring friendliness towards her enemy, Sparta.

Athens invented ingenious fables in honor of those divinities—rude at first and half barbarous—the red Phœbus, with his deadly bow, and Hercules, the dull hero of the club. Minerva herself, who received Hercules at his birth, saved him from Juno. Later she watched and defended the Heraclides who had taken refuge at the hearth of Athens. Theseus, the friend of Hercules, was protected by Apollo. The god of the day illuminated for Theseus the gloomy windings of the labyrinth of Crete, and saved the children whom the Minotaur would have devoured. Those children went yearly to thank him at Delos.

In return, the Dorians, a little humanized, adopted the ancient religions, and the cherished gods of Athens. Sparta, in spite of her savage pride, adopted the Ceres of Attica. Hercules caused himself to be initiated at Eleusis by the goddess, and carried her mysteries to Sparta, but not her peaceful spirit.

The blind prejudice of Tacitus against Germany, the French Anglo-mania of the last century, appears to meet in the strange infatuation of the great Utopians of Athens for rude Sparta. When they speak of her they are like children. The austere outside deceives them. Those silent Spartans, with great beards, wrapped in their miserable cloaks, coarsely nourished on black soup, keeping for themselves poverty, and leaving riches to the serfs, appear to them wayward philosophers. They set them up as models. Plato, in his long witticism which he calls the *Republic*, copies and exaggerates even their absurdity. Xenophon borrows from them what he can for the romantic education which he ascribes to his Cyrus. The great Aristophanes praises Sparta and scoffs at Athens. Aristotle, so earnest at moments, imitates them, and, in so doing, he is no wiser than the others.

It is true that when Aristotle reached the point of settling the high formula, decisive and true, of the commonwealth, he was decidedly anti-Spartan. He says that the commune, even in its unity, must not be less *multiple*, not composed of men of one kind, as in Sparta, but of "*individuals specifically differing*," as at Athens.* Differences which allowed the play of the various forces, the exchange of mutual services and benefits, the happy reciprocal action of all over all. Thus the State is for itself and for the individual the most powerful education.

At the centre of motion we do not see the motion, we scarcely feel more than the fatigue. Those thinkers, in order to weave ingeniously the subtle thread of their long deductions, required the calm and the silence, which the agitated life of Athens scarcely afforded. They envied, as a sojourn of peace, the apparent harmony of Sparta, a contracted and terrible life, fixed in a deadly effort, in which their genius would have been paralyzed and made useless.

In the false municipality, strictly one and monotonous, in which all would bear resemblance to each, the citizen, annihilated as a man, would live only for the State. The hero, who is the rich, free expansion of human nature, would appear there a monster, if perchance he could be produced.

At Sparta every one was a citizen. Not one was a hero in the full sense of that term.

---

* ARISTOTLE: *Politics*, vol. ii., p. 90. M. B. Saint-Hilaire's edition.

Divine genius of Athens! Her greatest citizens were heroes.

This beautiful peculiarity is seen in other places besides Athens. In a less degree it is found in other towns. It is the glory of the Greek world, and it constitutes its joy.

Strong through the Agora, the laws, the civil activity, the soul felt itself great and elevated, in a harmony even superior to the State : *the Greek life.* Through Homer, the games and the festivals, through the initiative of the divine educators (Hermes, Apollo, Hercules), the soul soared higher than the atmosphere of the local country, in the ether of liberty.

Hence it came about that Greece, except in rare moments of trouble, had this beautiful attribute of human energy—which the East, and still more so the mournful middle ages, did not possess—the characteristic of the strong : *joy.*

She had wings on her heels; nimble, sure of herself; through combats and unheard of labors, she was evidently gay, and smiled with immortality.

Nothing endures. The State, this work of sublime art, will pass away. The gods will also pass away. Make man eternal.

Man is the principal of all. Before the social organization, he was. After it, he will be. A day will come when nothing will be found of Sparta but briars ; of Athens but a few broken marbles. The Grecian soul, the light of Apollo, and the solidity of Hercules, will endure.

This soul feels and knows that it is divine ; it was blessed at its birth, rocked by nymphs, and favored with goddesses. The child, on parting its lips, found the milk mingled with honey which a divine bee had deposited. He was born pure. Pure the maternal bosom.* It is said

---

* The Greek woman, who can exercise the functions of the priesthood, is not the unfaithful Eve, credulous to the serpent, and fatal to her children, to whom she transmits the sin in the blood, and so ruins them all, except the

and repeated that Greece despised woman. It does not so appear to me. She was associated with the sacerdotal office. She was a Sibyl at Delphi, priestess at the great Mysteries, and pontiff in *Iphigenia.*

This alone changed everything. The mother was pure ; nature was good. Consequently education was possible, a natural education, which for the infant was liberty itself. The infant was started, the career was opened to him, he was emboldened, he was launched. " Run. . . . Go in the light. The gods call thee and smile on thee."

The East had no other education than its sacred disciplines. The West had for its education the crushing of the memory. It carried the anterior, heavy worlds, which do not accord.

Greece had an education. An education living, active, free, and not of routine. Education for herself, original, springing from her genius, and adapted to her. Education, in my opinion, of infinite value, because it was light, happy, and which, being life itself, was carried unconsciously, and without being burdensome. The robust person knew nothing of it. He marched with high head, he went on serenely.

The insurmountable obstacle to the Oriental, priestly education, was the miracle. Miracle and education are deadly enemies. If a ready-made god, a living miracle, can come from heaven, the art of making him is useless, even rash and impious. What would such an education be but a daring attempt to create by human means that which only prayer could obtain from on high ? The idea, that God may any day descend and untie all the knots of earth, stupefies the Hindoo soul, whose activity becomes

extremely small and imperceptible number of the chosen. The fable of Pandora has not at all the same bearing. Pandora does not corrupt generations. The child is not impure before its birth, nor doomed beforehand. Education will not be, like that of the middle ages, *Punishment*, a discipline of severity, of whips, of tears, a preliminary hell.

lost in fictions, and getting more and more childish, wears itself out in the doting Christmas carols of the *child* Chrishna. The infant-god extinguishes the infant-man.

On the contrary, Greece, not quite credulous of miracles, does not trust the gods; in her imagination she preserves her good sense. If she allows Jupiter to descend and create Hercules, it is on the condition that the hero will make himself still more a hero. Far from helping him, Jupiter is his obstacle—harsh, unjust toward him, submitting him to the tyrant Eurystheus.

From the archaic periods Greece occupied herself with the child. But in her male ideal, she feared the tenderness of the mother. For teacher and preceptor, Greece gave a hero to the hero. Achilles had for teacher Cheiron and Phœnix; Apollo and Hercules are the pupils of Linus. These gods themselves, together with Hermes, are the teachers and the educators of Greece. They represent the three periods—the child, the adolescent, and the man. Happy outline, harmonious and gentle, which leaves full scope to natures so diverse. The young soul, with a free step, following the indicated path, from Hermes to Apollo, from Apollo to Hercules, will attain through Minerva the summit of wisdom.

Greece had had Hermes, the god of the ancient races, for preceptor, educator. It was by a turn of dexterity and genius that she, transforming the new gods, reconciled them with Hermes, and confided the young men to their care. Hermes guarded the infant.*

Hermes abandoned his solemnity, and was no longer dreaded as he had been in Arcadia. He was the amiable god of the public schools, of social intercourse, and of instruction. He made himself exceedingly young, and became as a boy of sixteen or eighteen years of age,

---

* In regard to Greek education, besides the high authorities of Plato, Xenophon, Aristotle (*Politics*), there are numerous texts collated in CRAMER'S *History of Education,* and especially in the *Manual* of F. HERMAN, vol. iii., 2d Pt., p. 161. (Heid., 1852.)

nimble-footed, and winged. He was a delicate messenger, but not of the effeminate elegance of Bathyllus, except his beautiful hands. His hat and wand were winged; and on the death of any person he flew with speed to the under world to mitigate the severity of their reception by Pluto. Yet he was always on the highway to direct travellers, and was ever to be found at the door of the Gymnasium. The youth, who had just left his mother and nurse, was intimidated on his arrival at the Gymnasium. Poor little one. It is the most momentous step of life. Yes, the *Fall* of man is to leave woman, and for the first time to approach a stranger. The charming young deity knows just how to reassure him. He is motion, diversion, language, and grace in the highest degree. The child is perfectly captivated with him, and entirely forgets the dull fireside, the fond mother, and the tender nurse. He knows nothing but the Gymnasium ; he dreams of it and of Hermes. It is his mother and his divinity.

This god asked him precisely what his age demanded, what he loved, and would like to do. What? Simply two things : gymnastics and music—*harmony and action.*

Liberty and amusement, exercise and the sun—such is life. He browns and blooms. He soon obtains that slender plumpness which is indicative of agility, and which attracts the gaze of the gods themselves. It was delightful to heaven and earth. It was a holy work to exhibit beauty to the sky. In thanksgiving for her victory of Marathon, Athens ordered Sophocles, but fifteen years of age, the most beautiful of the Grecians, to lead a choir of boys, and to dance in the presence of the gods.

The finest thing at this age is the race. True moment of masculine beauty ! Females of this age are awkward, and, I had almost said, sluggish. While the boy, already a conqueror, is at the goal and laughing, the girl is still hesitating and getting ready.

Happy child ! Hermes desires to do still more for him, and calls Castor to his aid. What prize will be given to this victor ? Can you conceive ? A tripod of gold ? To him ? What would he do with it ? He blushes, he trembles, he is agitated in anticipation of what he is to receive. Never again will his heart beat so quickly ; not even on the day of his wedding, when the veiled maiden comes to him. A marvellous being that Neptune drew from the foam of the sea with a stroke of his trident, an animated tempest, but manageable, terrible and mild, ardent, darting fire from the nostrils and lightning from the feet . . . behold that which is to be given to him. He does not believe his own eyes. . . . When he is mounted on horseback, he and the horse move with the same soul. The heroic horse will go against the sword, although on the whole he is wise. In his most animated movements he exhibits moderation and judgment. He can follow with the young girls in the pageantry of the festival of the *Panathenæa.* Have no fear for the girl and the boy. The animal knows that the child he carries, although unsteady, is his friend. In the head of this most spirited of animals there is nevertheless an emanation of the moderation, and of the wisdom of Athens.*

At this time it is well to be seated. It is noon. The cavalier makes his repast on clear water and a few olives, and with them lunches on the *Iliad.* Each person remembers a portion of the epic, perhaps a canto of a thousand verses.†
Each person has his favorite canto, his favorite hero.

---

* See Xenophon, and a charming, exquisite book by Victor Cherbuliez, *On the Horse* (Geneva, 1860), in which he explains, in an admirable manner, how the horse participated in the benignant education of the Athenians (p. 127). In the harsh middle ages there was no horsemanship (p. 128). The horse was treated like man. It was not trained, but used only as a drudge.

† This is the ordinary retentive power of moderate memories. It is so in Servia to-day. This extraordinary poem, the *Iliad*, was written out as soon as commercial relations were established with Egypt, when papyrus could be obtained ; between 600 and 500 years B.C. There never was so *instructive* a poetry for the training of the energy of a people as that of Greece. The glory of it belongs exclusively to man. Olympus is so insignificant in it, that, when Achilles withdrew from the combat, Jupiter, to

The fiery esteem Ajax; the gentle, Hector; the affectionate, the friendship of Achilles and Patroclus.   From
among these diversified characters they choose, they compare, they plead in behalf of this one or that one.   Such
is the true Grecian spirit.   Some begin to speak.   Hermes
smiles.   Behold those orators.   The Gymnasium is an
agora.

Thus, very early, the language, in those young mouths,
is formed and made pliant.   True sons of Ulysses, they
are born sagacious and inquisitive, acute of hearing,
careful of good speaking, calculating.   In their rivalries,
and even in their rage, they aim to speak well, as though
they were already thinking that eloquence is the queen of
commonwealths, the mighty arbiter of combats more
serious, to be decided to-morrow.

This finest of human languages, compared with which
all other languages are barbarous, is naturally so well
made that he who uses it correctly, and follows it strictly,
will, by it alone, attain his highest aims.   Without speaking of its literary grace and melody, of its variety on all
the chords of the lyre, notice these essential points : its

counter-balance this hero, sent all the gods thither in one body.   It never
refers to the most ancient of Grecian antiquity.   Æschylus is so much more
pervaded with the spirit of the ancients, that he seems to be older than
Homer.   It contains, however, many things that are old and of great value.
Also, many things that are modern, and drawn with an admirable delicacy,
as, for example, the coolness of the beautiful Helen, her indifference, when
she thinks that Paris, or Alexander, who has been her lover for the last ten
years, is about to be killed, and the thoughtlessness which makes her inquisitive, and almost disposes her to return to the bed of Menelaus.   There
are also additions, entirely different in character, very coarse and very lamentable, and evidently inserted for the purpose of making the court of tyrants
laugh, and for the amusement of the Pisistratides.   In the xxi. canto of the
Iliad, the gods pommel each other in a vile manner, and are as grossly
insulted and reviled as in Aristophanes, but not with the same warmth,
spirit, and profound sense.   These blemishes do not prevent the young
and strong *Iliad*, and especially the *Odyssey*, the poem of patience, the
admirable epopee of the isles, from being the most wholesome food for nourishing, refining, and renewing the heart.   They are the inexhaustible sources
of eternal youth.

power in deduction, analysis, and synthesis, and in expos-
ing and facilitating every form of reasoning.

This language was a logic, a guide, as a teacher without
a teacher. In the Gymnasium, this language, refined and
easy, invited to discussion. But, on the other hand, its
remarkable clearness, simplified, elucidated the debates.

A perfect language makes the mind serene, harmonious,
peaceful; dispels numerous prejudices of ignorance which
engender hatred and perpetuate discord. Hence the great
calmness, the charming docility, which we admire in the
youthful interlocutors of Plato and Xenophon. This
beautiful language was their Hermes, the amiable con-
ciliator, and peacemaker.*

Apollo.—Light.—Harmony.

The most glorious day to the Grecian, at the age in
which memory is strongly impressed with great things,
was when he could join the sacred procession, which
was sent to Delphi, and mingle in the crowd. This
crowd was the greatest spectacle in the world. Twelve
peoples at once, from all parts of Greece, even from
hostile towns, marched peacefully, crowned with the
laurel of Apollo; and, singing hymns, ascended the holy
mountain of the god of harmony, of light, and of peace.

Delphi, as we know, was the *omphalos*, the centre of
the world. To assure himself of this, Jupiter one day dis-
patched from the poles two eagles, which met each other
on the summits of Parnassus. All this country of rough
rocks, of precipices, of obscure grottos, inhabited by
spirits unknown to the earth, was, between the human
countries of Thessaly and Boetia—a separate world, a
savage sanctuary, which the gods had reserved for themselves. At the entrance, in the defile of Thermopylæ,
was the dreaded temple of the ancient Demeter and her

---

* See STEINTHALL and BAUDRY's *Science of Language.* (1864.) I shall
return soon and often to this grand subject.

sombre daughter, who guarded the door of Greece. Over the narrow valleys, often black and deep, the rocks that crop out from the great chain in promontories, exhibit in the light, their eyries of eagles, which are towns, glistening fanes, and temples encircled with columns.

The combats of the day and the dawn recall to the traveller or the excursionist that he is in the memorable places in which the glorious day-god, with his silver bow, vanquished the dragon of darkness, Python, whose noxious breath spread night and death. Apollo still sits in the place of his victory, over the rocks which witnessed it, a place of soothsaying and austerity, the aspect of which alone elevates, enlightens, and purifies the mind.

A place less great than grand. In Greece everything is proportioned to the human compass. Parnassus is imposing without being gigantic, and, with its double summit, is lord over the beautiful plane which extends toward the sea. From on high flows down Castalia, a fountain, pure and cold, of transparent water, worthy of supplying such a temple, chaste as the muses, and their god. Phœbus is a celibate god. If he loved Daphné (the laurel), it was in vain. From that time he had but the two loves, of Melody and Light.

Midway of the mountain, above the town of Delphi, the temple is poised in majesty. All around it is the sacred terminus, an enclosure filled with monuments, which all the Grecian peoples, and foreigners, in their acknowledging devotion, erected without order. There are a hundred little chapels, or treasuries, in which the Grecian States have placed their gold under the guard of the god. In irregular groups, there shone a whole people of marble, of gold, of silver, of copper, of bronze (twenty different varieties of bronze, and of all tints),* thousands of glorious dead, scat.d, standing. Veritable subjects of the god

---

* QUATREMÈRE : *Olympian Jupiter*, p. 60, etc. In regard to this people of statues, and of Delphi in general, I follow the description of Pausanias.

of light. By day all these statues resemble a volcano of
blazing reflections which the eye cannot bear. At night,
sublime spectres, they dream.

Immortality is felt here, and the glory is palpable. It
would be necessary for a young heart to be totally deprived of the sense of the beautiful not to be affected. The
first feeling is the benign disposition of the deities. The
Grecian gods are on a level with the historical or mythological heroes, without pride, on friendly terms. All have
an expressive air of common relationship. Ulysses chats
with Themistocles, and Miltiades with Hercules. The
blind Homer is royally seated in the presence of standing
gods. Pindar, with the sacred lyre, the triumphal robe,
and pontifical decorations, again sings. Around him are
those whom he has celebrated, the conquerors of Olympia
and Delphi. Greece is grateful to them for the beauty
which they displayed during their lifetime ; she thanks
them for having, by the continuous work of the " human
form divine," in admirable features, realized Hermes,
Apollo, or Hercules, and who else ? Pallas ? Jupiter ?
Statuary perpetuated this, transmitted it in immortal images, to preserve forever the very rapid flashes in which
man for a moment saw the gods.

When the eyes became somewhat accustomed to this
splendor, having considered these divine heads one
after another, exquisitely outlined on the deep azure
of a pure sky, what must have been the impression
of the *Via Sacra*, of the ascent to Delphi ! And what
momentous words must the heart have heard from
those silent mouths ! What delightful and forcible lessons, and what encouragements ! From the victors of
Olympia to their singer, Pindar ; from the great soldier of
Marathon, Æschylus, to Aristides, and Epaminondas ;
from the brave men of Platea to the seven Sages ! Strong
and sublime chain in which the heart grew great. The
heart well understood this lesson : " Draw near and fear
nothing. Consider what we were, whence we originated,

and where we are. Do as we did. Be great in acts and
in will. Be comely, adorn thyself with heroic forms and
generous works which fill the world with joy. Work,
dare, attempt! A wrestler or a lyrist, a singer, an
athlete, or a warrior, begin! From the games to the
combat, mount, oh youth!"

Greece, in her most fervent and most real worship, preserved so much reason, such aversion for the absurd and
incomprehensible, that instead of imparting the terror of
the unknown, she marked the way by which the god was
deified, the progress which placed him so high, and the
various efforts, works, and benefactions through which
he obtained his divine rank. A graduated ascent, not
effeminate, but austere, was open to all. It may be arduous and difficult, but there is no precipice, no leaping, no
pointed rock, which prevents the steady ascent. The
novice, entering the temple, before the imposing image,
standing even in the presence of the deity, by no means
forgot the popular narrations which the people made of
the infancy of the god. Phœbus was born passionate, a
severe god, revengeful. In' the savage Thessaly, where
he appeared, his bow was often bent, and inflicted deserved punishment. The surly shepherd of Admetus, and
rude artisan at Troy, whose wall he built, he had not then
become the god of the Muses. Although originally a
demi-barbarian and a Dorian, the Ionian genius and the
Greek elegance adopted and invested him continually
with divine attributes. The Athenians commemorated him
at Delos. Every year the vessel, which brought back the
rescued tributes of children, took them to their savior,
Phœbus, whom they worshipped with the mystical dances.
They danced before him the labyrinth and the conducting
thread ; entangled and unravelled it. They acted even the
infancy of Apollo, the deliverance of Latona, his much beloved Delos, that rocked him in the midst of the waves.*

---

* HOMER: *Hymn to Apollo.* "The Muses, answering with melodious

Thus the god of the arts is himself a work of art. He is constructed by degrees, from legend after legend. He is on this account all the more dear and sacred. He acquired more and more the human heart, this large and benignant justice, which, seeing all, understands, excuses, acquits, and pardons. The suppliants, the involuntary criminal, victims of fate, even the truly guilty, had recourse to him. Orestes, despairing, appealed to him, when reeking with the blood of his mother, which his father had required him to shed. Closely following, pressing upon him, were

---

voice, sing the gifts imperishable of the gods, and the sufferings of men ; who, with all they have received of the immortals, are unable, nevertheless, to procure counsel and resources by which to keep off death and ward off old age. The fair-haired Graces also dance, and the Hours, Harmonia, Hebe, and Venus-Aphrodite, the daughters of Zeus, each holding the other's hands by the wrist. And with them sport Ares (Mars), and watchful Hermes; and Phœbus-Apollo strikes the harp, taking grand and imposing steps. Both golden-tressed Leto (Latona) and deep-planning Zeus are delighted to perceive the mighty Mind (*Noos*), their dear son, thus sporting among the gods."

M. Michelet is in error in imagining that the dance was for diversion. It was symbolical and imitative ; and Lucian declared it to be "a certain knowledge, an exhibition, a showing of things arcane (*aporreta*) to the mental faculties, and the expressing of things which are occult." The same writer describes the heavenly bodies as moving in like measures : "The dance of the stars in chorus, the concert of the planets in an established order, their united and harmonious movements together or by a single impulse, constitute the exhibition of the dance of the First-Born."

The Amazons instituted the dance of the gods. Indeed they appear to have been the introducers of the worship of Demeter and the other Hippian deities into Greece ; Plato says that Eumolpus, who instituted the Eleusinian Mysteries, was their leader, and Clement instances him as one of the Hyk-sos of Egypt. Their country was called Assyria, and they built Ephesus, where they instituted the worship of Diana; also Smyrna, the birth-place of Adonis, and Paphos, where they worshipped the heavenly Venus. The wife of Cadmus was one of their number. Callimachus states that the queen of the Amazons had daughters, known as the Peleiades, who were the first to institute the circular dance, and the *Pannychis*, or watch-night, or Nyktelian rites. It is evident enough, therefore, despite our author, that the Mysteries and other parts of the Grecian religion, whether Pelasgian or Ionian, were uniform with the Asiatic worship, and doubtless were introduced from Assyria and Phœnicia ; undergoing modifications only to conform it to the prevailing spirit of the people. Human sacrifices were offered in Greece on important occasions, and the rites were equally sanguinary as elsewhere.—ED.

9

the Eumenides.   He heard the hissing of their whips of vipers.   The merciful god descended from his pedestal and conducted the unfortunate to the town, which alone possessed an altar of mercy, the generous Athens, and committed his judgment to Minerva.   The powerful goddess, unexpected miracle, calmed the Eumenides, made those dreadful sisters sit down in quiet repose, who, till then, had wandered hither and thither over the earth, and filled it with terror.

The worship of Apollo originated neither by accident, nor by the vague popular instinct.   In its most ancient forms, it had the character of an institution of order, of humanity, of peace.   At Delos, he was offered only fruits. The Athenians, during his festivals, allowed no capital executions.   The games of Delphi, in their character, bore no resemblance to any other.   They breathed the sweet spirit of the muses.   The festival was inaugurated by a child.   Beautiful child, wise and pure, kept worthy by his father and mother to represent the god.   He was led in procession to the sound of lyres and citheras, into the groves of laurel which were near, where the *young Apollo*, with his virginal hand, cut the boughs of the sacred tree for the ornamentation of the temple.

The contests were but a competition of lyre, of song. Above all was sung the victory of the god of light over the sombre dragon of night.   Women, in the happy freedom of primitive Greece, mingled with the concourse. In the treasury of the temple was exhibited the gracious offering of a young maiden, who, against Pindar and other great poets, pleased the gods and won the prize.

The only gymnastic exercises were originally those of the adolescent youth, whose age and elegance represented the god of Delphi.   Veritable games and not struggles, foreign from the passionate violence of the combats of the athletes, which at a later period united with them.   Still later, and in spite of himself, Apollo accepted the noisy

races of the chariots, their tumult, the frequent bloody
and tragical accidents, which they occasioned.

All these were imported from abroad, as well as the intoxication, the orgies of another worship ; as was also the
flute with seven stops, the instrument of Phrygia, whose
boisterous sound imposed silence to the lyre. The latter,
weak and pure, had this superiority, that it did not drown
the human voice. On the other hand it sustained it, embellished it, and marked for it its rhythm. It was the friend,
the ally of the noble language in which Greece saw the
superior sign of man ; the *articulate*, the *distinct* language.*

The *barbarian* is the *stammerer*. Neither barbarians
nor their gods spoke ; they howled, or blew through this
instrument, which confused the mind and rendered the
soul boisterous. It was at the sound of this flute, complicated, jarring, of lugubrious, tempestuous, and feverish
effect, that men were led to the field of slaughter. The
bloody orgies, which incited to violence, were abhorrent to
the gods of harmony.

As soon as the sacred ground of Delphi was touched,
harmony entered the heart. Even the silence was full of
music. On the plains and on the mountains, in the sacred
woods, everywhere it was felt. In the temple, at the feet
of the god, before his silent lyre, the sweet echoes of a
heavenly concert were heard by every heart. At night,
when the doors had been closed, there were heard outside
the building melodious sounds, as though in those solitary
hours the lyre was quivering vaguely, and vibrating with
heavenly thoughts.

But the great lyre of Apollo was Greece herself, reconciled by him. All the Hellenic peoples came before him
and sacrificed together, mingling together their words and
their souls. The distinctive dialects, the light Ionic, the
grave and strong Dorian, the Attic, approached and

---

* HOMER : *Meropes Anthropoi.*

modified each other, as the worshippers communed
together in the *language of light.** Light removes mis-
understandings, is a powerful means of peace. It reassures
and renders the soul serene. We scarcely hate, we never
kill, the man with whom we can agree, in whom, through
the ideas and the feelings common to all, we have found
our proper heart.

If anything could bring near together the people of the
several States, and blend friends and enemies in one, it
would be the witnessing before the peaceful altar, the children singing together, adorned with the fraternal laurel.
Full of eager delight, the people contemplated this young
world in which there was no hatred, nor even the knowledge of old dissensions. Even they themselves almost
forgot them. They were enraptured with the charming
spectacle of this future Greece, which was making its first
endeavors, which was vying in strength and elegance, in
grace and beauty. This spectacle lorded over everything,
and banished every other thought, except those of admiration, of art, and of fraternal good-will. Some would even
praise the sons of their enemies more than their own
children.

The effect was admirable. Each town sent with its
young combatants, numerous deputations of grave men,
who sustained them, and were umpires of the games.
These deputies (*Amphictyons*) sitting together, constituted
a considerable body, which seemed like Greece herself.
In the controversies of either men or States, they were
often umpires. The weak, the oppressed, voluntarily
applied to them to intervene. Thus in time they became
the supreme judges of Greece. They were considered as
deriving their authority from the god. They sat at his
altar, and spoke as in his name. They were also supported by the dreaded authority of the two goddesses,
Ceres and Proserpina, whom they honored at Thermopylæ.

---

* I give this designation to the Greek language.

He who despised Proserpina died. This fortunate superstition, very powerful at first, restrained and disarmed the
unlike commonwealths that would otherwise have depopulated Greece. The oath of the Amphictyons appears to
have been dictated by the horror inspired by recent
exterminations, the utter extinction of the towns Helos
and Messena. The Amphictyonic oath obligated the
belligerents "never to destroy a Grecian town—and never
to divert its running water." In Greece, dry and cracked,
where water soon disappears, it was regarded as the very
life itself, and was placed, as in Persia, under the protection of the gods.

This was the prototype and exemplar, faint at first, but
potent in its influence of fraternal federation of States, the
great social lyre which, leaving to each chord its distinct
independence and power, united them in friendship, destroyed discordances, and, in the event of unexpected
hostility, was able, by a gentle ascendency, again to unite
them in harmony.

Nor was Apollo satisfied with this. Even on the theatres of the most cruel wars, in the fields still reeking, of
the States of Peloponnesus, he tried to establish peace—
at least the fleeting peace which the festivals and the
games could give. He inspired the Eleans, to whom he
appeared in a dream, to erect an altar to the god of their
enemies, to Hercules, the tutelar god of Sparta. They
obeyed.

By a praiseworthy sacrifice of hatred and ill-will, the
altar of the Eleans, every four years, united Greece at
Olympia, as she was united at Delphi. Conquerors and
vanquished, Grecians of the mountains and Grecians of
the islands, Sparta and Athens went there, to honor their
respective gods. For several days, at least, there was no
war. This appeared so agreeable that they made a god
of *Truce* itself. Amiable deity, who changed the minds,
and often brought with him his daughter, *Peace*, the
charming, the adored.

These general festivals, and the particular festivals which were very nearly general, as the *Panathenæa* of Athens, brought together an immense concourse. The roads were thronged with people, curious travellers, pilgrims, athletes, and strolling minstrels. Here, also, met the gods themselves, who sometimes travelled,* and who were importuned by one friendly town to honor another, or to protect it from some scourge of pestilence or civil war. Great movement, reciprocal hospitality, commingling, exchanges of festivals and of ceremonies, of songs and of fraternity.

Over the men and gods, over these crowds and festivals, over all this movement in which there was no jarring, three lights crossed and made the unity. To the inflamed, dusty splendors of Olympia, the subtle ether of virgin Attica responded. Over all hovered in divine charm, the warm, golden ray of Apollo.

Hercules.

Over this beautiful light of Delphi there still rests a shadow. I would remove it. It follows me. Is it certain that the god of the day has forever vanquished, in the serpent Python, the old powers of night?

In the dark defile of the narrow valleys of Phocis, along the precipices, before the grottos of remarkable echoes, the fantastic figures of Pan always appear to me. Further off, in the country of the Centaurs, those monstrous forms still dare, at morning, at evening, to show themselves in the low meadows. Even at Delphi, in the temple, without respect for the lyre of the god, strange noises are heard, the barbarous timbrel, the Phrygian flute, the dull cries of intoxication and unworthy sobs.

A witness, who cannot be disputed, tells us that when Greece was reassured by her great victory over Asia,

---

* Travels and hospitalities which drew the gods near, mingled them, gradually prepared the great *divine unity*, which Greece attained unaided, and without the need of any assistance from the East. See A. MAURY, ii., 28, *On the Theoxenies*.

another war, restrained hitherto, burst out with violence —
that between the flute and the lyre.*

The first, with great noise, was introduced everywhere,
and with it the *Horned* one of the East, god-goat, god-bull,
and god-woman. This new-comer, Bacchus, had already
glided into the Mysteries of Ceres, as her son, the innocent Iacchus. He grew great by the force of a fable
which begot weeping, the child dead and resuscitated.†
On this account he soon became the lord of the Mysteries,
and even of Demeter herself. An unwholesome vapor
appears to float about. All that nature had of secret
storms, all that which a sick heart had of fever and of
fancy, all that which the light of Apollo and the lance of
Pallas had intimidated, got free and no longer blushed.
Woman, whom the wars kept at the hearth, lonely and a
widow, came forth from her home and followed Bacchus.
The long robes were abandoned; she ran about in the
orgies with hair dishevelled and the bosom naked. Strange
delirium! What? to weep for Bacchus, is this pointed
iron, under the deceitful vine, necessary? Are night and
the desert necessary; those races in the forest; those cries
and those sighs, while a mournful music covers with a
fictitious grief their transports?

---

* ARISTOTLE: *Politics*, vol. i., p. 159. Ed. B. St. Hilaire.

† Mourning was a characteristic of the Asiatic worship. The Egyptians bewailed, with Isis, the murder of her husband and brother, Osiris ; the women of
Syria, Palestine, and Phœnicia wept with Venus-Ashtoreth for the untimely
death of Thammuz-Adonis; the worshippers of the Syrian goddess Atargatis,
or Rhea, lamented for her only-begotten ; and the Phrygians commemorated,
with noise and a tumult of grief, the anguish of Cybele, the *magna mater*, for
Atys; the Samotracians deplored Cadmilus, or Hermes, slain by his brothers.
Repeatedly do we find in the Hebrew writers a reference to this annual
festival of Mourning for the Only Son. "Make the mourning as for the only
son," *Jeremiah* vi. 26. "I will make it as the mourning for the only son,"
Amos viii. 9. "They shall look upon me whom they have pierced, and they
shall mourn for him as one mourneth for the only son ; and shall be in
bitterness as one that is in bitterness for the first-begotten" (*Protogonos*),
Zechariah xii. 10. The only son was the Syrian Bacchus, under whatever
name, slain inopportunely, mourned, and finally, after three days, restored
to life. In this particular the old religions were substantially alike.—ED.

The same witness relates to us that the fury of the flute (*i.e.*, of Bacchus), after the Median wars, invaded Sparta,* whose robust and mannish girls, neglected by the men, avenged themselves in love. They took a leading part in the orgies over the rough Taygetus. Athens was not less degraded by this folly. Everywhere the flute and frenzy. Everywhere the furious *Thyades.* Those of Athens even went in groups to Delphi, under the eyes of Apollo, and of the chaste muses, to carry off the girls of Delphi to take part with them in the frenzied enthusiasm. They ran about hither and thither all night, and did not return with them till morning.†

The surrounding air is no longer the same. The savage virtue of Hippolytus, in which the conquerors in the games sought their sovereign energy, now flagged and softened. Those males are too proud to seek the females. They have an overwhelming contempt for the Bacchantes. Nevertheless, distressing miracle of Bacchus, this noise troubles, enervates, renders languid. It is like the atmosphere before an impending storm, which oppresses. The thought wanders after them in the woods. "Where do these Bacchantes go? What do they wish? I would not follow them, but I desired to know. . . . Is it true that

---

* ARISTOTLE: *Politics*, vol. i., 159. Ed. B. St. Hilaire.
† "Fruitful Athens was aroused
By the chorus of the sleepless Luaios :
And many a group of revellers shouted ;
The assembled multitude, with many-colored robes,
Thronged all the streets ; and Athens everywhere
Was covered with vine-leaves to honor him
Who causes plants to grow and fructify:
Women placed iron on their bosoms,
And bound phalli to their breasts,
Thus celebrating the Mysteries.
Young girls danced in sacred measures,
And crowned their hair, braided upon their temples,
With ivy-blossoms. The Ilissus carried to the city
Water imparting prophetic powers, in honor of Dionysus;
And the revellers dancing on the shores of Cephissus
Shouted aloud the Evian hymn."—Ed.

the fawn, torn with their nails, is bitten with their teeth, that the warm blood in long draughts intoxicates them, swells their bosoms with love for this god-woman, who made them hate man, who made them put Orpheus to death?"

What matters this to you, young man? Rather go with me. Let us sit down at the feet of those heroes of bronze which the rising sun of Delphi emblazons. All the mountains are crowned with strong and pure light. Their summits, finely indented, as of polished steel on the azure, pierce the sky. One of these, calm and strong, which looks from on high, on all its neighbors of Thessaly, triumphs in its glory. It is Mount Œta, the pile of Hercules.

May the heroic legend strive against Bacchus! May the good, the great Hercules strengthen this wavering young man, and keep him firm in the holy party of the Lyre. Hercules, who is generally regarded as coarse, knows nothing but the lyre. If he has occasionally been the rival of Apollo, he is all the more his friend. He is the hero of the West, whom the Eastern Bacchus, the furious one, persecutes.*

Would you wish to know that which the noble god of the day needed to sustain him in waging this great war? My son, it was pain, grief, death; it was the funeral pile! Apollo, who is only light, could not descend into the dark kingdom. He had not struggled vigorously against death, against love. He had not undergone the misfortunes, the involuntary crimes, the expiations of Hercules, the flame, which when traversed, places him pure, and a conqueror in heaven.

---

* It is lately, very lately, and only by Diodorus, that we learn of this hatred of Bacchus, who, on the whole, had a stronger grudge against Hercules than had Juno. True and profound revelation, which simple good sense ought to have made us conjecture. It was a dangerous secret which no one would have dared to reveal so long as Bacchus was the master, and had under his command an army of the initiated. A single word dropped by Æschylus put him in danger.

But what Apollo most needed was work. He had tried, he even became a mason ; but his hands, too soft, would have been compelled to abandon the lyre, and could not have felt any more its delicate strings. He left to others the labors, the sweat ; the race to the winged feet of Hermes ; the struggle to the arm of Hercules—the despised works in the great struggle against the earth. He left the better part, perhaps, to Hercules, my son ; the hard labor, the great viaticum of life which keeps it serene and strong. The ethereal art, the muse, are these enough ? I doubt it. Are they sufficient to sustain us against the assaults of nature ? No. Believe me, the fatigue, the labor, of all the hours are necessary. I am thankful for this. It has served me, led me, better perhaps than anything else. I shall die rich in works, if not of great results, at least of great purposes. I lay them at the feet of Hercules.

There were a hundred heroes in Greece, but only one whose exploits were LABORS. Strange, astounding fact ! Greece has such strong, good sense, a reason so marvellously adequate, that even against her prejudices—the scorn of labor which she calls servile—her great deified hero is emphatically the WORKMAN.

Consider that it is not a question of elegant, noble, or altogether heroic works, but, of course, that which was vile and unclean. The magnanimous goodness of this hero, however, considered nothing base which was of benefit to mankind. He fought hand to hand with marshes and poisonous hydras. He compelled rivers to aid him ; here dividing them, there uniting them in those stables of Augeas which he flooded, swept, and purified. What could the bow of Apollo have done here ? In order to destroy Python forever something more than arrows were necessary. Perseverance and the humble heroism of Hercules were necessary.

The great deliverer of the Persians, as we have seen, was the blacksmith. Gustasp, their great hero, in making

choice of a trade, selected that of the smith and the anvil.*
But the iron ennobles. The hammer is an arm as well as
an implement. Persia would not have dared to give her
hero so low a place. The Grecian genius is so bold, so
free, and free of itself, that it has not feared to debase its
Hercules, and he becomes greater by his debasement. It
realizes the Persian ideal better even than Persia was able.
A benefactor of the earth, Hercules purifies and embel-
lishes it. He banishes its morbid torpors. He compels
it to work, and creates fruitful fields. He pierces the
mountains of Thessaly, and the stagnant waters are drained
away. Behold a paradise, the valley of Tempé.† Everywhere pure and rapid waters, large and safe roads. He is
the workman of the earth ; the artisan who fashions it for
the service of mankind.

This conception of Hercules astonishes on every side.
It greatly excels both the *Iliad* and the *Odyssey*. Hercules has the fury of Achilles, but greater goodness. When
he has done evil, he repents, and repairs it. His heroic
simplicity removes him far from Ulysses. This perfect
Grecian of the islands, so deceitful, is very far from the
immense heart of Hercules. By land and sea Ulysses
looks for his little country ; Hercules for the great, and
wishes the welfare of all, the establishment of order and
justice over all the earth. Hercules is the great victim,
the living accusation against the order of the world, and
the despotism of the gods. His mother, the virtuous

---

* *Shah Nameh.*

† A similar tradition exists in Cashmere. Humboldt states "that its primeval name was *Casyapamar*, signifying the habitation or Casyapa, a mythological personage by whose agency the valley was drained." Indeed, the par-
allel holds much further. The population of that region, the Candaharians,
seem to reappear in the Centaurs of Thessaly ; both agreeing in custom as
much as in name. They procured their wives by carrying off virgins by
force ; they doted on horses ; their chief bore the title of Charon or Cheiron.
Hercules, who is the hero of so many exploits in and about Thessaly, is apparently a Heri-culyus, a lord, or protector of the people, whose cause he
champions and vindicates.—ED.

Alcmena, faithful as a wife, intended her son to be legiti-mate, but he was, instead, a *bastard.* Conceived the first, he was born a *cadet* to the inferior estate of a younger son, by the injustice of Jupiter. At length he became a *slave*, the slave of his elder brother, the feeble, the dastard Eurystheus. A domestic slave and sold ; he was slave to his strength and to the intoxication of blood. He was the slave of love, because he had nothing else here below.

His enormous strength was his fatality. He was not adjusted to the feebleness of the world. Often, when he intended to touch lightly, he killed. This benefactor of men, magnanimous defender of the oppressed and feeble, lived overwhelmed by involuntary crimes, repentances, and expiations.

He was depicted as small, squat, and very black. He was possessed of the kind heart as well as the strength of the black man. Antar, the Arabian Hercules, is black. In the *Râmayana*, the Indian Hercules, Hanuman, so good, so strong, who carried the mountains, is not even a man.

Thus, everywhere, the popular instinct has taken for its hero the lowest, the most humble, the victim of des-tiny. The consolation of the oppressed crowds is to op-pose the grandeur of the miserable and of the slave to the severity of the gods—Hercules to Jupiter.

Legend of the inferior tribes, touching but sublime and facetious. Hercules is made after their image. He has enormous appetite. He eats an ox. But he is kind-hearted; he allows the people to laugh at him. He likes to laugh himself. When he had taken alive the terrible boar of Erymanthus, which Eurystheus required of him, he bound him, he carried him bristling, the black head showing the white teeth. The King, affrighted by such a gift, fled from his throne, and hid himself in a cask or cellar of brass. One imagines that he is reading the German scene of the bear which, in the *Niebelungen*, Sieg-fried amusingly unloosed.

Hercules, being force itself embodied, the strongest of men, the Dorians adjudged him to themselves, and made him the ancestor of the Kings of Sparta. But he is just the opposite of the Spartan temper. He is the man of mankind, beyond the exclusive egotism of a State so completely wrapped up in itself.

He went among the Athenians, who graciously assured him that at his birth Minerva had received him in her arms. They established him at Marathon. They made him the friend of Theseus. Nevertheless his legend is far from being Athenian. He humiliated Athens in saving Theseus from the domain of Hades. He is appropriately the hero of the country of the Athletes, of the good and the valiant Boetia, very unjustly despised by Athens, the rural country of poets and of heroes, of Hesiod, of Pindar, of Epaminondas. He is a Theban, unless he came from the strong Argos. He grew great around Elis and Olympia, in their rich plains. When young he fought in the dense forest of Arcadia. He was the adopted child of those of whom but little is said ; of inferior tribes which the city eclipsed ; of a Greece less brilliant, but strong and generous, which had less of art, and perhaps more of heart. This obscure, voiceless world survives in Hercules.

Three or four alluvions of ancient races, in some way superposed, exist together in this young god, who appeared very late in mythology. The Pelasgians had not all gone, nor the glorious Achæans, who conquered Troy. The subjugated masses who cultivated Thessaly, who performed the labors under the name of Hercules, were certainly extant, and probably contributed to form the great legend.

Hercules, in his statues, has the traits of the Athletes, the striking disproportion between the chest, enormously large, and the head, very small. The same inequality appears in his moral nature. He partakes qualities in common both with god and the beasts. When the inhuman judgment of Jupiter declared to him that he, the strongest of the strong, must become the slave of the coward, he fell into a terrible frenzy, and went mad with grief. He no longer recognized his children, but imagined them to be monsters, and killed them. Yet he was the mildest among men, and the most submissive to the gods. Without a domestic hearth, without family, he began, from the moment of his recovery, the great solitary, arduous, and prolonged labors which were to save mankind.

The first of these labors was peace, which he, by his own arm and prowess, established all over Greece. He strangled the monsters, the hydras and lions of the old world. The new tyrants, the brigands, felt the weight of his club. The dangerous forests, the gloomy defiles, became safe; even the untamed rivers were vanquished, confined, and compelled to flow in their channels. They became highways. Greeks now freely communicated together, and assembled at Olympia, where Hercules had established before the altar of Jupiter the contests of peace, superseding the old bloody conflicts. He himself taught the exercises which made others resemble him, which created calm heroism, which built up the indestructible man, and made him firm like iron in the service of Justice. No violent competition, no animosity, was permitted. The olive was the only crown which he gave to the conquerors in those games.

Greece was too small. Hercules set out for a larger field of achievement. He wished to extend the peace which he had established, to institute everywhere the new rite. The ancient custom on every shore was to immolate the foreigner. At Tauris, a virgin cut his throat at the altars. In Thrace a barbarous King threw men to furious horses, glutted them with human flesh. In the north, the cruel Amazons made light of the blood of males. The same ferocity in Africa, where Busiris gave to the shipwrecked the hospitality of death. At the extremity of the world, in Iberia, Geryon devoured men. These were the adver-saries of Hercules, who searched for them beyond the seas, found them, captured them, and dealt with them as they had dealt with their guests. The law of hospitality was established from Caucasus to the Pyrenees.*

Hercules boldly entered the adytum or sacellum of the mysteries which made the strength of the barbarians. He faced the gloomy sea of the north, sanctuary of storms, which no one dared to enter—the turbulent, inhospitable Black Sea. He called it Euxine (hospitable). The queen of the frightful shore, the Amazon Diana of Birmo, was subjugated, like the sea itself. He forcibly carried off her belt, and hence her ferocious pride. Before him nature everywhere lost her virgin savageness. At Gades he broke the old barrier; with a shove of his shoulder he

---

* Jacob Bryant, in his *Analysis of Ancient Mythology*, proposes a more intelligent explanation of this custom. The practice of offering human sacri-fices, common alike to Greece, Rome, Asia, Africa, and Europe, was denoted by these customs. In Hebrew story, Abraham was commanded to sacrifice his "only son;" the book of *Leviticus* provided for such cases, and Jephtha is said to have actually immolated his daughter. Erectheus, at Athens, Marius, the Roman consul, and the Carthaginians, when Agathocles besieged them, sacrificed their children to propitiate divine power. The worship of the goddess Hippa, the antitype of Cybelê, Astartê, Iris, and Demeter, was thus characterized. Hence Diana at Tauris, the same as Brimo, was so worshipped; the Black Sea was called *Axenus*, for this cruelty to strangers, who were put to death in preference to citizens; Diomedes, the Thessalian, cast strangers to his horses, or rather gave them to the *hippai*, or priests of Hippa, for sacrifice; the Amazons, who worshiped Mars and Diana, and insti-tuted the rites of Ceres in Thebes and Attica, were *Oiorpata*, or immolators of human beings; a man was annually torn in pieces and his flesh tasted at the orgies of Bacchus, till an animal was substituted; and in Crete, Sicily, and elsewhere, the priests were disciplined in boxing and other athletic exercises, that they might overcome strangers and visitors, and have a pretext for im-molating them. The stories of Polyphemus, Busiris, Antæus, Eryx, Cycnus, Andromeda, Lycaon, Echetus, Geryon, the Sirens, and Læstrygones, and doubtless all cannibalism, were examples of this practice. Indeed Hislop, in his *Two Babylons*, derives the term "cannibal" from *cahen*, a priest of Baal, the sun-god of the Hamitic nations, who was worshipped by such offerings. It was believed that the gods hungered for blood, and could not communicate with man till it had been tasted or inhaled by them. It is still a custom in Africa, and certain islands of the Pacific, to immolate all strangers and criminals; and the practice of capital punishment, which is still preserved, is a relic of the old pagan rite.—ED.

parted two worlds, opened the strait. By him the small Mediterranean became the woman of the great ocean, and turning its back to Greece looked towards the distant Atlantis.* Its azure, salt wave, emancipated, bounded in this immensity which the heaven of Homer had not seen. Olympus was surpassed. What will become of the gods?

This rash one did not stop. The gloomy infinity of the Celtic forest did not affright him. He entered into its depths. He penetrated the glaciers of the Alps, the eternal desolation. He laughed at the black firs, he laughed at the avalanche. Through this place of terror he made, without difficulty, a highway, the great thoroughfare of mankind. Henceforward all, even the feeblest, the poor, women, old men, bowed over their sticks, follow without fear the high road of Hercules.

He had accomplished mighty achievements. He left behind him enduring monuments. He thought it time to be seated and to rest himself at the base of Ætna, at the foot of the great altar which smokes eternally. He breathed, he peacefully contemplated the blessed, sacred fields, always adorned with the flowers which Proserpina gathered, and he thanked the goddesses. His heart vibrated with joy. In his heroic simplicity, always

---

* An accomplished writer, not a professional geologist, suggested to the editor, in a private letter, that perhaps at a former era a salt sea extended through Middle Asia, dividing Scythia and the Turanian or Tartar races from those of the South and West. This would, if true, account for the existence of salt lakes and deserts in that region, as well as for the fact that the Tartar races are not known in the Hebrew and other old records. If the Mediterranean, by some convulsion, forced its outlet to the Atlantic, thus draining away that region and reducing a continuous body of salt water to lakes and barren deserts, the hypothesis would be a probable fact. The Dead Sea was a part of the Red Sea, ages before Abraham, Nimrod, or King Menes; and Lower Egypt was a part of the Mediterranean. Hercules was actually a. Libyan and Phœnician, rather than an Aryan or Grecian divinity. His name was the Sanskrit synonyme of Melkarth, and he held no place among the divinities of Olympus. The Grecian Herakles was probably another divinity, and probably was the appropriate deity to innovate upon the order of things.—ED.

free from pride, he pronounced this sentence: "It appears to me that I have become a god." *

The gods had waited up to this moment. Nemesis heard him.† This savage goddess and her ominous genius, Até, fly incessantly over the whole earth and gather the imprudent words of prosperity. The cry of boldness or of audacity which unluckily mounts to our lips gives to the jealous ones on high a pretext to punish us. They allot to men, but with niggardly reserves.‡ They give little and withhold much. They release certain favors while they limit, refuse the surplus, *the too-much, the excess.* This too-much is the glory, the genius, the greatness of man—that by which he can become a god, and it is that which the gods withhold. Dædalus, Icarus, and Bellerophon were punished for having taken wings. In Homer, the too bold, too happy ships were changed into rocks by Neptune. Was not the good and pious Æsculapius struck by lightning for having saved man's life?

Hercules was still more culpable! He had forced *Terra Mater,* the charming and venerable mother of men and gods. It is in vain that he says he did it out of love; that by piercing its mountains and draining its marshes, by rooting out the black tufts of its humid forests, he emancipated Ceres. The earth remains disturbed on account of it. If formerly, according to the fable, Ceres wept by reason of the assaults of Neptune, how much deeper her indignation against Hercules, who is only mortal? But is he only mortal? Is this bold one, with his superhuman labors, mortal? This is what it is essential to know. Between the old outraged deities of earth and the jealousies of the young Olympians a strange covenant is

---

* These sublime things, although only found in Diodorus and other writers, comparatively modern, are certainly ancient traditions, or rather adaptations of the older Phœnician legends of their Fire-god and tutelar deity.

† *Nemesis,* or *Moira,* signifies *distribution, division.*

‡ There is nothing more instructive on this subject than the treatise of MR. TOURNIER: *Nemesis and the Jealousy of the Gods.* 1863.

10

made. The last-born, Bacchus, an illegitimate brother of Hercules, undertakes his ruin. What says Jupiter? He allowed him to act—to test his son? or, was it from ill-will against humanity, too bold? He yielded to his favorite Bacchus; he yielded to the gods. *Hercules must die.* He must be convinced that he is mortal.

The effeminate Bacchus, who passed his life in long robes, in the half-sleep of an indolent woman, dared not face Hercules. He went to find the Centaurs. This odd race, of indomitable fury and strength, had sprung from a strange mother, the *Cloud*, inconstant deity, sometimes like smoke or fugitive fog, sometimes pregnant with lightnings, filled with thunder-bolts, of an elasticity more terrible than the thunder-bolt itself, and of such formidable expansion as to hurl mountains to the sky. The sons of the *Cloud*, the Centaurs—unbridled horses in their lower parts, hasty, of furious rut—are men of folly, of caprice, inflammable as their mother. Moreover, through her magic, they had something of the coarse phantoms of the middle ages, monstrous apparitions, fantastic terrors, bad dreams, frightful nightmares, which frenzy and make mad.

A people so much the more dangerous because they were very diverse, of contradictory spirits. Cheiron was a wise one; another, Pholus, a good Centaur, was the host of Hercules and his friend. It was Pholus, simple and credulous, that Bacchus deluded. He brought to him a terrible drink (the brandy of the savage?), and told him not to open the cask until the day that he entertained Hercules at his house. Scarcely had the cask been pierced before the vapor spread itself. All the Centaurs were delirious. Pride? Hatred? or Envy? Vain and light folly? Whatever may have been their thoughts, they flew into a passion, they assaulted the peaceful Hercules. The rocks fled, the forests were uprooted and flourished in the air, the oaks of a thousand years were brandished. Horrible hail-storm! The firm hero, with his calm, stout heart, was not dismayed. He responded with advantage, and hurled

back at them their oaks and rocks, but with an arm much
more sure. The earth was strewn with the bodies of those
monsters. At evening all was over. No one has since
seen the Centaurs. Not having been able to ensnare him,
to assassinate him, the gods sentenced him. He must
undergo everything. Jupiter decreed, Eurystheus an-
nounced it. He must die in obedience. The tyrant an-
nounced to him the fantastical wish that he should go to
the underworld, and bring back to him the three-headed
dog. Bitter derision towards a mortal, who could only
obey by entering the world of death, with the hopeless-
ness of being able to do no more, not even obey.

How bitter is death! But especially for the strong,
for those who feel in themselves all the energies of life!
Death is deliverance to the feeble and the sick. Hercules, the most alive of the living! for him it must be an
enormous effort to submit to die. We see that in his
heart he would say : " Suffer this cup to pass from me ! "
but he does not. He goes in search of Ceres, the benign and forgetful ; and having been initiated into her
mysteries, he humbly prays her to strengthen him.

He visited again the places of his youth, of his first exploits, in that Thessaly where he had created Tempé.
The king Admetus, though he was overwhelmed with
sorrow, received him as a guest, and bid him welcome.
Hercules learned that the Queen Alkestis, in order to
save her dying husband, and to preserve to her son a
father more useful than herself, had embraced death, and
bravely descended into the gloomy kingdom of Pluto.
Hercules was moved. This great deserted palace, the
husband in despair, the son drowned in tears, a whole
people around a grave, all this pierced his great soul. He
no longer thought of death. He would go to Hell, the
world of the dead, face Pluto, vanquish death, bring back
to the husband the adored spouse. Admirable folly of
compassion ! But the strongest are the most tender-
hearted !

In all this legend little has been said of Minerva. But luckily she followed him. It was not in vain that at his birth she received him from the womb of his mother. Minerva, at the solemn, decisive moment, reappeared. I am now reassured. Behind the sublime folly I see the eternal wisdom.

He went to Tænarus, he descended into Hell. Hell was afraid of Hercules. Cerberus came to lick his feet. Pluto was amazed; but Proserpina took the part of the bold hero. Pluto consented. He let him go,—let him triumph over death! Hercules did not ascend from Hell alone. A veiled woman accompanied him. She also entered her home, the house of Admetus. He did not suspect her identity, but rejected her. But immediately the veil was removed! Enough! let us not describe this unique scene, which no one can read without weeping.

What is hell, the underworld, henceforth? A trifle. We laugh at it. The Furies have been frightened. Charon has obeyed; a living person has passed and repassed on his boat. Cerberus, in a cowardly manner, his tail between his legs, crest-fallen, followed the conqueror, but, at the sight of light, disappeared. The brother of Jupiter, the King of the ghost-world, and of Tartarus itself, has been outraged with impunity, and appears, in these days, to have withdrawn into the profound abyss, the doubtful fog of the great deep. Great, terrible blow to the gods, who will surely avenge themselves. This last victory brought inevitable misfortune to Hercules.

Strange destiny! His only impiety was that he was worthier than Olympus. His gentleness of soul, his magnanimity, had led him to avenge the outrage which had been received by the wife of Eurystheus, that unrelenting persecutor, that cruel tyrant over him. The gods of Homer were disparaged, humiliated, by this contrast. Such excessive virtue had been never heard of among them.

The maxim, "Render good for evil," which was en-

joined on the old monastic East, is perhaps too easy
to the feeble. But that Hercules, the strongest of the
strong, should exhibit this extraordinary goodness, is
novel and marvellous. It is the very heaven of the Greek
genius. The heaven of the heart destroys the heaven of
the imagination.

Hell, the underworld, Olympus, all the gods have
sunk in this contrast: one thing remains, the greatness
of man.

Well, if thou art a man, it is by that that thou wilt be
assailed. Thy courage is invulnerable, but not thy love,
not thy friendship. At first Hercules lost his brother,
whom he loved. He lost the companion of his labors,
the courageous friend who followed him everywhere, who
bore his arms. Henceforth he must go alone, and fight
alone over the earth.

The strong are very sensitive to pain, and allow themselves to be afraid of it. Hercules had once been delirious ; and, after his descent into hell, when he had been in
the very presence of Death, his head was disturbed. His
heart, full of grief and trouble, invoked relief from the
dangerous physician, Love, who scoffs at our ills. He
yielded to Love, and followed meekly as a bull blindly
goes to meet the deadly blows. He loved Dejanira, the
dangerous and the jealous. He loved Iolé, and found
nothing to come from such a love but outrage. The
brother of Iolé repelled the bastard, the serf of Eurystheus ;
he irritated Hercules, who killed him. Frightful misfortune ! He was inconsolable. He pined away, he drooped,
and, sick, he went to consult Apollo. This was the severe oracle : " Pay them the price of blood ! "

" But I have nothing in the world ! "

" Thou hast thy body. Sell thyself as a slave in
Asia."

Hercules obeyed. In this indolent Asia Minor, in this
effeminate Lydia, where man is a woman, he had not a
master but a mistress, a woman, the Queen Omphalé. Was

not this enough ? No. The fable adds that, by a double servitude, his soul was also enslaved, wretched by loving the
cruel woman, who amused herself with him. She exhibited
the deplorable spectacle of Hercules disguised, Hercules
in the garb of a woman ; most terrible burlesque ! Men
were horrified at the sight, but she laughed pitilessly, and
exacted, in order to complete the humiliation, that her
slave should work cheerfully, that he should spin, and exhibit himself to all less as the captive of an overmastering
fate, than of a dastardly love, and of a feeble heart.

So men and women laughed, and Olympus sang. Hercules was delivered, only to suffer still greater calamity.
He returned to Greece, and rejoined Dejanira. After such
misfortunes, the humiliated heart willingly hides itself in
love and solitude. He took her into the desert. But, on
the road they met with a strange adventure. A river debar-
red the way. A young Centaur, the only one who had
escaped destruction, offered himself to carry Dejanira over
the stream. Did he wish vengeance ? or was he, according to the blind instincts of his race, mad for Dejanira ?
It is not known. Having landed her on the bank, Hercules still being on the opposite shore, he proceeded to
satiate himself with her. Hercules had his terrible arrows,
poisoned with the Hydra of Lerna, and yet he hesitated,
fearing to wound Dejanira. At last he let speed the arrow,
pierced the monster, who, in the double crisis of pleasure
and of death, pouring out his life, love, rage, mixed with
infernal poison, violently tore off his soiled tunic, and said
to Dejanira, " Take this. It is the soul of Nessus. In it
is love and the eternal desire."

This caused the death of Hercules. He soon after put
on this murderous tunic, having received it from his too
artless spouse, who expected to be loved the more. The
horrible poison burned in him. In despair, he refused to
wait for death. He anticipated it. He enfranchised himself, and threw aside his tormented body in which he had
done so much, suffered, undergone the humiliating miseries

of our nature. He made, with trees heaped up on Mount
Œta, a colossal funeral pile, and desired his last friend to
apply the torch.

He was enveloped by the flame and ascended. It is
said that he ascended to heaven. But what heaven?
Was it Olympus? His very career had killed the Olympians.

What is added, and what is certain is that Hercules
espoused Hebe, the goddess of eternal Youth, in other
words, he lived and remained young. Two or three thousand years are of no consequence. Other mythologies
have been introduced. Other saviors have varied the
great, eternal theme of the Passion. The incarnated
(*avataras*) of India had for their Passion to go through
human life and to experience its miseries. Those of
Egypt, of Syria, and Phrygia, the Osirises and Adonises,
the Bacchuses, the Atyses, the mutilated gods were torn
to pieces, suffered, and endured. But their *passive Passion*, far from giving us strength, has been discouraging,
and their legends have created sterile inertia. It is in
the *active Passion*, the Herculean, that there is the exalted
harmony of man, the equipoise, the strength which makes
him fruitful here below.

Persia had this intuition, but vague, quite elementary.
The Grecian Hercules was exact, strongly marked, and
of such a positive personality that we can portray him
much better than the historical heroes. His compact
solidity placed him apart from all the gods, and it is he
who, by contrast, makes us feel their transparency. As
to the restless Bacchus, who disputed the ground with
Hercules, he is lost in the troubled vapors of night, of orgies, the reeky exhalations of the East.

The shadow of Hercules, the remains of Hercules, his
remembrance, his Olympian lessons, these accomplished
the great and substantial realities—Platea, Marathon, Salamis.

But that which made him survive in Greece, and constituted him the spouse of the goddess of eternal Youth, the young and the living, and the hero of future time, was his humble and sublime part of laborer, the heroic workman.

He dreaded nothing, he disdained nothing. In establishing the sacredness of peace between man and man, he civilized the world; in piercing the mountains, emancipating the rivers, he subjugated, purified, created anew the earth.

He is the strong arm, the great, patient heart, the courageous workman, who prepared the earth for the second creator, the artistic Prometheus.

Prometheus.

Æschylus alone, among the poets, had the good fortune to be at once the singer and the hero, to have the deeds and the writings, the grandeur of a complete man. His tragedies fifty times won the crown.* He, like Homer, had rhapsodists who sang his verses on the roads. He never died; he was always sustained in the theatres, which played only the pieces of the living. He remained in a statue of bronze in the square of Athens, as a censor, a pontiff, and a prophet, to watch the people, and to constantly warn them. Aristophanes, the great scoffer at the gods, respected only Æschylus. He had seen him in the underworld seated upon a throne of brass.

In the noble epitaph which Æschylus made for himself, he remembered only that he fought at Marathon. He forgot his hundred tragedies. There never was a more valiant family than his. He was wounded at Marathon, and was the brother of the most glorious soldiers of Salamis. One of these was Ameinias, the bold pilot who first struck the fleet of Xerxes, and won the prize of valor at Salamis.† The other was the stubborn Cynægirus, who allowed himself to be cut to pieces as he held the vessel with his

---

* It is said that Æschylus won but thirteen dramatic contests.—ED.

† HERODOTUS : viii., 84, 93.

hands, which were severed, one after the other, and then he still kept hold by his teeth.   The sons, the nephews, the kinsmen of Æschylus would have done as much, if they had had like opportunities; they made up, however, by a torrent of tragedies, good or bad, composing and writing with the furor of the great old man.   One of his sons had the peculiar good fortune to win the prize over Sophocles, over his masterpiece, *the King Œdipus.*

The magistrates of Athens carefully preserved a complete copy of the works of Æschylus, lest some rash actor should change any of his sacred words.   Nevertheless, in spite of this vigilance, only seven dramas remain to us, of which there is but one complete trilogy, the *Orestcia.*   Of the three parts of the Prometheus, only one survives. Enormous and colossal remains !   As the traveller, who, finding in the sands of Egypt the foot of a Sphinx, or its granite finger, attempts to calculate what must have been its prodigious size, we in like manner, viewing these remains, seek to conceive the dimensions of this colossal Æschylus.

Aristophanes admirably says that the verses of Æschy‧lus are strong " as the closely-fitted planks of a vessel," as the indestructible frames of those conquering ships, which dashed to pieces the fleet of Asia.   He placed him above Sophocles, far, very far from the feebler Euripides. But his true place is between Isaiah and Michael Angelo.

In the sombre Prometheus there is more than simple art ; there is the true essence of grief; nothing which softens or consoles as in Sophocles.   The tragic utterances of the heroes of the past seem dreadful warnings, mournful forebodings on the present.   Above all Æschylus reminds us of Michael Angelo.   The Italian prophet, in the midst of the splendors and of the conquests of Julius II., painted terror on the ceilings of the Sistine Chapel, while the prophet Æschylus appears to have been filled with grief in the midst of the prosperity of Athens.

Both had seen beforehand the terrible trials, the cruel

blows of destiny, and at the end, the *judgment*, the high victory of justice. This was the greatness of Æschylus which Aristophanes could not appreciate. Against the despotic arbitrariness of the mythology of his time, and of all other mythologies, he invoked, contained, brought forth the principle of *justice*. His Prometheus proclaiming the overthrow of Jupiter, also foretold the death and impotency of every myth of the future, not established on the inflexible right. His Caucasus was the rock on which the Stoic was soon to fix the Organon of Impartial Justice, against the tyranny of gods in heaven, and of kings and priests on earth.

The future unknown, veiled. The severity of the prophet, his grief, fills with astonishment. Æschylus, in his fortieth year, began the series of his threatening tragedies, in the smiling moment in which the triumphant city was pursuing, and crowning her victory, and appeared the Queen of Greece. She was brilliant, she was fruitful. In every sense she was radiant. She was young, and in her twentieth year in her two admirable geniuses, two adolescents, who just then began to give indications of their wonderful faculties, the beautiful Sophocles, the powerful Pheidias. The latter, first a painter, by the test-stroke of his chisel, sculptured the soul of Athens in his Minerva Polias, haughty, sovereign, and colossal, who, with her dazzling helmet, ruled at the Acropolis and in the temples, and overlooked the distant sea and islands.

Moment of immense expectation! Between Themistocles and Aristides, between the generous Cimon and thr sagacious Pericles, the struggle appeared equal, and their contests even seemed to constitute the harmony of liberty.

Æschylus saw nothing of this. His soul dwelt in the preceding century, in the disasters and dangers. He, like Herodotus, had the presentiment of the Nemesis that hovers over our heads, and takes revenge on our prosperity. The prodigious Babylon has indeed fallen. Massive

Egypt, so strongly seated, is also prostrate.   The good
Crœsus, the cunning Polycrates, and delightful Ionia, all
have perished !   Athens remained the dike which arrested
the torrent of barbarians.   But how many and rapid the
changes in Athens herself !   Æschylus, when an infant,
saw the Peisistratidæ, and the vindication of liberty, the
valiant act of Harmodius.   Grown up, he won the great
glory of his wound at Marathon.   Greece for the moment
found herself carried to heaven by the great wave of Salamis.   She descended again, and a new age began.   That
of heroism had gone forever.   That of harmony now
began—the reign of the arts, of the beautiful.   An immense radiancy of inventive genius and of fruitful intelligence, a world of grace and light was ushered in to
astound all coming times.   In a single century was prepared the work of two thousand years !   Is it thus that
men live ?   How is it that we do not foresee the coming
days of exhaustion ?   What a beautiful play will Nemesis
have in return, when she brings hither her barbarians, not
this time from Asia but from Macedonia, in the gloomy
day of Cheronea !

Certainly the bow of steel had slackened, and the lyre,
enriched with new strings, took not its harmony except
from abandoning the rough and strong tone which it had
in the time of the heroes.   Sophocles tells us that Hercules, civilized, abandoned the club ; that he studied and
taught the choir of the stars, and conducted their concerts.*
The second Minerva, less colossal, no longer extended her
threatening look over the seas.   Pheidias, this time made
her meditative, of a deep and penetrating mind, closely
resembling the effigies of Themistocles, " of him who
alone *saw* and *foresaw*," says Thucydides.

At what is she looking ?   We do not know.   But she is
certainly looking at something immense, infinite, and sub-

---

* In other words, the Phœnician Hercules, the sun-god, had taken the
place of the Grecian hero.—ED.

lime. More than Athens herself. It is rather the long career of centuries which Athens will illuminate. She contemplates the eternity of art.

Who marvels that Greece, in her wonderful beauty, admired, adored herself? wished for immortality? Observe that before all statuary, the living statue existed; that the powerful gymnical and harmonical creation had made out of the real the most perfect ideal ever dreamed of. Art at first copied; it began with portraits.* It did not amuse itself by sculpturing gods at hazard. It made the likeness of those it saw. Beauty appeared divine in itself, and more divine as a revelation of the soul. Pheidias became a sculptor by witnessing, on the Olympian course, a beautiful boy, coming off conqueror in a race. Another youth of sweet beauty, at fifteen years of age, led the chorus of thanksgiving to the gods, after Marathon; he was applauded by the Athenians . . . his soul burst forth. . . . It was Sophocles.

All this is grand and pure, very noble, and yet lively and fruitful. The gods humanized, or, rather, made divine by the soul imparted to them by Pheidias, left the adyta of the temples, and seated themselves under the porticoes, and even in the public squares. So the cities had two classes of inhabitants side by side and living together, men and gods. The strange idea of Winckelman that all was motionless, beautiful without but destitute of expression, is daily more and more completely contradicted.† These marbles everywhere palpitate with life.

---

* In 558 B.C. the custom was introduced of erecting statues to the conquerors at the Olympian games. This is an important observation of M. de Ronchaud in his beautiful book on *Pheidias*, page 59. From that moment sculpture began to soar.

† Compare the brilliant genius of the Renaissance. Jean Goujon, where he is sublime, as in a river, a nymph (*Cluny Museum*) has made fluid bodies, of a fantastic undulation, through which life runs, and which plunge us in a profound revery. . . . Death and life, what are you? The longer I remain here absorbed in looking at this, the less I know about it. The Greek, on the other hand, gives a conscious, strong, and eager feeling of life! The

Before Euripides, and already in Sophocles, it was apparent that, far from being cold, this art was endangered by its tenderness. I admire Sophocles, but not without revolt, when he dwells too long and sadly on physical evils, like the wound of Philoctetes; when he unnerves Hercules, and exhibits as feeble the strongest of the strong. Leave to me the entire beneficent legend, for I shall soon need it. Consider that Zeno will soon oppose the philosophy of Hercules to the glory of Alexander the Great.

His *Œdipus of Colonus* is also very exciting. The subject is " the necessity of death," the remedy of errors, and the recovery of life, the sweet expiation which awaits the victim of fatality in the long-wished-for sleep under the generous shelter of Athens, the profound security in the woods of the Eumenides. The two adorable girls carried away, brought back, produce the highest emotion. . . . See ! all the great people weep.

I understand very well that the hero, Æschylus, who saw the beginning of that age of emotions, those affecting marvels, and other of refinement, of sublime analysis, was alarmed. What did he think when that wonderful reasoner, Zeno of Elea, who first formulated logic, went to Athens? With remarkable skill, Zeno, overwhelming the haughty sophists of Ionia, proved to the Athenians, in that centre of activity, that motion did not exist. Pericles and all listened. They were passionately fond of such tests of skill.

The centre for thinkers was soon transferred to the residence of a young lady, one of those Ionian women, whom the overthrow of Miletus sent to Athens. These Milesian women, all charming, exciting attention because of their painful shipwreck and the sale and enslavement of many, became the more the queens. The voluptuous Thargelia, the delicate and impressive Aspasia had a court, and what

fainting women, who, from the fronton of the temple, are gazing to see if the child delivered to the Minotaur is coming and do not see him, are striking and tragical in the highest degree.

courtiers !   The undulatory genius of Ionia, with its fleeting grace, which made Olympus and its metamorphosis of
old, was Aspasia herself.   Pheidias, and his young school,
at her court, got the inspiration of that exalted irony
which mocked and arraigned the gods.   Pericles, the reflecting and cautious orator, learned from her the art of
mimicry and the imposing comedy, which fascinated the
people.   The sophists studied her insidious words, the
art of entangling, unravelling, and remixing the fine-spun
threads of women, which even the keenest could not discover.   Protagoras learned from her to doubt everything,
and Socrates, later, to doubt doubt.

Strange refinement, and how rapid !   How many centuries in twenty or twenty-five years !   Yesterday, it was
the coarseness of Marathon ; to-day, all is elegant, refined,
subtle.   Where is the robust spirit which made Greece
victorious ?   I see lodging with Pericles his teacher, an
obscure man renowned for volatilizing the gods.   This
Anaxagoras, the Ionian, was surnamed " the NOUS," or
spirit, because he believed there was no other god.   Sublime and pure idea which, centralizing the deity,* but
drowning the energies of the nation in æther, caused Pallas and Hercules to disappear, and conducted all Athens
straight to monarchical tranquillity.

Unity in heaven, unity on earth, was the dream which
brooded in secret.   Many would have a monarch to
represent Jupiter, not with the " Spirit " of Anaxagoras, but by their favorite Bacchus-Dionysus, a god
wholly eastern, who wore the tiara,† and the effeminate
dress of the women of Asia.   He had taken the thyrsus,
and the ivy of the god of vintage, the ancient, rural
Bacchus.   He drew after him women and slaves, a
troop of *orgiasts*.   The Athenian slaves, who were sub-

---

* Anaxagoras styled the Divine Being " *Nous autokrates*,"—the Mind or
Spirit that by itself rules all.—ED.

† SOPHOCLES.

stantially free, bold, like our *Frontins* and our *Lisettes*, admitted to the spectacles, to the Mysteries, had their god, their tyrant, their Savior, in Dionysus. By his affiliation, he was worshipped at Eleusis. He had occupied Delphi, dug for himself a subterranean tomb under the temple, from which he was resuscitated. He compelled Apollo to play in his comedy. Nor was this all. He aimed to eclipse all the little gods of Greece and to be the leader in great things, as in the conquest of Asia and of India. When was this to occur? and in whom was this great god to make his appearance? To each *tyrant* the people exclaimed : " It is he ! "

By a strange coincidence, Gélon, the glorious ruler of Syracuse, on the same day in which was achieved the victory of Salamis, had subdued Carthage, and imposed on her the law that she should no longer offer human sacrifices. He felt so secure that, on his return, he laid aside his sword, and went about without guards. He was chosen *tyrant* a second time, and hence for life. The *tyrants* were revered like gods, chiefs of liberty, the liberty of brutishness. They appropriated the name of the celestial ruler *Dionysus*, or the name which pleased the vain hope, *Savior* (Sôter) ; or were called Demetrios, the name from Demeter. These Saviors were terrible; they crushed the idiots who expected liberty from the ruler.

Gloomy future, which at the time of Æschylus was scarcely distinguishable. The orgies of Bacchus had but recently been instituted at Sparta.* The Spartan Pausanias, the vanquisher of Platea, thought he could make him the Gélon, the Bacchus Savior of Greece. The enlightened Athenians laughed at this. Those dark-laid schemes seemed impossible. The old men, however, who observed Pericles, were of opinion that they could trace in him the features of Pisistratus.

But let us return to art. Under the dominion of Bac-

---

* ARISTOTLE.

chus, in the constant fermentation of the mind, the theatre became the controlling demand of Athens. It became radiant, and abandonded all its elementary forms. All gradually changed, the stage, the plays, and the actors.

Up to this time the stage had been built in frame-work, and temporarily for the hours of the festivals ; it was extemporized for improvisation. The poet would not entrust any one with the oversight, the effort, the danger of·the performance. He represented himself the part of the hero. Tragedy required an act of courage, of devotion, in which all the energies of the man are staked. He rushed fearlessly on the trembling boards, from beneath which proceeded threatening echoes. With all the energies of his physical being, his soul, and his voice, he defied the caprices and the ridicule of the audience. Was the face masked, and thus sheltered from outrage? Not always, for Sophocles, because of his extreme beauty, played the part of the beautiful Nausicaa in one of his own pieces.

But this was a severe trial to Sophocles, and the people, who were passionately fond of him, spared their favorite this painful task, and assigned him other and more congenial characters, that of a priest, for example. They thought that he was "so beloved of the gods " that they attributed to him a miracle. One day, during a storm, a hymn of Sophocles was sung. In an instant it became calm. Neptune and the sea listened.

He felt that he was beloved. In his twentieth year he competed for the tragedy. He produced a graceful pastoral, *Triptolemus*, doubtless to the praise of Eleusis and of the new Mysteries. It contained this line from Pindar : "This is true happiness: to see them, and then die !" These words excited, delighted, and carried away all that were initiated. The admiration, the furor for the young poet went so far that they sacrificed to him one of the grand tragedies of Æschylus. The old partisans of Æschylus, heroic and patriotic, struggled in vain. There was a general misunderstanding. The matter was referred

to the generals, to the glorious Cimon, who, having returned from a new victory, brought back the ashes of
Theseus, a most acceptable gift to the Athenians. The
son of Miltiades could not be hostile to the old soldier of
Marathon. But the valiant Cimon could not be brave
before the people ; he recognized their wishes and turned
his back on Æschylus.

Æschylus, henceforth, had everything against him, his
age, his long successes, and the progress of art, which
pursues its own path, independently even of genius. The
art required more of the tragic and less of the lyric—a
more complicated plot, which seizes the heart, keeps it
uneasy, in suspense. This was the peculiarity of Sophocles.
Æschylus did not decline it. He followed it in the *Oresteia.*

This is the grandest production of the Greek theatre, or,
rather, of any theatre. Shakespeare, with all his resources
and varied effects, his magical and profound complications,
has not surpassed it. So exceedingly simple, it dispenses
with all ingeniousness, and without subtlety, without
twisting, without trickery, it takes a stronger hold of us,
clasps us and captivates us.

The three pieces of *Orestes* advance in terrific crescendo.
It was customary, during the festivals, to play from morning to night. The three pieces could be represented in
one day ; the *Death of Agamemnon* in the morning, that
of *Clytemnestra* at noon, and the *Eumenides* in the evening. One drama after another, terror after terror, the
audience could not breathe. The firmest trembled. Women swooned, and it is said that many miscarried. At
night there was general consternation. Æschylus alone,
who had acted Orestes, was undismayed.

Agamemnon had taken effect. A cold chill seizes us
when his perfidious wife receives him with tenderness and
wraps him in her veil. The Clytemnestra (*Choephores*)
from the beginning causes the hair to bristle with terror ;
the shivering of the parricide, even the anticipation of the
remorse. Orestes realizes his destiny. The gods wished

11

him to murder, and then sought to punish him for doing
their will. This is the audacious plot of the *Eumenides,*
making plain the inconsistency of the gods. They pursued the gods no less than Orestes, overwhelming them
together by their mutual contradictions.

Æschylus was very bold. He expressed the popular
belief; but it might produce irritability, indignation, when
it was beheld so clearly exposed. This has never been
stated, because it has never been made apparent what
was the moral condition of the mind, the inclination of
the Grecian Olympus at this period of its rapid descent.

With the overthrow of Ionia, Jupiter and Apollo fell
into notorious disrepute. Their oracles were disregarded.
Crœsus, who had paid them immense sums, who expected
to conquer the Persians, and became their prisoner, outraged the god of Delphi by offering him his chains. This
god was surnamed *Loxias,* the ambiguous, the equivocal.
When he was consulted before Salamis, he evaded an
answer, and was ridiculed. The only god left was Themistocles. Æschylus evidently remembered the uncertain
oracle, which occasioned the loss of Lydia, and poor
Ionia, and the unfortunate Miletus so much regretted by
Athens. In the *Eumenides* he boldly said: "Behold
the temple of Delphi! . . . How it drips with blood!"

Apollo outraged, Jupiter outraged (as he had done),
was not his most dangerous act. The mortal danger in
his production was what he made the Eumenides say, and
contemptuously repeat over and over again: "*The young
gods.*" If this sentence injured Phœbus, it fell much
more directly on Bacchus, the last-born of Olympus.*
The terrible goddesses crushed this profaner of their
secrets with all the sacredness of their antiquity.

Æschylus, who was an Eleusinian, who, according to a
fragment, loved, as a son, the Eleusinian Ceres, knew better than any one else the significant changes in the Mysteries, in which Iacchus, who was first introduced as

* HERODOTUS.

a child, grew up, became Zagreus dead and revived, and
finally the triumphant Bacchus, who subdued poor Ceres,
and became for good or bad her husband.*

This revolution seems to have occurred between 600 and
500 B.C.† But things rush on. To the Eleusinian Bacchus, who preserved some decency, was gradually mingled
the ignoble product of the Asiatic Bacchus. (Sabazius
Atys, Adonis, etc.) All this before the year 400 B.C.
The great Bacchus, who tore Orpheus to pieces, the Savior, as he was called, of women and of slaves, god of
liberty (of drunkenness and of frenzy), this great Bacchus
upheld by the masses, was a tyrant in Greece. He inspired terror everywhere.‡

Even at Athens, the city of incredulity and laughter,
the very compact masses of the initiated, the women and
the slaves were very daring, and especially at the theatres,
where their numbers gave them boldness. Slaves were
admitted.§ They dared not speak, but they could mur-
mur, roar, and it sounded like thunder. Women attended.
Their regard for this tender Bacchus sometimes made them
furious, and almost assassins. Æschylus came near experiencing this. For a word which he said of the Mysteries in one of his pieces, he would have perished under
their fury had he not embraced the altar which was on
the stage.

We can realize the extreme danger to which he exposed
himself by that terrible and clear expression : " *The young*

---

* Yet Clement of Alexandria says that when he was tried on Mars Hill for
having divulged the arcane wisdom, he exculpated himself on the ground that
he had never been initiated. His brother, Ameinias, the hero of Salamis, is
said to have secured him from the rage of the populace.—ED.

† More properly between 500 and 400 B.C Æschylus was born at Eleusis,
525 B.C.—ED.

‡ Herodotus, who, as we know, read his history at the Olympian games in
452 B.C. (four years after the death of Æschylus), was so fearful of this
tyranny that, whenever he met with Osiris, the Egyptian Bacchus, he declared
that he held his peace and did not dare to speak.

§ GORGIAS.

gods." But, in braving the fanatics, was he assured of the support of the opposite party, the strong thinkers, the sophists, those who followed Anaxagoras and his disciple Pericles, *who wanted no God but the Spirit?* By no means. This party of religious liberty was attacked by Æschylus on account of their tortuous ways with respect to political tyranny. He made the Eumenides say : *" Revere justice, honor the laws. Take care not to give yourselves masters."* The entire piece, doubtless, was a transparent attack against the intrigues employed by Pericles. Some one, instructed by Pericles, had instigated the people to suppress the Areopagus. Æschylus interposed the bold drama, in which he exhibited Minerva instituting, for the trial of Orestes, that irreproachable tribunal, which had long made Athens the centre and the temple of law.

The Areopagus was not abolished. The people recoiled. But so much more certain was the ruin of Æschylus. They dogged his steps. Under twenty pretexts he was persecuted and calumniated. They whispered in the ear that, although in the *denouement* of his tragedy, he dared not kill his victim before the spectators, he did it behind the scenes ; and that thus in the frenzy of success he offered human sacrifices for the favor of the gods of heaven or hell.

Such charges as these ingeniously prepared the way for the great blow, *the accusation of impiety.* We know but little of the details. Did he defend himself? We are ignorant. It seems that, for his defence, he only exhibited his wound. The accusers remembered Marathon, his brother and Salamis, blushed, were silent.

Not being able to strike him they struck the theatre, but the blow was aimed at Æschylus. One morning, it fell. The old theatre of wood that so often had shaken under his feet and resounded with the thunder of his voice—fell. Manifestly the vengeance of the gods. He had tired their patience. They had imposed silence on his impious fury, on this Ajax, on this Orestes, on this gigantic blasphemer.

He had destroyed himself, and also his theatre. Another edifice was erected, beautiful, of marble, surrounded with statues. But it did not suit Æschylus. It did not, like the other, vibrate and breathe, impregnated with the ancient spirit. The images of the gods, marvels of art, divided the attention, the regard. The most prominent of the statues was the pensive, sleepy, and voluptuous young god Bacchus, a masculine Venus, the beloved of Athens.

All this reminded the old hero of the sentence in his own drama, which the Furies repeated to Orestes: "It is all over with thee. . . . Thou shalt never more speak."

I think that it was at this time * that, just as he was leaving these scenes forever, the old Titan erected his own Caucasus, caused himself to be bound, nailed, and thunderstruck by Jupiter, in order to hurl at him the great word of rebellion, the prophecy of the future.

Colonus, a little *demos*, or market-town, not far from Athens, a place of most tragical interest, is known by Æschylus's tragedy of *Œdipus*, his death, the mystery of his grave. It had near by the woods of the Eumenides and the altar of an outcast, the Titan Prometheus. While the Sacred Highway to Eleusis was day and night peopled, noisy, Colonus was deserted. Its old, ill-famed divinities did not attract the people. Its forbidding woodland affrighted. The passer-by avoided it and turned his eyes away.

Prometheus, as is known, was the personal adversary of Zeus, who denounced him, caused him to be nailed up on Caucasus. In spite of the gods he had given us fire, and with it the Arts. The Greeks dared not forget him, and half-worshipped him. The economical honor of a little race was paid annually to this benefactor. But few patronized it. Aristophanes complained of it. While people crowded one another in the equivocal Mysteries, "no one knew how to bear the torch of Prometheus." This torch,

---

* This is the very reasonable opinion of Ottfried Müller.

kindled at an altar at Athens, had to be carried to the altar of Colonus. The rapid, sparkling or smoking fire with which the wind sported, sad image of our destinies, passed from hand to hand, but scarcely reached there. The gloomy altar remained obscure.

Strange forgetfulness! Culpable ingratitude! Prometheus was the primitive emancipator, and all free energy proceeded from him. Through him, and not Vulcan or Hephaistos, who was not yet born,* has sprung forth Wisdom, the elder daughter of Jupiter. The god of the thunderbolt, among his black clouds, was oppressed by her, felt her brooding under his brow. The industrious Titan, with a blow (the most beautiful and sublime that was ever struck,) pierced his temple. A luminous ether shone, serene, pure, virginal, the eternal virgin who was the inspired soul of Athens, still alive, and who will live and survive all the Jupiters.

This is certainly the most exalted legend of antiquity. Noble product of genius and of grief! It is the immutable lesson of man, that of emancipation through effort, the only efficacious justice. It teaches each one to draw out of himself his *Pallas*, his energy, his Art, his true Savior. It is directly opposed to the gloomy Saviors of the different faiths, the false liberators. It alone is the Liberator.

This ether of Pallas seems to be the same fire with which Prometheus kindled the human soul. The Titan took it from Heaven to place it in us. Till that had been done, man was as heavy clay, and dragged himself about, herding with his kind, scoffed by the gods. Prometheus put in him the spark. This was the crime imputed to the great Titan. " And, behold, he begins to gaze at the

---

* Prometheus was doubtless an older deity than Zeus, being Pelasgian or Æthiopian, and not Aryan or Ionian. The scholiast to Sophocles declares him to be " first and older, holding the sceptre, and Hephaistos or Vulcan new and second." Most likely he pertained to the worship which the Olympian gods superseded. Jacob Bryant declares him to have been a god of Colchis, which would render this account very plausible.—ED.

stars, to mark the seasons, to divide time. He combines letters and fixes memory. He finds the high science, the numbers. He digs the earth and surveys it, makes cars, vessels. He understands, he foresees, he pierces the future." Prometheus opened to man the road to enfranchisement. He was the *anti-tyrant* at the time when Olympus, in its young *Jupiter-Bacchus*, was more and more the *tyrant*, a type too well repeated by the tyrants of earth.

I am much mistaken if the Titan Æschylus did not frequently come to ask, as Œdipus, a seat of the Eumenides of Colonus, if he did not sit down at this deserted altar of the great forgotten benefactor. At this altar, and not elsewhere, could the poet learn two things which the Titan alone could reveal. Æschylus knew the name of Prometheus's mother, knew that he was not the son of a certain Clymenè, as it was absurdly said, but the *son of Justice*, of the archaic Themis, who had witnessed the birth of all the gods. The second thing, altogether divine, which neither Hesiod nor any one else had suspected, was the true motive for which Prometheus sacrificed himself. In Hesiod, the benefit conferred by the Titan was a trick of malice : he wished to play a trick on Jupiter. In Æschylus, he had compassion on the miseries of man. *He had compassion.* This constituted him divine, this made him a god above the gods.

Compassion! Justice! Two most powerful levers which gave an incredible force to the old fable. Thirty-thousand spectators were captivated, bound more tenaciously than Prometheus on Caucasus, when he uttered the cry, " O Justice! O my mother ! Thou seest what they make me suffer ! "

What heart was not pierced when with a profound voice he repeated this bitter sentence, " I had compassion ! This is why no one has had compassion on me ! "

If, as it is believed, the tragedy of *Prometheus* appeared about the year 460 B.C., Æschylus was then sixty-five years old. I believe, however, that in spite of his age, Æschylus really appeared at this time on the stage. No one would have dared to perform those very dangerous pieces but the author. Aristophanes found no one but himself to perform the piece in which he stigmatized Cleon. Æschylus, after the *Eumenides*, in which he braved at once both the party of Pericles and that of the *young gods*, could scarcely find an intrepid actor to play the Titan, the impious, the solemn enemy of Tyrants, of *Tyranny*. It is this word evidently which opens and explains the drama. (Τυραννίς.)

Notwithstanding this, it is said that the *Prometheus* is obscure. It is too clear. On one side there was bound and nailed the Son of Law. On the other hand, quite powerful in heaven, there was the Tyrant, the enemy of Law, the Lord, the arbitrary one, the favor or Grace. This one was called Zeus, or Jupiter. But Jupiter, at that time, was mingled with Bacchus, and soon after lent to him the thunderbolt and the eagle.*

There was the especial danger. Æschylus alone could act, acted, gave his arms to the chains, his hands to the nails, and his head to the hammer. Extraordinary spectacle, which had all the effect of a personal execution !

Not a word in the first scene, while the cruel slaves of Jupiter—Force and Strength—compel Vulcan to rivet him fast. These left him only this decided and audacious order, " Respect the *tyrant*." He opened not his mouth. But when left alone, his heart burst, and from the mask of brass escaped a terrible sigh.

Æschylus, in the *Seven*, and in the *Persians*, appears sometimes exaggerated and emphatic, but not at all in *Prometheus*. It is nature, it is grief, true explosions of grief, a feeling at once both general and personal. There is no distinguishing. It is the Titan, and it is Æschylus. It is man as he was and as he will be. Does humanity complain,—humble itself? No. From the depths of

---

* In the statues of Polykleitus.

grief it raises itself in its strength. We feel that heroism in man is nature.

To the nymphs of the ocean, who came to weep with him, he explained his destiny, but with a greatness and haughtiness which made them shudder. He spoke in the same way to his feeble friend, the Ocean, who wished to give him cowardly advice. He indicated forever the great traits of the Tyrant: "*He who rules by HIS own laws,*" ('Ιδίοις)—peculiar, individual, personal,—savage and not civil—unequal caprices, love for one, death for another. And he adds this strong sentence: "*He has the right in himself,*" and he is its proprietor.

But the deepest trait of the caprice which best marks the Tyrant is the outrage, the cruel *débauche*, the barbarity in love itself. What Æschylus himself, when a boy, saw under the Peisistratidæ, and which occasioned their fall, he portrayed in Jupiter. The unfortunate Io, deceived by Jupiter, delivered to the fury of Juno, stung by the atrocious hornet, goes distracted over the seas, the precipices, from one region to another. As she ran along, she accidentally drew near for a moment to the fatal rock of Caucasus. The two wretched personages, Io and Prometheus, the eternal motion and captivity, the eternal immobility, looked for a moment upon each other.

The hapless Io wished to know her destiny. She asked the enigma of the world, "Who rules destiny?"—"The Parcæ, the Fates."

Cruel sentence, which however is but a cry of grief over the disorder of this world. This fatalistic form * recurs very often in Æschylus, like bitter complaints, roarings. It is a weapon rather than a dogma. He employed Destiny, as a yoke of brass to make the Gods bend, to

---

* Quinèt and Louis Ménard have well said that the Greek Fatalism had been infinitely exaggerated. It is absurd to think that the people who, of all other, made the strongest use of liberty, did not believe in it. The fatalism of the Mussulmans, the fatalism of Christianity, made the middle ages sterile. If Greece was so fruitful, it is because she believed in liberty.

break the caprice of the Homeric Olympus. But look at the bottom, the true thought and the soul. Living liberty is everywhere seen in his dramas. It circulates in them, and enlivens them with an extraordinary breath. In the *Seven*, and in the *Persians*, it breathes and is the country, the free genius of Greece. In the *Eumenides* it is the right, the judicial debate of Law and Nature. *Prometheus Bound* is, in the highest degree, the *freeman*— the liberty, all the more strong that it is the *daughter of Justice*. It is not Titanic fury, a vain *escalade* on heaven, but *just liberty* against the unjust heaven of Arbitrariness (or of Grace).

Prometheus is the true prophet of the Stoic, and of the Jurisconsult. He is the anti-pagan, the anti-Christian. He leans on law, he invokes nothing but his works. He proclaims only Justice, no privilege of race, no predestination, nothing of the archaic primogeniture of Titans over gods. The deliverance for which he waits will come to him sooner or later from the hero of Justice, Hercules, who will set him free and will kill the vulture which gnaws him. Jupiter then will yield to the Right, will submit to the return, the triumph of Prometheus.

But all must be expiated. He will not escape altogether. A terrible successor will come, a dreadful giant, armed with an avenging fire, to destroy that of Olympus and his little thunderbolt. Jupiter, bound in his turn, will become the *sufferer*. At the moment in which we think that Prometheus is on the point of telling the name of this conqueror of Jupiter, comes Mercury and interrogates him, but draws from him nothing but scorn. The thunder mutters. . . . In vain. Prometheus, with firm foot, waits, defies. . . . The thunderbolt falls. We remain in ignorance of this deep mystery.

The land of Athens, after the play of Prometheus, could no longer endure Æschylus. He voluntarily exiled himself. The people breathed easier.

A prophet is the honor and the scandal of the world.

Isaiah was sawn asunder. The unlucky Cassandra, in whom Æschylus appears to have painted himself, victim both of the people and of the gods, goes through outrages to find the deadly knife, under the fatal laurel. People are implacable toward those who force them to see. They bear a grudge to them for having spoken, and yet would compel them to speak more. If they do not explain themselves, they are impostors. " Die, or explain ! Thou breakest the public peace. Thou art the enemy of the commonwealth ! " This is the inward torture of the prophetic spirit. From those frightful peaks to which his flight had borne him, he sees the immensity, the *terra incognita*. But how can it be described ? This troubled vision, which can neither be illumined nor removed, overwhelms the seer. Æschylus, who had taken refuge in Sicily, survived a short time. Death came to him from heaven : " an eagle, holding a tortoise, looking for a rock on which to break it, took for a rock the head of Æschylus, his great bald forehead." The eagle was not deceived.

After Æschylus there came no prophet. In his hundred tragedies, in which he is so antique, and by far the elder of Homer, he had made, if we may say it, the *Greek Bible*, the *Old Testament*. All the Hellenic world, even in its remotest colonies, as long as it endured, played Æschylus at the festivals, as a religious duty.

To him alone was given to see, beyond the great age of the Arts and the Sophists, the road of brass from Pericles to the thirty tyrants. He speaks of it in the *Eumenides*. " Beware ! make thyself no master." In the *Prometheus*, exalting himself, embracing heaven and earth, he indicated the tyrannical ways of the " *young gods*," the orgies of the *god-tyrants*, who, by apotheoses or by incarnation, gave us the tyrant-gods.

Athens was shocked, and averted her eyes. She fell back on Sophocles. The beautiful and sweet geniuses of harmony, who delighted this century, took pains not to imitate the troublesome, the unrelenting Æschylus. Sophocles and Pheidias, far from denouncing the frailty of the gods, and their sad discordance, accorded to them in the marble and in the drama, if not a powerful life, at least the Elysian dignity of great spirits. Sophocles treats them with gentleness and respect, and vindicates them. By a happy turn, the disorder of the world was evaded, veiled. The dreadful Sphinx which Æschylus dared to exhibit, be assured, will be seen no longer. Sophocles, and his offspring Plato, who will soon appear, turn away their eyes from it. Does this monster still exist? Who could see it? A sacred forest of laurels, surrounding it, has become dense with underbrush, trees, leaves, and flowers!

The fencing of the Sophists, their amusing encounters, vie with the theatre. Under the porch, and in the gymnasia, the people encircled them. This people, laughing and inquisitive, values the Socratic irony more than any of the games of the athlete. They are proud, refined, subtile. Who would dare to entertain them with coarse novelties, which come from Thrace or Phrygia; with those little Mysteries, which the women play among themselves in the evening; with the orgies of weeping, in which, for the pleasure of lamenting, they mourn for the murder of Zagreus, who never existed, for the death of Adonis, lying on a bed of lettuce, or the wound of Atys, who is neither man nor woman? People scarcely deign to speak of it. So much the more easily did the obscure outflow of the follies of Asia gain stealthily, and infiltrate itself.

It is asked how Asia acts so slightly on Greece through her purest genius, Persia, while she acts so strongly through the lowest, the mad blindness of Phrygia, through the charlatans of Cybelè, through the gloomy and unclean genius of Syria. Had she become so fallen, so enfeebled? Had she in her decline deserved such disgrace? This has been said, but wrongfully. Greece had no decay whatever. She died young, like Achilles. Her strength

and her fruitfulness were the same. Plato and Sophocles
had passed away. But the genius of Science opened to
her a new career, not less great, and more firm. Hippocrates, and Aristotle, those two remarkable observers,
began a Greece of adult and manly genius, armed with a
better method, with superior light, and more certain pro-
cesses, which was going to stride over two thousand
years, and approach the age of Galileo and Newton.

The internal wars of Greece could not have destroyed
her. She would have found in herself powerful renewals.
The strife of faction could not have destroyed her. The
incentive of competition, which stimulated effort, carried
energy to the highest degree, and was a part of her life.

Slavery, whatever may be said about it, did not destroy
her The Greek was not weakened by it ; he reserved to
himself the works of strength. There never was a people
more generous toward slaves. These frequented the
theatres, and were even admitted to the Mysteries. Their
condition was tolerable. Diogenes, the slave, would not
be enfranchised. An Athenian proverb tells how changeable was the condition of the slave : " The slave of to-day
will be a denizen to-morrow, and soon after a citizen."

Were the altered, corrupted customs of Greece her
ruin ? Not at all. The unclean Venus-Astartè of Phœnicia, who flourished at Cyprus, at Cythera, at Corinth,
had really very little place in Grecian life. The most ordinary sense, the most elementary physiology, show that
he who incessantly expends an enormous amount of
strength in all kinds of activity, has but little reserved
for vices. If I were assured that an artist worked
twenty hours daily, I should be fully persuaded as to his
morals.

The Greeks were talkers and laughers—often cynical.
Far from concealing anything, they have exhibited too
plainly miseries and shames which had rarely existed.
The Grecian morals, of which so much has been said, at
which the Greeks themselves jested, are to be seen in a

single district of Christendom which we could name, more than they ever were in the entire Grecian world.

The little that was really bad among them came very late. In the first rapture of Art, when Pheidias proved "that the human form was divine," the sublimity of the discovery raised the soul to a great height. It must be acknowledged that the extreme beauty of perfect harmony astonishes and stupefies more than it inspires love. Gymnastic life is chaste and sober. It is not at all probable that it made false women like those of Asia; on the contrary, it made hardened sinews and stony muscles, imposing and powerful males.

Woman was honored in Greece. She always had her part in the priesthood, and was not excluded from it as in Judea, and among many other peoples. Haughty, exacting citizen, much more than man, in all the solemn honors, she dominated over the house, frequently influenced in the State. The comic writers, and the incident of Lesbos in Thucydides, demonstrate this. She had her distinctive Mysteries,* her bonds of union very strong, which constituted a feminine republic. The jests of Aristophanes are most serious. The public evil was that women did not follow men, but remained stubbornly apart from them. Will Greece, in her Olympian course, in her burning chariot, over the wheels on fire, degrade this weak companion ? A life so strained ! Beyond all moderation, so many works and combats ! Woman is dazzled, frightened, and no longer sees man. What is this ? A fire from heaven ? . . . She fears the destiny of Semelè.

To this too brilliant light we must add the strange hilarity which comes from all excess of strength. It is the ardor, the youth, the triumphal pride of life. Woman is wounded by it and humiliated. Her eyes are downcast. She takes refuge in night. She ought not to have been left there. Easily she makes discreditable friends.

---

* The Thesmophoria.

Surely, this sister of Alkestes and of Antigoné, with such
a heart, admirably adapted to the devoutness of Nature,
deserved that her noble spirit should be opened to the
high life of Law.   She would have returned much.
Greece herself, with all her genius, had not been able to
conjecture that which the tender, assiduous culture of the
spouse, the fathoming of love, would have added to her
of heroic delicacy.

Woman was driven towards the mournful gods of the
East,—Bacchus, Atys, Adonis.   In the spring festivals,
thoughtless youths, in scoffing orgies, sang of the forsaken
beauty, whose void widowhood Bacchus alone could fill.

Can it be said that she had taken no step toward the
higher life ? Oh, no ! The immortal memory of her who
was calumniated, but who was a heroine as well as a sublime poet, still existed.   Alcæus reminds us of her in this
beautiful and touching line : " Dark hair ! sweet smile !
innocent Sappho ! "   Innocent ! *   This poet, proud and
strong, penetrating, uttered in this a beautiful truth :
Genius is innocence !   Profound mystery of great artists.
They preserve their purity whatever occurs.   Sappho
was born pure and very gentle.   Plato places her among
the seven sages.   We see her astonished and afflicted at
the news that her brother had purchased in Egypt a very
celebrated courtesan.   She was indignant at tyranny ;
she hazarded her life to overthrow the tyrant of Lesbos.
She lost her country, but found her genius in exile.

She changed all music.   She invented the song of tears
(*mixolydien*).   The lyre, under the hand, was insensible ;

* She was born at Lesbos in 612 B.C., conspired against Ptolemy at the
age of sixteen, and retired to Sicily.   She was a rich, married lady, and
mother of a son.   Her native country atoned for her exile by stamping her
image on the money as that of the genius of the town.   Sicily erected a statue
to her.   She was called the tenth muse.   Her memory was worshipped.   A
century or two after a songstress of Lesbos (either from love or enthusiasm)
took the name of Sappho.   It was she who made the leap at Leucadia.   (See
Visconti, etc.)   Toward A.D. 1822 medals have enabled us to distinguish
between the two Sapphos.

she made the bow, which causes it to sigh and groan. At
last (this is the great stroke) the uniform cadences which
had been in use, appeared emotionless to her passion.
She found the rhythm which darts the thought, and which
is named Sapphic. In a recitative of three verses, the
bow is straightened. . . . A short line relaxes it. . . . The
arrow is at the heart.

Nothing is more rare than to find rhythm. Homer and
Shakespeare had none. Of this ardent, good, tender,
astonishingly fruitful Sappho, who had inundated Greece
with flame and light, there remain but a few golden
words, simple sentences, which move our passion. Who
can say that with all this, she, the unfortunate, had not
found love ? That she had loved in vain ? That the
world had fled from her ? That she had no consolation
but the tenderness of her affectionate female pupils, who
wiped away her tears, and whose tender-hearted friendship has been aspersed ?

The tears and despair of Sappho constitute the accusation of Greece. The Greek genius, it must be confessed,
passed between two worlds, it lived in the midst of things,
neglecting the two extremes, the poles, the great perspective, which opened on one side or on the other. It
fathomed neither love nor death.

These are two schools and two great paths, through
which the soul studies herself, penetrates herself, in herself and in the All ; and in this loving Soul, that, through
these two harmonious forms—Death, Love—makes her
eternal beauty.

At the entrance of these two paths Greece turned aside,
went on, smiled. Her Love was but a child, a new-
fledged bird. Death, if not heroic, does not attract attention. Death is adorned, nimble, and crowned as at a banquet. The beautiful Proserpina descended below, but did
not part with her flowers.

It is a regret to us. Greece, manly and pure, very
lucid, had alone the right and power to lead us, as

another Theseus, to the double labyrinth, in which one is so easily lost. The effeminate, mutilated, enervated gods of Asia have conducted us thither through equivocal paths, greatly to our injury.

An entirely new, disagreeable host entered this world, *the weeping Death*, enervating and disheartening, exactly contrary to the harmonious Death, which greets, adopts the divine order, and is illuminated by it, as in the *Thoughts* of Marcus-Aurelius. This weeping, feminine spectre came to us, and in the midst of strong labors and manly resolutions, the heroic soaring, sighs near us, and says : " To what purpose ? "

Listen to this equivocal, vague, and effeminate preacher, swimming in the wave of reveries, mingling with grief, I know not what, that is loved : is it the sweet and holy tears of sorrow ? of pleasure ? We do not know.

Virgin of Athens ! Proud Pallas, so pure ! What must have been thy prophetic scorn when people dared to offer thee the feverish instrument, the stormy and mournful flute of the worship of Asia ? . . . Thou didst throw it into the fountain.

Hercules treated it in like manner. The day in which he heard the pathetic festival of Adonis, the enervated, the woman-god, he was indignant, and cursed the coming shame. But the supreme condemnation of these two *sexed-gods* is Prometheus, father of Fire. He taught us another process, which was unknown in Asia. How through the iron and the steel, the effort, Art brings forth this immortal daughter, Reason, Wisdom—the ether of clear thought, the only inventive and fruitful thought— exactly contrary to the dreamy torpor of the marvellous Orient.

But the East proceeds, invincible, fatal to the gods of light, through the charm of revery, through the magic of *chiaro-oscuro*, the clare-obscure. No more serenity. The human soul, this curious Eve, digging in the unknown, is going to rejoice and lament. It will doubtless find strange

12

depths. The strength and the calm? Never. It will have joy—violent, often mad, tart and gloomy. It will have tears; yes, many tears, the contrast between these two things, their struggle and impotency, and the melancholy which follows.

Part Second.

CHILDREN OF THE TWILIGHT, OF THE NIGHT, AND OF THE LIGHT REFLECTING AGAINST THE DARKNESS.

——:o:——

CHAPTER I.

EGYPT—DEATH.

EGYPT is certainly the greatest monument of death on this globe. No people on earth has made such persevering effort to preserve the memory of those who are no more, to continue to them an immortal life of honor, of remembrance, of worship. The whole length of the valley of the Nile is a great mortuary book, indefinitely unrolled like an ancient manuscript. Not a stone on which there is not a writing, adorned with figures, with symbols, and enigmatical characters. Tombs on the right, on the left; temples which appear to be sepulchres. Nothing more imposing to us than this long funeral path.

Very different is the impression on the African. The Nile is the joy of Africa, her festival and her smile. This great river of life which, from unknown mountains, brings its tribute so faithfully every year, is the idol, the fetish of the world of blacks. As soon as they see it in the distance they laugh, they sing, they adore. In this thirsty land the constant concern is water. From the great sand desert of Libya, or from the frightful chains of granite which lie on the Dead Sea and toward the desert of Sinai, for what is the vow, the prayer, and the sigh? A drop of water. A trifling oozing under a palm-tree is called emphatically an *oasis;* people flock to it and bless it. What must have been the love for the great oasis, Egpyt? Thou didst ask water. Behold a sea, an immense sheet of water, in which the land disappears, soaked, flooded, and dissolved. Toward the north it is but ooze. It is precisely this ooze, this Delta saturated with water, which is the paradise of Africa. All desired to live there. All wished the joy of it at least after death. Their bodies were conveyed thither in boats. The tombs were piled on top of one another. This low Egypt, luxuriant in productions, is the triumph of life, like an orgy of nature.

Behold, then, two aspects, decidedly different, of this region. Our Europe admires it for its mortuary aspect; Africa and the South for its river, for its possessions of water and food. We would willingly think of it as an immense female Sphinx of the length of the Nile, a colossal nurse in grief, exhibiting a beautiful face, noble and gloomy, to the world of whites, while, before its breast, and around it, the blacks kneel.

This is the first glance. The impression at the second is no less great. Nowhere, in the solemn accord of heaven and earth, is the drama more striking. The Nile, pontifically, on a fixed day, descends and rolls, expands, refreshes, and fertilizes. It scarcely subsides, before man, equally regular, without losing time, measures, re-establishes everything, ploughs and sows, and so accomplishes the agricultural round of the year; while, from above, the sun, almighty benefactor, no less punctually vivifies, quickens, and blesses.

Life of immense labor! But still more immense was the conservative force, the effort against death, the admirable perseverance to preserve, in spite of it, all that was possible of life. The family is exhibited there in its most affecting aspects. Unique example! An entire people, during many thousands of years, has absolutely had nothing else in view than to assure one another of the second life of the sepulchre. We cannot think, without emotion, of the privation with which the most poor purchased it. Each tomb is for two—the husband and wife. This was their common aim. The man by excessive work, and the woman by the most extreme economy, gained and hoarded the little sum necessary to purchase what was needed in order to be embalmed together, to sleep together under the stone, and so be resuscitated again.

The contrast is very beautiful. Egypt is admirable for death and for life ; both of which contribute equally to this greatness. It is a region by nature harmonious, and, quite artlessly, a system. There is nothing elsewhere to be compared to it. The great Carthage, for example, her monstrous empire, scattered here and there in fragments, is entirely different. This is also the case with Syria. She has two faces, like Egypt, but they are by no means in harmony.

Egypt, on the contrary, in her institutions, and in her diverse characteristics of art as well as of nature, was a unit, perfectly blended, both by the natural gentleness of her profound, peaceful spirit, and by time—the enormous duration. She participated in the majesty of the tomb. All came to honor her as the great mistress of death. All—even Greece, came to her school, and interrogated the Egyptian priests. Their enigmas and their symbolism, their purifications, their great festivals, their continual judgments on the dead, the constant lamentations of female weepers, and of male weepers likewise—for man also wept at funerals—all this was imposing, affecting. In spite of himself the observer imitated—not all, but this or that particular ; and often awkwardly. Phœnicia, opposed by nature, Judea, opposed by profound hatred, notwithstanding, appropriated some parts, as did also the Christians. Though the Christians denounced Egypt, they followed her, and still follow her. In their ideas, their rites, their festivals, their calendar, their funeral dogmas, their great dogma of the death of God, they follow with so

many other people, behind her sepulchral boat, and in its
eternal track.

Champollion has well said : " Egypt is altogether
African, and not Asiatic."

The official monuments, in their monotonous solemnity,
do not, any more than the priestly Pantheon in its dreary
doctrines, speak clearly on this point. But the popular
religion points it out distinctly. It is altogether African,
without mystery, in broad daylight, all love, sensitive goodness—voluptuous goodness. What can we do with it ? It is
Nature, the mother of us all, venerable as well as impressive.
Whatever she does, we must love and respect her !

The poor people—in their laborious life, in this monotonous climate, with a culture always the same, a weighty
enigma of dogma, of incomprehensible writing—would
have failed a hundred times without the good genius of
Africa, her Isis, the divine female, tender mother and
faithful spouse. In her they lived.

If goodness exists anywhere on earth, it is in those
races. Their types, remote from the dull people of the
negro countries, and no less differing from the dry Arabian or Jew, have an extreme mildness. The family is
very affectionate, and the welcome is good and sympathetic even toward the stranger. Egypt knew little of
human sacrifices. It is true that annually a girl was
thrown into the Nile, but it was a girl of wicker. No
Harems and no Eunuchs. Neither eccentric love nor
mutilation of infants, as in Æthiopia, in Syria, and everywhere. Monogamy was general and voluntary. A man
could have many wives. The spouse had great ascendency, and maintained it. On the upper Nile she had the ·
peculiar felicity of never looking aged. She preserved the
beautiful forms which are seen on the monuments, the
very full bosom, erect, firm, elastic.* It indicates, as in

---

* CAILLAUD, II., 224. This author speaks also of the charming piety of one
of the female Æthiopians, who, seeing our travellers completely exhausted,
asked them how long it was since they left the Nile. "Four months ago."—

the sacred paintings, eternal virginity, and continually holds erect the vase of immortal youth.

The Kings of Asia, who often had, like the Xerxes of Herodotus, a profound sense of nature, preferred the Egyptian to all other women, asked her from the Pharaohs. They loved her better than the servile Asiatic, or than that haughty half-male, who was called woman in Europe. They believed her to be ardent, capable and yet teachable, especially rich in goodness ; in a word, that she would return the most love and obedience.

Woman ruled in Egypt. She could mount the throne, and was a queen in every house. She transacted every kind of business. Man acknowledged her genius, did not forsake his work, and tilled or wove.* Diodorus goes so far as to say that the husband swore to obey his wife. Without her skilful government, neither could have reached that difficult aim of the poor, the common embalmment, the union of eternal rest.

Egypt was delighted with her Isis, and saw nothing but her. Not only did Egypt adore her as a woman, as enjoyment, as happiness, and as goodness ; but all that was good was Isis. The wished-for water ; the river, the good liquid female (Nile is feminine), was not distinguishable from Isis. The fruitful Earth, which brings water, even all Egypt was Isis. The good, motherly cow was so much loved by the goddess that she took its horns for her ornaments. The horns or the moon-like crescent ? Isis was the white moon, which comes so agreeably in the evening after the intense heat of the day, which imparts rest to the laborer and his beloved wife ; the moon, sweet companion which regulates duties, which measures the work to man, the love to woman, and marks its return, its epoch and *its sacred crisis.*

"Four months !" said she, fixing on us her beautiful black eyes, full of mildness, and, stretching her arms toward us, again said : "Oh, my friends ! Oh, my unhappy brothers !" She gave all she had, dates, water.—*Ibid*, p. 242.

* HERODOTUS.

This Queen of the heart, the good genius of Africa.
without mystery, was enthroned as woman, simply
adorned with her beautiful breasts, and all the attributes
of motherhood.   She carried the lotus in her sceptre, the
pistil of the flower of love.   She bears royalty on her
head, in the form of a diadem, the greedy bird, the Vulture, which never says " Enough."   The Vulture, em-
blem of Death, austere procuress, which imposes love, the
maternal renewal.

The badge of the Cow-Mother, which, strange head-
dress, is erected above the Vulture, indicates all that love
wishes : *to renew life incessantly*.   Beneficent fruitfulness, infinite, maternal goodness, constitute the innocence
of the passionate ardors of Africa.   Soon love and grief,
the eternity of regret, will more than sanctify them.

In the Universal Mother (Isis-Athor, or Night) were
conceived, before time, a daughter and a son, Isis-Osiris,
who, being two, were yet but one.   They had loved each
other so much in the maternal womb, that Isis became
pregnant, and before her birth she was a mother.   She
had a son named Horus, who is but the father formed
again, another Osiris of goodness, of beauty, of light.
Three therefore were born, mother, father, son, of the
same age, of the same heart.

What a joy !   Behold them at the altar.   The woman,
the man, and the child.   Bear in mind that these are persons, living beings.   Not the fantastic trinity which India
makes out of the discordant marriage of three archaic
religions.   Not the scholastic trinity which Byzantium
has subtly woven into her metaphysics.   In Egypt, it is
life, nothing more.   From the burning jet of nature
comes forth the triple human unity.

No other myth had such strength of reality and truth.
The mother was not a virgin (as that of Buddha, of
Genghis, and so many others) ; she was indeed a woman, a
true woman, full of love, and her breast full of milk.
Osiris is a true husband, whom no one can scoff at ; real

and active, of assiduous generation, so enamored of his Isis that his superabundant love fecundated all nature. The son was a true son, so like to his father that he was a solemn testimony to the union of the parents. He was the living glory of love and marriage.

As all was strong and true, beyond the false and the doubtful, so the result was also strong and positive. The human Osiris religiously conformed to the One above, fecundating his Isis, Egypt—fertilizing woman and earth, generating incessantly from his work fruits and the arts.

These gods had not the impersonality, the obscurity, and the terror of certain religions of Asia. They were venerable and affecting, and they did not affright. If the Hindustanic Siva were not careful to close his eyes, he would unconsciously burn all with his devouring glance.

In Egypt human nature itself was at the altar, in the mild aspect of the family, blessing creation with a maternal eye. The great God was a mother. I am greatly reassured! I feared that the world of the blacks, too greatly dominated by the bestial life, had been struck in their birth by the terrifying images of the lion and the crocodile, and would never make but monsters. But behold them tender-hearted, humanized. The amorous Africa, from her profound desire, has given birth to the most attractive object of the religions of earth. . . . What ? The living reality, a good and fruitful woman.

Joy bursts forth, immense and popular, and altogether natural ; a joy peculiar to thirsty Africa. It was water, a deluge of water, a prodigious sea of sweet water, which came from I know not whence, but which overspread the land, drowned it in happiness, infiltrating itself, insinuating itself into the least veins, so that not a particle of sand had cause to complain of thirst. The small, dry canals smiled in proportion as the murmuring water visited and refreshed them. The plant laughed heartily when this salutary water moistened the beard of its roots, besieged the stalk, ascended to the leaf, inclined the stem which was softened, and moaned sweetly. Charming spectacle, immense chain of love and of pure voluptuousness ! All this was the great Isis, flooded by her beloved.

But nothing endures. How can we deny this ? All perishes. The Nile, the father of life, dries up, becomes parched. The Sun is tired. Behold him obscured, turned pale ; he has lost his rays. The *living Sun* of goodness, who sowed in the bosom of Isis his seed—every wholesome thing, had been able to create all things out of himself, except time, duration. One morning he disappeared. . . . He had been immolated by his cruel brother Typhon, who divided him with the sword, dismembered and scattered his body. The honor of man, his pride and his strength, his manhood, had been harshly mutilated. Where are these poor remains ? Everywhere, over the earth, in the waves. The stormy sea carried part of them as far as Phœnicia.

Here we leave the domain of fables. It is a living reality, an excruciating recollection of the mutilations which were made (and are made) to prepare false women, young eunuchs, for the markets, who were sold for the Harems of the East. For a long time Phœnicia was the centre for these sales.

Isis tore her hair, and went in search of her Osiris. With true African grief, the most ingenuous in the world, Isis, abandoned, without pride, confided to all nature the painful tortures of her widowhood, her regret, her poignant desire, the heart-breaking impotency in which she was to live without him. At last she found some of the members which the waves had carried off. She went as far as Byblos, in Syria, to recover them, and obtained the pledge that they should be returned. Only one part was wanting.* Profound despair ! " Alas, this missing part is life ! Sacred power of love, if deficient, what becomes of the world ? Where can I find it ? "

* The אלב, *pala*, or phallus, which being the physical *agent* for procreation, was made the symbol of Life.—ED.

She implored the Nile and Egypt. Egypt was unwilling to surrender that which would be for her the assurance of eternal fecundity.

But such great love and grief well deserved a miracle. In the violent contest of tenderness and of death, Osiris, although dismembered and cruelly mutilated, by a powerful will, revived and returned to her. And so great was his love, that by the strength of the heart, he found a last desire. He came back from the grave to make her again a mother. Oh! how eagerly she received this embrace. . . . Alas! It was nothing more than a farewell. The ardent bosom of Isis will not warm this icy germ. No matter. The fruit born of it, sad and pale, indicated no less the supreme victory of love, which, fruitful before life, is still so after death.

The comments which have been made on this very simple legend lend it a deep meaning of astronomical symbolism. And certainly the coincidence of the destiny of man with the course of the year, the decadence of the sun, etc., was early felt. But all this is secondary, observed later, and added. The first origin is human; it is the real wound of the poor widow of Egypt, and of her inconsolable sores.

On the other hand, we must not be deceived by the coarse African coloring. There is here something more than the regret of physical desire and unsatiated passion. With regard to such suffering, Nature would have had a ready answer. But Isis did not wish simply a male, she wished him whom she loved; *her own, and not another;* him, and him only. It was a feeling entirely exclusive and *individual.* It is to be seen in the infinite care she takes of his mortal remains, so that not one atom shall be wanting, and death shall make no change in them, but some day shall render, in its integrity, this unique object of love.

In this most tender, altogether pure and ingenuous legend, there is an astonishing zest of immortality which has never been surpassed. Be hopeful, ye afflicted hearts, sad widows, little orphans. You weep; Isis also wept, but she did not despair. Osiris, the dead, still lives. He is here, renewed in his innocent Apis. He is now the shepherd in the underworld of souls, the complaisant keeper of the world of ghosts, and your dead are near him. Fear nothing, they are there. They will return some day and reclaim their bodies. Let us envelop with care their precious mortal remains. Let us embalm them with perfumes, with prayers, with burning tears. Let us keep them near us. Oh! the delightful day in which the Father of souls, coming out from the dark kingdom, will return to you the cherished souls, rejoin them to their bodies, and say: "I have preserved them for you."

Up to this point all is natural. A beautiful popular tradition added to it an incredible excess of goodness. It was said that Isis, in her melancholy excursion, when she was looking for the remains of her husband, found something black, bloody, and shapeless,—a little newborn monster. She knew by its color that it was an offspring of the black Typhon, her enemy, her tormentor, the ferocious murderer. This child was Anubis, the figure of a grave-digger, with the head of a dog or a jackal, as seen on the monuments. But the adorable goddess, in the presence of this feeble creature, that was crying or yelping, felt only compassion. Goodness was stronger than love and grief. She raised it from the ground, and took it in her arms. She could have had it brought up and nourished by another; but Isis is all tenderness and mercy. She could not do anything by halves. She pressed the odious nursling to her bosom, to her deeply-lacerated heart; in tears she smiled on it, and magnanimously ended by giving it the breast. Spectacle truly divine! Let all the earth behold! The widow of the murdered one nourished the child of the murderer. Satiated with the milk of goodness, bathed with the tears of love, the monster became a god.*

This is the most tender conception of the human mind. I do not see anything in either the myths of India, or the Christian myths, that can be compared to it. The myth of Egypt declared that race innocent which the middle ages believed to be devilish, damned; it established this fact, that crime was not transmissible; that the child of the criminal (black as his father) is no less worthy of celestial compassion; that divine goodness admits him to rise, to mount to God.

The result is beautiful. This black child, this son of crime, by his illegitimate birth doomed to death, and yet consecrated to life by his nurse, became the genius of the passage between life and death, the good genius who interpreted the two worlds.† He understood everything, knew all mysteries, created all art. It was he who fixed memory, in which the fleeting generations will be preserved and consecrated. He formulated and calculated the year. He invented writing, which chronicles the remembrance of the months and years. His art gives to our mortal remains that stability which enables us to await in bonds the day of resurrection. But the supreme office of Anubis, and his highest benefaction, was to welcome, to reassure, and to lead the poor soul at the moment that it left the body. The soul, a sad bird, wandering, entered a strange world. Did it sleep? Was it awake? This is well exhibited in a magnificent copy of the *Book of the Dead*, on a mantel-piece of the Louvre. The soul, represented as an interesting young man, does not know what to do, but is in good hands. The dear Anubis touches his heart, and strengthens it. " What dost thou fear? I answer for thee. . . . Fear not the Judgment. . . . If I, the black

---

*Anubis is declared by Plutarch (*Isis and Osiris*, 14), and other writers, to have been the offspring of Osiris and Nephthys, wife of Typhon.— ED.

‡ He was styled the פתח, *peter*, or opener, because he opened the mysteries of the underworld.—ED.

son of Typhon, have passed in safety, thou, innocent, pure in thy white robes, hast not reason to be alarmed. Come ! the good Osiris awaits thee."

While writing this, I glanced over the plates of the grand Descriptions—those of Champollion, of Rossellini, and of Lepsius. With my heart filled with these sublime myths, I was anxiously looking for images of reality to bring them out clearly. One plate arrested my attention, and made me think.* It was that in which a sub-farmer, at the head of his cattle, was going to render his account to a scribe, who notes the number, and writes down whether the flock has increased or diminished. The peasant, still young in appearance, beardless, as all Egyptians, stands with arms folded over his breast, in the posture of religious respect. The scribe, by no means imposing, is the agent of the king or the priests. It is known by the beautiful history of Joseph, that all the land of Egypt belonged to the king, except one-third, which, according to Diodorus (i., 40), belonged to the sacerdotal order. Property, in Egypt, was scarcely anything more than a tenantry. From the Pharaohs to the Ptolemies, to the Sultans, to the Beys, the sovereign had the land cultivated by whom he wished. He was at liberty to make each generation pay, to compel the son to redeem the land which his father had occupied. The results of such a system are known. It made misery perpetual in the richest country in the world. At the death of the father, the family knew not its destiny. At the moment in which the embalmers entered, with the chisel in their hands, the son and the mother fled in tears, and abandoned the body and the house. The next day another proceeding took place. The scribe of the king, or of the priest, entered, pen in hand, and reckoned the animals ; and from his report it was decided whether the family had increased the cattle and deserved to be continued. I think the plate, to

---

* ROSSELLINI, in folio, vol. ii., plate 30.

which I have referred, exhibits a scene of this kind. At the foot of the scribe is seen a prostrate female figure, so very humble, as to appear terrified—as if praying and entreating. Is she the wife, or the mother of the tenant?

The poor family underwent at once two judgments. Could the survivors retain the occupancy? Would the dead person be judged worthy to enter the sacred tomb? The priest alone decided.

Enormous privilege, which, among people so tender in their family attachments, accorded to the priests unbounded terror.

Overwhelming servitudes carried the men away incessantly. Everything was performed by manual labor. Rameses employed one hundred and twenty thousand men at one time to erect one of the obelisks of Thebes.* To cut and smooth the basalt, the granite, and the porphyry, with the rude tools of that time, how many men and centuries were necessary? A man taken in youth, recently married, wasted his life in the quarry, and did not re-enter his home until bowed with age. Oh! how many human lives, chagrins, and tears, in the building of the Pyramids, those true mountains of grief, in the enormous cemeteries of the low lands on the side of Libya! And how much despair in the subterranean perforations of the mountain-chains on the Arabian side, in those rugged rocks which eternal labor changed into funeral bee-hives! Thousands of living men, in order to hollow those abodes of the dead, have lived by the lamp-light only. Dead themselves, if we may so say, having no day, no sky, but in the smoky vaults of the sepulchre.

"The sacred characters were only known by the priests,† and ignored by the people, by those numerous masses whose years were wasted by engraving them on the granite. All the complications of the three Egyptian styles of writing are known: symbolism, short-hand, and ordinary

* LETRONNE : *Acad.*, xvii., 34.
† DIODORUS.

alphabet. Is this figure before me a man, or an idea?
Is it a sentence or a letter? Overwhelming enigmas,
which surely the head of the stone-carver could scarcely
have unravelled. Admitting that he could have read those
terrible inscriptions, and pierced the mystery under the
obscurity, what would he have found? The obscure
meaning of the sacerdotal religion, the hidden doctrines of
emanation, by which the gods, issued one from another,
easily re-entering one another, mingled and confounded
one with another, precisely as in the black conduits which
had been pierced in those mountains, the funeral labyrinth
became entangled and confusing.

Neither the characters nor the thoughts were intelligible
to the people. But the harshest thing is that Egypt had
for ten thousand years* pined away in this enormous
work, without even the consolation of understanding its
sense and purport. Alas! where is 'the good, popular
religion, so touching and so clear, summed up in Isis?
What has become of it? Isis is still seen in the monuments near the kings, as adviser, as protectress. But in
reality the active and master spirit in all this was the wise
god Thoth,—an elevated, refined form of Anubis. This
religion of goodness, which issued from the heart of a
woman, was changed by him, and became a system, a
laborious system, pervaded with dogmas and observances,
a scholasticism of priests.

Death was the only hope for the man and woman so
frequently separated. In that hot region where the sun
splits the stone at mid-day, the poor laborer prayed

---

* PLATO: *Laws*, ii., 3. " This doctrine has been known among them from
antiquity ; . . . they exhibit them in their temples ; and except there, it is not
lawful either for painters or others who work out forms, or whatever else
there may be, to introduce any innovation, or even to think of any other than
those of the country ; . . . and you will, by observing, discover that what have
been painted and sculptured there *ten thousand* years ago—and I say ten
thousand not as a word, but a fact, οὐχ ὡς ἔπος ειπειν μυριοστον αλλ' ουτως-
are neither more beautiful nor more ugly than those turned out of hand at
the present day, but are worked off according to the same art.—ED.

this sun to give him, by its liberating stroke, rest forever with and near his wife. On her part, the woman cultivating the earth, with her son, subjecting herself to many fastings, thought of nothing but of the accumulation of the little money for the embalmment.

If either of them failed in this end! If he was so unfortunate as to be judged unworthy of the sepulchre! and his wife condemned to eternal widowhood! . . . Painful thought which troubled the mind and spoiled even death!

The soul, the best soul, could not attain a second birth, except through a laborious series of transformations.* What, then, would become of the doomed soul, which, alone and without a god to conduct it, took this terrible journey? Horrible and unclean, it was changed into a swine, which was detested by the Egyptians as well as by the Jews. Fantastical monsters intervened to debar the way. With these the soul had to fight. To crown the whole, it was scourged by malevolent guardians. Query, Ape-demons? Leopard-demons? †

Behold the swine into which, according to the gospel, Jesus sent the demons. Behold the Middle Ages, the beginning of the elements of those traditions of terrors, which have so cruelly narrowed and perverted the mind. The agony was frightful. As in the dark Christian centuries (the tenth, eleventh, and so on) the dying man, believing that he would be carried away by demons, had recourse to the invocation of saints, and had himself covered with relics, so the Egyptian was so frightened that the one guardian, Thoth or Anubis, could not reassure him. He feared for each limb, and for each claimed the aid of a special god. He caused himself to be upheld, not by four, but by fifteen or twenty divinities. A god

---

* In an inscription, Ahmes, chief of Mariners, intending to say: "*I was born,*" said "I have accomplished my transformations."—DE ROUGÉ, *Acad. of Inscrip. M. des savants étrangers*, 1853, vol. III., p. 55.

† I cannot distinguish which of the two by the plates of Champollion. (In folio, vol. III., plate 272.)

13

was responsible for his nose, and kept it secure. Another
warranted his teeth, another his eyes, another his neck.
The terror was so excessive that he was not satisfied with
having the arm protected, but must also have a guardian
for the elbow ; and so with the leg and knee.*

Spirits did not *appear* by day, so that the living could
act.   At night they walked over the earth, even the bad
spirits.   Hence a thousand fears, a thousand spectres.
No safety at the hearth.   The innocence of animals, their
peaceful manner, sometimes gave assurance.   Hence,
probably more than from anything else, the excessive at-
tachment to these good companions ; hence the touching
small talk, the worship of the sacred animals, the gentle
friends of man, that cared for him in life and death.

Where ends the animal ?   Where begins the plant ?
Who can tell ?   Sensitive plants, Ampère remarks, in this
powerful climate, approach the animal.   They have their
fears and their dislikes, as if they were delicate women,
fixed by fate to a single spot ; without language, without
the means of flying or escaping.   Palm-trees evidently
love.   In all ages, in Egypt, the people assisted them in
their loves.   The male plant, separated from its love, was
drawn near by the ready hand of man.

The tree moans and weeps, as with a human voice.
The French in Algiers, who were cutting trees in 1840,
were surprised and almost frightened at hearing them
groan.   An illustrious, learned man was present, and was
troubled, moved, as the others.   What must have been
the impression of those sighs of the tree, of those heart-
rending complaints on the mind of the poor Fellah !   How
could he doubt that a wretched soul, like his own, was

* Champollion had already given one of those rituals of the dead, in the 4th
vol. of *Cailliaud's Journeys.* Lepsius published one complete in 1842, in
quarto, and M. DE ROUGÉ has given another, in folio, in this very year, 1864. I
see in it the most curious things.   The soul has to fight the fantastic animals.
It is forbidden to work in Ker-neter, to leave (the Amenti) the infernal regions during the day.   When it rises again it will recover its heart, etc.

under the bark? The tree, being rare in Egypt, is so much the more loved and cherished. He who had the happiness to have one at, or near his door, lived with it. He related everything to it, confided to it his fears and his griefs, the exactions of the scribe or the overseer, the excessive work, void of consolation, and alas! sometimes other wounds, cruel and from the beloved hand. In brief, *he trusted it with his heart*, deposited it, hid it in the tree. The *Mimosa*, which shudders and feels everything, sometimes received this heart; also the Persian laurel, the tree of Isis, admirable tree; its leaf a tongue, its fruit in the form of a heart.*

But what part of the tree is sufficiently discreet to receive this delicate deposit? The trunk? perhaps, because, when cut, it moans. Or, is it the branch, which, between itself and the trunk, can press and hide, unite maternally? Or is it simply the flower? In the cases of the mummies, the painted flower is half open, permitting a small head to pass, the pretty soul of a woman. If such an Acacia closes its flower at evening, it is to preserve the heart of man.

Great and profound secret. This Egyptian tree is not like that of Persia, the sublime Tree of Life. It is a restless tree. It may be ruthlessly cut down to-morrow for a boat, or a palace. What then becomes of the heart? The man trusted the secret of his deposit to only one person, to his unique, beloved spouse, putting his life in her hands. We may imagine with what veneration the woman regarded the tree, after the death of her husband! How sacred, and what a confidant! How consulted, how listened to in those hours of security when alone. It was the successor; it was a husband, a lover, an altar, a dead and living god, often bathed with tears.

Such things only happen in true love, in monogamy, the holy, solemn, and tender marriage, as it was in Egypt. The tree did not fail to be moved and to answer. The

---

* PLUTARCH,

wife often lived on the tears shed by the tree,—tears of its own kind, vegetable tears doubtless, of the pine and many other trees. Was this friendly compassion? Was this really the soul of the dead imprisoned under the bark, pressed, suffering, which, in order to reveal itself in its poor language, wept this sentence to her: "I still love"?

This touching faith, which has made the tour of the world, had its primitive, its purest type, in Egypt.

The sepulchral boat of Isis, searching for Osiris, landed at Byblos, in Syria. I know not what, in the bottom of her heart, told her that he had stopped there, and was in the palace of the King. In order to be received there, Isis, although a queen, humiliated herself, and represented herself as a servant. She observed and watched everything. The magnificent palace, supported by columns, had one column (Oh! miracle!) which wept. This was a pine-tree.* Isis had no doubt whatever that it was he. She divined the metamorphosis. It had floated to the coast, to the pine forest of Syria, and hidden itself in the sand; it became a pine-tree. Placed in the palace, it always remembered, and wept. Isis drew it from its position, embraced it, and flooded it with tears, and rendered it funeral honors.†

---

* At Teneriffe, the pines, which have supported the houses since 1400, still weep.

† This legend of the living tree, so sorrowful and sometimes comforting, appears to have had its origin in Upper Egypt, in the *Acacia mimosa* of the desert, continued in the *Persea Laurus*, in the pine in Syria, in the pomegranate and almond tree in Phrygia, etc. The unique literary monument, which, up to this day, we have from Egypt, very ancient in character, and certainly even more ancient in conception, starts from the acacia. It is a short personal story, which serves as the frame-work of the general and popular idea.

A very honest and laborious young man, named Satou, worked at his elder brother's, and made the cattle prosper. The wife of this brother, who was a beautiful woman, preferred Satou, because he was strong, and wished one day, at the burning hour of rest, to keep him with her. Despised, she accused him. He would have perished if his ox and cow, which loved him, had not put him on his guard. He swore his innocence, and assured it forever by a cruel mutilation. Very desolate and alone, he retired into the desert *and put his heart into an Acacia.* The gods had compassion on him, and made for him a more beautiful and admirable wife, whom he loved so much as to entrust to her the tree in which he had placed his heart.

This beloved but ardent woman, eagerly desiring an efficacious love, grew weary, and allowed herself to be carried off. The Nile bore her to Pharaoh. Remorse went with her. She thought she could end it by cruel means, by cutting down the tree of Satou. In vain. The poor heart became a magnificent bull, which groaned and roared at her. It was killed. Two drops of its blood had fallen on the ground. Out of them sprang two trees, not the wretched acacia which was cut, but two sublime trees, two gigantic *perseas*, which chatted together of love, and sighed. The queen was frightened, and caused them to be sawn down; but a splinter separated and touched her so intimately, that she became with child. Satou had conquered her in spite of herself. He was restored to the human form, was glorified, and became *Phra*, Pharaoh, Sun. (All the same.) Now master of this cruel wife, he did not avenge himself, but only related to her what she had caused him to suffer. See the translation and the very interesting notice, which M. DE ROUGÉ has given of this manuscript of the fifteenth century B.C.—*Athenæum Français,* vol. i., p. 281. 1852.

CHAPTER II.

SYRIA—PHRYGIA—ENERVATION.

IN the funereal monotony of Egypt one feels his soul alienated, cramped (during a hundred centuries), and stifled, as under the tree of grief. The contrast is very striking when one gets out of such a place and enters the stirring world which lies round about it. It seems to him that a sea, a tempest of sand, like the whirlwind in the desert of Libya, or in that of Suez, is floating before his eyes. Among the blacks of the Upper Nile, in the encampments of the Arabs, in the world separated from Syria, even in those great empires of the profligate Babylon and the barbarous Carthage, the mind seemed to be led astray, and to be in the midst of a chaos.

The myths, which are luminous in Greece, harmonious in Egypt, and which maintain an appearance of wisdom even when most fantastical, here seem to whirl as the simoom of the desert. It has not been spoken enough of how much this south-west between Africa and Asia, where all is fragmentary, divided, unorganized, looks in its whimsical worships, like a real dream.*

---

* In the conscientious Egyptian paintings, which strike the beholder with their truthfulness, one may see what difference in countenance there was, seventeen centuries before Christ, between the Syrian, the Assyrian, the Arabian or the Jew, the Negro, and the European (the Grecian as it would seem). Those paintings are masterpieces indeed. The Grecian, who looks like a man of modern Greece, is the mariner of the islands, with a profile harsh and cunning, and with a piercing look. The Negroes are lively. In their excessive and unconnected gesticulation it is very well shown that they are not stupid fellows, but that, on the contrary, they are too lively, of rich blood, unsettled in their convictions, hot-headed, and half-mad. A precisely opposite type is exhibited in the stiff and unyielding Bedouin, the angular though not ignoble Arab, the rough and unprogressive Jew—pebbles of Sinai cut fine as with a sharp instrument. I am sure these will live and defy the action of time. But

Syria felt her god in the swarming sea, whose waves seethed and bubbled up a flood of living foam, oily and permeated with myriads of fishes. Like the Euphrates,* she had for her ideal the fish and the Female-Fish.

Certainly, if the infinity of inferior love, of fecundation shows itself anywhere, it is undoubtedly in the fish. Fishes could fill the sea. They swamp it literally at certain times, make it white and illumined with a fat, thick, and phosphorescent *sea of milk.*

Behold the Venus of Syria! It is Derceto, it is Astarté or Ashtaroth, who is male and female, the dream of generation. The Hebrew, at the skirts of the desert, living poorly, dreams of a people as numerous as the whirling sand. The Phœnician, in the rich towns of badly-smelling ports, dreams of the infinity of tide, a people of amphibious beings, who stir and swarm from Seidon to Carthage and to the ocean.

In the inland, the poetry of the amorous Syrian women, who are pretty and who woo lasciviously, was to dream

---

the ephemeral and spurious figures of Babel and Phœnicia are short-lived, and, like insects, continue their species through the ceaseless renewal of generations. The man of the river Euphrates is a fish; the man of Tyre is a frog. The low backward inclination of the forehead in the Babylonian figure reminds us of his god, and belongs to the aquatic world, the Magian fish. The man, however, is not repulsive, nor is he void of grace in his movements; he inspires us with confidence, and seems to bid us "Welcome." And thus is it that the gods of every land, and men of all nations, were attracted and fused together helter-skelter in Babylon, because of the easy and accommodating manners of the Babylonians, who freely welcomed and admitted all on equal terms. Unlike the Babylonians, the Phœnicians are not dressed in beautiful and closely-fitting robes, but with short jacket (of esparto ?) and naked arms, like a sailor, leaving their limbs free for action. Their eye is clear, and they seem like men accustomed to look at distant objects on the great plain of the sea. This picture, however strange, is beautiful and serious. More wonderful: they have no neck. Singular abortions, their precocious vices have arrested their growth. Their faces indicate cruelty and indifference, which fit them for their profession as merchants; a horrible traffic in human flesh being the chief article of their commerce.

* See the monuments in RAWLINSON (1862), v. 1st, page 167, in BOTTA, AUSTEN, LAYARD, etc.

of numberless doves, a people obscene and charming. Their violent caresses, their love-intrigues, very irregular, whatever may have been said to the contrary—were the spectacle and the lesson. And their consecrated nests, increasing day by day, could at their leisure whiten the sad cypress of Astarté.

The Phœnicians carried away with them Astarté * on their ships, that they might have a good voyage. They worked on her behalf. Their great commerce consisted in carrying off doves—women, girls, or pretty boys—and taking them to the seraglios of Asia. Their religion was to raise, in every settlement which they founded, an altar to Astarté, a convent of soiled turtle-doves, who fleeced the foreigners.† Cyprus and Cythera were defiled by this worship to such an extent that the girls of these islands underwent, each of them, the sacred blemish before their marriage. ‡

They were lucky enough to get off at such a price. For this Ashtoreth or Astarté, the Venus of pirates, was not always distinguished from the other god of the Phœnicians, whom they called the King (Moloch), and who was so fond of boys that he stole some of them every-

---

* Venus Euplæa, the goddess of prosperous voyages by sea.—ED.

† Jacob Bryant describes the Sirens and Lamiæ of Italy as a Canaanitish priesthood, whose women, by their music and personal charms, seduced travellers and sea-faring men to repair to their temples. The Jewish *Scriptures* make frequent mention of them, קדשים and קדשות, men and women consecrated to the sanctuaries. The *liaison* of Judah (*Genesis* xxxviii.) with his daughter-in-law, Tamar, was induced by the religious consideration that she was a *holy woman*, a minister of the temple, and not a harlot. All Syria, from Hierapolis and Cappadocia to Arabia and Egypt, swarmed with these votaries of Astarté, both male and female.

‡ HERODOTUS: i., 199. "The Babylonians have one most shameful custom. Every woman born in the country must once in her life go and sit down in the precinct of Venus [Mylitta or Astarté] and there consort with a stranger. . . . A custom very much like this is found in certain parts of the island of Cyprus."—ED.

Also, *Baruch*, vi., 46. "The women also with cords about them, sitting in the ways, burn pastiles for perfume," etc.—ED.

Also STRABO: xvi., and *Ancient Symbol Worship*, page 87, note.—ED.

where. This king, god of blood, god of fire, war, and death, delighted himself in an execrable manner in clasping living bodies to his iron bosom, heated to a white heat. If the boy was not burned, he was mutilated. The iron made a woman of him.

These Molochs, these cruel merchants, masters, and sultans everywhere, with their ships crammed with wretched, living human flesh, and with their caravans, who led those wretched beings away in long herds, had nothing whatever to do with Syrian women. The latter were widows. At night, on the high terrace of their house, or on the dry wall which supported vine-plants, they cried, dreamt, and told their griefs to the moon, the equivocal Astarté. The sulphurous breath of the swallowed-up cities blew from the South, and from the Dead Sea.

They dreamt. Never were dreams so powerful. The *Parthenogenesis*, the force of the desire, which is fruitful without a male, burst out in the Syrian woman, who alone had two children.

One of them was the Messiah-woman, who freed Babylon, which till that time had been a thrall of Nineveh, the great Semiramis, who was born a fish, and became a dove, who married the whole earth, and at last wedded her own son.

The other child was a god of sorrow, the Lord (Adonai or Adonis). He was born out of incest, and his worship, mixed with tears and amour, was also impure and incestuous.

The great Syrian legend, the incest under its three forms, Semiramis, Lot, and Myrrha, ends in this feminine creation of immense importance, *Adonis dead and risen.* A sensual and weeping worship, and very fatal too, through which the world miserably went down the declivity of enervation.*

---

* It is necessary to trace it to its source, and to say a word about the remotest antiquity to give a clear idea of this worship. The foreigner is regarded as unclean and abominable by the spiteful morals of those small tribes,

At all times, burials have been the occasion of the saddest follies.* *Male and female mourners*, feigning despair, blinding themselves with wine and tears, became utterly delirious, and ended by acting as if they had been dead themselves, cutting their own flesh, and outrageously staining it. Lot, who had seen the land sink into the flames, and lost his country and his wife, believed that everything, even the law itself, had come to an end. He was dead, he cared for nothing. They were at liberty to delude him as much as they wished.

The Lot of Byblos is affliction. *Gingras* or Kinyras, the funeral harp, in this bad dream, is a king loved too much by his daughter. This daughter is Myrrha, the

---

each of which thought itself to be the chosen people of God. To marry a foreign woman, to leave for her sake one's kindred, was held a crime, and as an incest. The only pure marriage, in their opinion, is with the near relative. For this reason the daughters of Lot, having seen their tribe perish, say: "There are men no more." Horror seized them at the idea of associating with a man of another tribe. But on the other hand the highest dishonor, according to Syrian ideas, would be to die a maid, without child, like a sterile fruit. They addressed themselves to the only man yet remaining, their own father; they deceived him and had by him two sons, Moab and Ammon. In the book of *Genesis* there is not the least blame imputed to them for having done so. On the contrary, the Jews trace from Moab the descent of Ruth, the charming Moabitess, from whom sprang their kings— David and Solomon. The history of Lot does not differ at all from that of Semiramis, and of the real queens, Anaitis, Amestris, Parysatis, etc. They wish to maintain the unity of their stock against the confused life of the seraglio. For this purpose they marry or wish to marry their own sons, according to the custom of the Chaldean magians. This strange marriage in a country in which woman becomes old so soon, was indeed a kind of celibacy. It was perhaps a symbolical marriage, the mother having the title of wife, that she might repel any foreign woman, and at the same time making her female slave take her place. This Sarah and Rachel did, as it is related in *Genesis*. This marriage concentrated in the family the mysterious tradition of the arts of the magians, their astronomical attainments and industrial or medical formulas and receipts, of which they were extremely jealous. Two very ancient historians, Conon (quoted by Photius), and Xanthus of Lydia (CLEM., *Strom.*, iii., 185), mention these marriages, as well as Euripides, Catullus, Strabo, Philo, Sextus Empiricus, Agathias, Origenes, Saint Jerom, etc.

* See books of *Leviticus* and *Deuteronomy.*

myrrh which is burned at funerals. Harp and myrrh, lugubrious things, have so much of affinity that they mingle themselves during twelve nights. At length Gingras becomes indignant. But she does not, and, disconsolate on account of her love, she weeps, and will continue to weep under the shape of a myrrh-tree.

" Was this tree a punished, an execrated one ? " By no means. The Syrian woman made of it the exquisite and perfumed being which made death charming. One of its beautiful, sweet-smelling tears was Adonis, who was such a pretty boy, that from that time there existed for her no other god. She called him " my Lord " (Adonaï), " my Baal " (proprietor, husband). She herself dreamed that she was his Baaltis, his Astarté, who must possess him, Astarté Hermaphrodite, Adonis wife of Adonis. And in order to reach the height of foolishness, her love-name was Salambo (*Samalkis*), the mad flute, which is dismal and furious, and which is played upon during the burials.

But by making Adonis her Baal, she had cruelly provoked Baal-Moloch, *the king*, the king of Fire, the king of War, and of Death (Mars or Mors). This demon takes the form of a demoniac beast. *He enters into a hog*, or rather into a wild boar, and wounds the beautiful boy in the sexual part, kills him, or kills his power of love.

Who could doubt about all this when his blood is still flowing? At Byblos there is a torrent, which, by a singular coincidence, becomes troubled and reddens at the time, described in *the Song of Songs*, when the season of rains is over, and the feverish blood runs quick in the emotion of a Syrian spring-time. " It is the blood, the blood of Adonis ! "

Tears are a relief. Those mourning women were insatiable of them. Every place echoed with their tears. At Byblos, they used to weep before the sea, while the warm wind blew from Africa, in the intoxication of spring-time. In Syria, at the end of September, when the vine mourned over the year, for it was the last month, they,

during seven days, till the first of October, used to rave
and to blind themselves with tears, over the vintage-tub. In
some places they could not wait for autumn, but during
the harvest, under the piercing rays of the sun (Adonis),
these mad female lovers welcomed him with abundant
tears in his supreme victory.

It was a rage for burials. They fancied, for everything
was confused in their minds, to have lost their lover as
well as their child. They made up an indifferent doll,
which represented a very effeminate boy.* Over this
wretched rag-baby, they, with heart-rending cries, performed the funeral rites and obsequies. They washed
that doll, opened and embalmed it. Afterward they put
it on a catafalque, and contemplated it for a long while,
especially its cruel wound, which was made on its delicate
side. They sat down in a circle on the floor, with their
hair dishevelled, sometimes chanting litanies, sometimes
holding their peace, and now and then heaving deep
sighs. From time to time one of them said: " Alas! my
sweet Lord! where is now your lordship?" They were
stifling. At the end of seven long days it was necessary
to put an end to all this, it was necessary to part from
each other, and to bury this unfortunate doll. And what!
To see him no more! His Astarté, his Baaltis, the desperate Salambo looked in vain for him. Was he dead?
. . . They took pains to make up a little miracle. In
some flower-pots, prepared beforehand, they set some of
those plants which heat causes quickly to blossom, and they
exposed them on the roofs of their houses, on the terrace,
where people sleep in Syria. These were *the gardens of
Adonis.* Precisely on the seventh day they went up to
see . . . and behold . . . the plant had burst out . . .
the plant had flourished. Shouts of love were heard from
terrace to terrace. " Oh! joy; the Lord had risen from
the dead!"

---

* I follow closely the ancient texts, which the reader will find in Movers'
Phoenicians, I., chap. vii., 190–253.

Everywhere the frantic Astarté seized again her young, living, entire, unmutilated lover. They reassured the world that it had lost nothing. They raised up the sign of fecundation (the phallus mephallityth or neuropast) as it was done in Egypt. But there was a great, a very great difference in the purpose of so doing in the two countries. As to Isis, the African wife, it was the over-excitement of mutual happiness, and her adoration of her husband. As to the Syrian Baaltis, it was the blind intoxication, the indiscriminate tenderness, which welcomed the unknown friend in the foreign guest, in the passer-by, in a word, in Man. Adonis would have it so. The woman who forebore to do all this, and shut her door, had, for penance, to let fall her hair, and thus, with her hair cut close and ugly, had to remain for a long time without daring to appear in public.

It seems that Baaltis-Astarté acted in antithesis to Moloch. This jealous, terrible *king* sacrificed men in order to keep, through dread, his colonies. She, on the contrary, opened the door of her house altogether to the passer-by, saying : " The poor foreigner ! " Moloch, the great seller, the great mutilator—everywhere prepared Adonises for the seraglios. Astarté, on the contrary, worshipped the maimed boy.

This seems to be a striking opposition, but indeed it is not. Unclean love is a kind of death. Moloch, in all his horror, was less dangerous than the deep abyss of Astarté. The amorous compassion, the effeminacy and the tears, the contagious delight of the rites of *Adonis* brought on the world the terrible and deadly fact : *the disappearance of manly strength.*

Look at this progress of weakness. In Egypt, Osiris died, it is true ; but he did not die altogether, because, even dead, he became the father of Harpocrates. In Syria, the male was nothing more than a weak adolescent, who did nothing but die. There was no paternity in him. Adonis had no child. He was himself the child. But in Phrygia, under another name, he sank still lower.

The Syrian woman, although she looked languishing, was at the bottom violent and terrible, and incapable of resignation. She was full of boldness and prompt in doing good as well as in doing evil. Jahel, Deborah, Judith, and Esther, saved their people. Athaliah and Jezebel were monarchs. It was the same with Semiramis, the famous Dove of Ascalon, who flew away from Syria to the Euphrates. The goddess-fish,—Derceto,—got with child by the god Desire, and was delivered one fine morning of this strange creature. From a slave having become a queen, and being lascivious and warlike, she got rid of a husband who worshipped her, became wife of Ninus, the great king of the East, took away his life and usurped his throne. She dethroned also Nineveh, and made of Babylon, with its hundred gates and gigantic walls, an image of herself, a monstrous gulf of pleasure, which opened to everybody the shelter of its impure brotherhood.

Babel was already the tower, the celebrated observatory of the Chaldean Magi.* She was the market, to which every year were brought from the upper Euphrates, and are still brought,† the wines of Armenia, which led to joyous festivity. She was an open city. The people of Asia were afraid of the walls and obscurity of cities.‡ The free chief of a caravan apprehended that if he stopped in a walled town he would be lost, robbed, sold, and perhaps killed there. When the conquest of Nineveh drove away its people to Babylon, this industrious people allured at any price all merchants and reassured them. The advice of Balaam (prophet of the she-ass or Baalpeor), as given in the book of *Genesis*, was followed to the letter— *to seduce through woman.* The haughty ladies of Babylon sat down at the gates, and invited the foreigner. What could be more reassuring? Whoso that passer-by was,

---

* Diodorus.   † Rennell.   ‡ Herodotus.

from the East, from the West; of whatever race, a merchant, a chief of a tribe, a savage Ismaelite, a runaway
perhaps, or a miserable slave, the great lady, in state
and seated on a golden throne, received from him the
small sum which he threw on her knees. The Venus of
Babel imposed this duty of humility and equality. He
seemed to buy her, for every marriage was a purchase,
and, as it were, to marry her. Let him command!
Was all this a merely symbolical ceremony? But how
proud must he have been in espousing Babylon, the
great Queen of the East, "*the daughter of giants,*" of
whom he has dreamed so much in the wilderness! He
felt himself beloved, adopted, and a Babylonian, himself
acquired and bought forever. Such was the snare of this
city. The foreigner, in passing over its threshold, lost
his recollection. With that small sum, given to the beautiful smiling lady, he found presently that he had also thrown
away into her hand his past, his country, his family, and
the gods of his ancestors.

All this went so far that he himself, in return, built and
enlarged Babylon, working eagerly to raise the walls of
his new country. As by a charm those walls rose two
hundred feet high. The Magians, by a stroke of genius,
had foreseen this, and had beforehand drawn astrono-
mically, according to the number of days of the year, a
city of three hundred and sixty-five stadia in circum-
ference. The bricks were baked in the sun. There was
plenty of asphalt. The whole was constructed at once,
with a true rage of love, by *the friends,** the paramours, of
Queen Semiramis, the symbolical personification of Babylon. The walls, a real chain of mountains, on which four

---

* It results from the combined narrations of Herodotus, Ctesias, Diodorus,
etc., that this enormous city, which *contributed the third of the revenue of
Asia*, was traced beforehand, *and built at one time;* that its walls, so prodigious, were the *spontaneous* work of multitudes who took shelter there under
the protection of the tower of the Magi. This reminds us on a grand scale
of some constructions of the Middle Ages, as the cathedral of Strasbourg,
which was built by the pilgrims, who worked at it day and night.

chariots could go abreast, suddenly lorded it over the country. The neighboring kings were in a rage, and threatened. But they ceased, when they saw that Babylon was unassailable. During two or three centuries it was the universal refuge, the ark of the arts of Asia, which wrapped them up and preserved them from the *floods* that lowered over the horizon.

What a great spectacle to see so numerous a people become the children of this strange mother, who, under her vast robe, welcomed and sheltered any man, whether he was black or white, freeman or bondsman. The slaves themselves had festivals, in which their masters attended on them. The captives also were so well treated that they throve as in their own home, as it is seen in the case of the Jews. In the midst of this great confusion, people easily believed themselves to be brothers. Women helped each other to husbands, the ugly ones receiving their dowry from the beautiful. Sick persons placed themselves confidently on the public squares and consulted the friendly multitude.

Babylon, by the purchasing of mercenary soldiers from the North, became a conqueror. Her Magi or Nabi (Nabuchodonosor) frightened for a while the world, by carrying away and conducting to the Euphrates whole peoples, as Israel, Judah, etc. But this grandeur was not strength. The heterogeneous masses could only increase the discordancy of Babel, the confusion of mind, of languages, which has become a by-word. Babel and Babylon seem to be synonomous words, as *barbarian* in Greece, to signify a smatterer, a mumbler, who mixes many languages. Such medleys are injurious to the mind and produce giddiness. Witness the great Nabi who *became a beast.** The women there being more sober and more dispassionate, and whom no excess can exhaust, found themselves to be more and more the only males. Babylon itself was woman. The

---

* *Daniel,* iv.

queens-magi, especially Nitocris, who governed gloriously, made in vain some immense works of defense, in
order to stop and delay the enemy.

Persia made light of such defence, entered, and thought
herself to be the mistress. But she was herself taken captive in the long run. The old, voluptuous city embraced
her, held her fast, and prepared for her a bed so voluptuous that she grew soft in it and melted. The genius of
the Magians, which was obscure, profound, unclean as
well in its origin as in cunning and lust of power, and
which had eaten the fruit of the tree of evil, perverted
altogether the conquerors. The queen-mothers imitated
the amours as well as the boldness of Semiramis. The
kings copied the pride, and the downfall also, of the
Nabuchodonosors. The Magians made up two idols, the
idol *King*, protected on every side by that comedy of
dread, which is seen on the monuments, the eagle-bull
with a human face, etc. The other, the idol-*Mother*, the
Great Mother Mihr-Mylitta, or Venus, in which character
they swallowed up all the gods of the East, and which
they boldly placed between Ormuzd and Ahriman, as a
Mediator, who domineered over Persia herself.

Personified Voluptuousness, Mylitta, the true conqueror
of Asia, sat, at the summit of Babel, on a throne, and
her lewd colossus wantonly reposed upon amorous lions.
Between those beasts was the King of kings, whom she
kept enervated and mild by the means of a Babylonian
seraglio, in which every year were incessantly placed
five hundred young creatures, a multitude "of fat children." *

Mylitta, in the lower part of Babel, and under the low
vaults where formerly the sacred dragons were fed, had
her young unemployed priests, gallant, rosy, with painted
faces,—counterfeit boys, counterfeit girls with false and
delicate voice, victims of shame, who were hired for

---

* *Daniel*, i.

money, and in their immolation, *saw* the heavens open and told good fortune.

This unclean religion spread fast. Mylitta gained ground in the West. In Lydia, in Phrygia, at the great slave-markets, at the manufactories of eunuchs, Mylitta was called Anaïtis-Atys; she was the Great *Ma* with numerous breasts, whom Greece called Cybelé. In this confused country of Phrygia, a veritable chaos, where people mixed everything without understanding, Atys, by a monstrous legend, became the little male, the Adonis of this large Cybelé. They imitated the *Passion* of Adonis, the holy week of Byblos. The *child* was always represented as mutilated, lost, recovered, and bewailed by women. The getting-up was still more pathetic, barbarous, grotesque, and very shocking. They did not take out a small image of wood, but a piece of bleeding flesh, which they set up as the head of Adonis, or his obscene relic. The horror was at its height. Then the tree of Atys appeared,—a pine-tree, as at Byblos,—enchanted, groaning, and full of sighs. The crowd, with dishevelled hair, prayed and called him up. At length a child burst out from the opened tree. Atys, in rising from the dead, was charming, worthy of admiration, in his equivocal gracefulness, both boy and girl at once, the uncertain dream of love.

This drama of giddiness and of fancy was highly remunerative. The priests of Asia Minor, like the ecclesiastical princes of Italy, traders in every way, speculated at the same time on piety, love, and fortune-telling. They drew from their Atys a lucrative brokerage; and so grew rich, became kings and popes.*

They pushed on their success, sending forth in every direction their missionaries and ·apostles, itinerant Atyses, mendicants, collectors with an ass, soothsayers, cunning merchants of prayers and expiations—true antique Capu-

---

* KREUZER by GUIGNAUT : book III., ii., p. 80, *et passim.*

chins. They were half-eunuchs, and therefore safer minis-
trants to lust, and they sold at the same time pleasure
and penance.* These queer fellows, as the Flagellants,
shamelessly exhibiting themselves under the lash, moved
tender hearts to compassion. They bled, and women
became delirious, and fainted away.

Behold the conquerors of the world. Antiquity will be
swallowed up in their Atys-Sabazius.

---

* PLATO: *Republic*, ii., 7. "Pedlar-priests also, and prophets frequent-
ing the gates of the rich, persuade them that they possess a power, granted
them by the gods, of expiating by sacrifices and incantations in the midst of
feastings, whatever injustice has been committed by any one, or his forefathers."

See also APULEIUS: *Metamorphosis*, viii.—ED.

CHAPTER III.

BACCHUS-SABAZIUS—HIS INCARNATION—THE TYRANT.

BY looking at Greece invaded, penetrated by the gloomy gods of the East, I feel the same dismay which Athens felt when the sea was covered with the fleet of Persia, commanded by the Phœnicians; the same dismay felt by Syracuse, when the vessels of Carthage brought thither its black Moloch. What will become of mankind, if the country of light is darkened with the worship of the Eastern gods?

They are all from Syria.* Everything passes through Syria, even that which is Egyptian or Chaldean. The uncouth gods of Phrygia, such as Atys-Sabazius, are the counterfeit of the Syrian gods, Adonis, Sabaoth. The Phœnician colonies are the great vehicle of this muddy torrent.

Nothing is so strange as the metamorphosis through which those savage gods creep, and diffuse themselves into Greece.

The stern Adonai of the desert, a mourner at Byblos, becomes the charming Adonis. Sabaoth, *the lord of the seven heavens*, of the myriads of stars, the ancient father of the Magians, and god of Sabaism, becomes Sabazius-

---

* The antagonism between Phœnicia and Greece is not less evident than that between Carthage and Rome. On *Adonis*-Atys, *Sabaoth*-Sabazius, *Mylitta* (Mithras)-Venus, *Baal-Peor*, the ass belonging to Bacchus, see the Hebraic and Greek texts, especially MOVERS, I., 350, 365, 383, 668, 695. On *Mithras*-Venus, see the *Investigations* of LAYARD, and especially his *Memoirs* (of vast erudition) on the worship of the cypress-tree. *Acad. of Inscriptions*, vol. xxii.

Atys, a young martyr, whose Sabazian sorrow and nocturnal festivals will last two thousand years. Quite close by him, not only in antiquity, but in the Middle Ages, will reign the other demon, not less tenacious, but more sly, the cunning Baalpeor of Syria, with long ears, the ass of wine, of lasciviousness, in an unmanageable manner given to Priapus. " *Orientis partibus—adventavit asinus—pulcher et fortissimus.*"

But those whimsical figures would have frightened Greece, if most of them had not passed through a great transformation, and had not been immersed, boiled, scummed, and fermented, not in Medea's caldron, but in the reeking vintage-tub of a rural god, who appeared to be innocent, a god whom one finds everywhere, the god of vintage, the god of the lively round,* and the coarse pranks which people play at vintage time. And hence springs up Dionysus, *Bacchus-Sabazius*, the *chaos* of gods, the false Mediator, the false Deliverer, the god of Tyrants, the god of Death.

In the India of the *Vedas* we have noticed the fermented liquor, the Soma, which was the offering of Asia. It was replaced by wine. In going toward the West, it met with the vine, which was preferred to it, and which seemed more divine. Each year, this god in casks started from Armenia, loaded on leathern boats encircled with boards, and an ass was placed on them. He went down the Euphrates. The Chaldeans, who had but their bad palm-tree wine, drank with devotion this nectar of Armenia. The boards were sold. The ass was loaded with the leather,† bringing it to the highland. This amiable ani-

---

* Bacchus comes from everywhere, receives all things, and absorbs everything. As the god of wine, of noisy agitation, of rounds and of *dancers*, he is a Thracian. (See LOBECK). Thracia and Phrygia are the classical lands of vertigo ; the *dervis-dancers* continue the round of Bacchus-Sabazius-Atys; most of them are venal drunkards, who *whirl* in order to drink, and drink that they may *whirl*. ED. GERHARD (*Griech. Mythol.*, I., 467-512) exhausts in an admirable manner the theme on the Thracian, Grecian Bacchus, etc.

† The commerce of wine in that country, in our own time, is the same as it

mal, the pride of the East, that each year, without fatigue and in triumph, like a magian king, entered Babylon with the cheerful vintage, was warmly welcomed and honored. The title of Lord, *Bel*, *Baal*, was given to him. He was respectfully called *Belpeor* (Lord Ass).

Respect even greater he received in Syria, where his lascivious gayety, and his amorous power, and his superiority over man, astonished the Syrian women, as the prophet says. He was himself a prophet, and spoke under Balaam. The mountain on which he spoke is still named *the Ass*. On the whole he was a demon, Baalpeor, an unclean and voluptuous demon, who serves everybody and all purposes, allows people to get upon his back, and to bridle him.

It is on the mountain of the *Ass* that the angels themselves, inspired by Baalpeor, burned in lust for the daughters of men.* Even in the wilderness, as Ezekiel says, the festival of *the ass* was already celebrated. However, he did not go to Egypt, where his neck would have been broken without mercy. He went toward the North, toward the West, solemnly preaching the cultivation of the vine from which people have wine, the cadet brother of Love.

The ass would have invaded every place, and would have been Priapus and Bacchus. His personality, quite a comical one, prevented him from being such. He could not have become the voluptuous Proteus of tears and of joy. He could not have played the child to affect women. He could not have made of himself a tortured beautiful boy. He could never have created the spectacle of the *Pathemata* (*Passion*).

This spectacle appears to have had its origin in Crete, through the tradition of the child given up to the Minotaur

---

is related in Herodotus to have been in his time. RENNEL, etc. See (besides MOVERS) the texts collected by DAUMER, GHILLANY, KREUZER, ROLLE, etc., on the ass of Babylon, of Balaam, of the Talmudists, of Bacchus, etc.

* ST. HILAIRE.

(Bacchus). The child represented Bacchus, the victim took the place of the god. This little Bacchus, or *Zagreus*, torn to pieces and immolated on the tumbrel of the vintages, made people first laugh and afterward cry, on account of his screams and his tears, the false blood which flowed. *The Passion* of Zagreus, a tragi-comical one, represented at Athens and everywhere, was the beginning of the Greek theatre, as the theatre of the Middle Ages began with the Mysteries, the kindred of *the Passion*.

Women, in their little Mysteries of springtime and autumn (*Anthesteria* and *Thesmophoria*) festivals, in which mother Ceres twice a year expressed *the rights of love*—women, I say, found it very gentle to have in their arms the fruit of love, to carry to those festivals a little child, whom they called Iacchus. Bacchus, under the form of a child, entered Eleusis, with his tragi-comedies, his Passion of a god torn limb from limb, his incestuous equivocation of obscure symbolism. Lamentable additions. The grain died and lived again, so also did Proserpina. Bacchus died and rose again. It was a drama in a drama, which made intricate this beautiful and great moral theme, without strengthening it.*

It has been said, not without some grounds, that this was the heathen mass. The initiated partook of the supper of Demeter, of the bread, and the mixed beverage, which she drank in her gloomy courses, in her motherly *Passion*. This was a communion under both species, to which, however, Bacchus did not add that of wine. But in his own

---

* LOBECK'S *Aglaophamus* is, and will be, the chief, most complete, and most critical book on this subject. All the *texts* are there brought together, judged and elucidated with peculiar strength. This *thaumaturgy* of Mysteries, confused and obscure, fumeous as it was, was not wholesome for the mind. Bacchus had spoiled the ancient and charming myth of Ceres. This is the reason why Socrates and Epaminondas would not be initiated in them. Nevertheless there could be no immodesty in the Mysteries at Eleusis. A serious lady, the hierophantides, superintended. At the altar a young boy was always present. Diodorus and Galienus say that people brought back from them always pure and pious ideas.

festivals he took an inferior name, the name of *Ampelos* (vine), and offered himself in funeral sacrifice. Bacchus-Vine gave up himself, and immolated himself to Bacchus-Pluto, and pretended to die for us.*

He is here evidently the *mediator* who mitigates the passage, and gently leads the souls from this world to another; who takes upon himself to plead for man and to pray for him. He could act on man's behalf because he had not been a god at first, but simply a hero, an *heroic* man. Humanity, at this strange epoch, seemed to think itself unworthy of speaking to God. It needed intermediate agents, guides, and interpreters. Mithras in the nether world, and Bacchus on earth, will already speak for us. God and man have two languages. Behold! they are separated! Man is deprived of the glorious privilege of a direct intercourse with God. Oh! what an immense fall! Is heaven higher? I do not know. But I am lower.

The wise had at first energetically struggled against Bacchus. We have seen the war of Apollo against him, the memorable contest between the flute and the lyre. The lyre killed Marsyas, the flute killed Orpheus. The followers of Pythagoras at first opposed Bacchus, aiming at purity, but nevertheless submitted to the vanquisher. They adopted him in their *Orphean hymns*, in which they wished to reconcile everything,—uniting helter-skelter the Phœnician Love (or Desire), the Greek Zeus, and the new Mysteries with Bacchus.

Thus the wise and unwise, the pure and the unclean, all took sides with him. Plato, against Socrates, and the Socratic spirit, wished to have a *Mediator of love*.† This

---

* KREUZER : *Symbolik*, iii., 1027.

† "Man, the eldest of the gods, is born of Love and Chaos." This is a piece of Phœnician doctrine which one wonders to see in the *Birds* of Aristophanes. But it had probably remained, together with the power of the Eastern Venus, in the islands and Grecian ports, and ancient Phœnician colonies. Philosophers rashly and too easily lay hold of these Asiatic ideas, which they understood very badly. Pythagoras copied Egypt, and Pherecydes copied Phœnicia. They thought to follow some ideas, and did not see that

is a great part, which *Eros*, the winged child, will never assume in Greece ; but it accrues altogether to Bacchus, ever since irresistible, all-powerful, carrying away everything.

Art contributed not a little to bring this about, followed the decline, and made it more rapid.

Bacchus, in his statues, at first was manly enough. A son-in-law, a son, a husband of Ceres, according to his various names, he was noble still, when, in the last act of the Mysteries, he lay beside the venerable goddess, on a triumphal bed. Equal to Jupiter of heaven in the statues of Polykleitus, represented with the eagle and the thunderbolt, and being the Jupiter of the nether regions, with the holy cup of the dead ; Savior in heaven, on earth, in the

---

they were following the sinking of the world, which had become general through the fall of the empires of Asia. Persia became effeminate, received the Mihr, the Mylitta of Babylon, a mediator of love. Will this dogma enter Greece ? Could not one hope that the logic, the school of analysis, and of the Socratic good sense would shut it out ? Socrates, a few days before his death, had, in his admirable *Euthphron*, formulated the inmost depth of the Grecian idea, the *Law, a queen of the gods themselves,* shutting the door of heaven to the tyrant gods of favor and of love. Now this very god of love, the true eastern tyrant, indifferent to justice (or rather an enemy to Law), comes in through a false door. Which ? The very school of Socrates, when it was divided and jarring. Plato, the great artist, willingly took doubtful and incoherent glimpses from the hypogea of Egypt, or from the smoking volcanoes of Sicily. The poetry of the *Mediator* of love troubled him, and also won him over. In the wonderful dialogue of the *Symposium,* a shocking, sublime, and austerely licentious dialogue, he puts into the mouth of Socrates, his teacher, a doctrine which was to undermine utterly the Socratic teaching. "What is love ? A god ? No ; for he has desires, and is not sufficient to himself. A man ? No ; for he is immortal. He is a being who stands between the mortal and the immortal. He is the Mediator, who is the link of all things. . . . Love is a *demon,* Socrates, a *great demon ! God not revealing himself immediately to man,* those spirits are his interpreters." (PLATO, *Banquet,* 229.) All this is said slightly, and with a laughing gracefulness. Then comes a charming story. Then follows a bold scene, which modern readers find to be shameful, but which the light cynicism of the Greeks surely relished, and which made this little book pass quickly from hands to hands. Its consequences have been incalculable for the ruin of Greece, and the impairment of the human mind.

10

underworld, and opening hope everywhere, he appeared the god of gods.

But he was indeed woman, and as such he appeared more and more. He became Adonis, Atys, and Sabazius, the womaned youth, whom Nature, by mistake, had dignified with the sex of man. Somnolent and with half-closed eyes, he seems to be only a lazy beautiful woman. This beauty asleep has the unwholesome charm of a marsh under flowers, and is quite different from Eros, the lively and wild boy, who is all sparks.* Art made him more and more effeminate, daring not indeed represent him with a woman's breast, but making him the indecent rival of Callipyges. All this by degrees till he became the young, fat, a little bloated, and gloomily unchaste Bacchus of the column of Nero's gardens. He fixes a sad and haughty look on the sun, but the sun blushes in seeing him.

Vain fables embellished this favorite. People without any respect for Homer, who had pointed out at the cowardice of Bacchus, made of him a Hercules fighting with the Titans. They made him a conqueror of India, giving him tigers to draw his chariot, instead of the ass, which is his riding animal. They sang his praise, as having strolled about the whole earth, amphora in hand, and overthrowing the strongest through the invincible force either of wine, or beauty.

I do not know how Aristophanes, the undaunted comic author, dared in his *Frogs* show the true Bacchus like a

---

* The ordinary model of Eros was evidently the eager, shining Greek boy, with a piercing look, in a word, a *Spirit.* This exalted all. The high admiration, which made him divine, felt in him the hero, and wished that he were such. The model of Bacchus, on the contrary, is a mild, feminine, soft, delicate beauty : that of the northern slave: there is no such thing in the South. Sometimes he lifts to the sky a look of sadness, and sometimes he closes his eyes. If one has a will to do so, one can make of him the Genius of Sleep, *at the Louvre,* or that of gentle Death, the amiable and hoped-for deliverer of the slave (*Bibl. Impér.,* engravings of ancient statues). Baleful conceptions of a very corrupting art, which softens the heart with amorous compassion for this dangerous son of dream and caprice, in whom is the heart of the Tyrant.

fat, unclean, cowardly woman, who is frightened to death for nothing. If he wished to vilify him, his attempt was a failure. Bacchus was the worshipped mistress, the popular darling. The Grecian peoples, among whom the enfranchised and the slave already ruled,—the false Athens which had replaced the true one,—acknowledged themselves in him, found him charming, and honored him precisely as a gluttonous and cowardly slave, especially as an enemy to labor, or as Idleness and Drunkenness incarnated. He was just the King, the Tyrant they dreamed of.

This was the terrible power of Bacchus. *He was the god of tyrants and of slaves.* He was the *good tyrant* of drunkenness and of hazard, of happiness and *Good Luck.* He was the Deliverer, who unbound and untied (Eleuthéreus, Lysios, Lyæos); he untied man from the cares of the year, of the works of summer, in order to enter in the vintage. In autumn, in spring time, he made the festival of the slave. He nourished him with hope, with the chimera of the kingdom of Bacchus, and of the *lawless* life, in which to drink and to sleep will be the only law.

A god who untied all, was, of course, himself unbound, and without girdle ; his Bacchantes also were so, in sign of ease. No more *mine* and *thine*, no more boundaries. Especially no more labor ; Bacchus had abolished it. In its place, he had instituted an eternal banquet, in which he will make the shares. His diadem seems to bear his name (*Isodctès*) *the Divider.*

If he untied everybody, will he not unbind woman ? At first he gave her the freedom of tears, sensual tears,—" the sweetness of crying." With his laughing train of Satyrs and Silenuses, he was pre-eminently a mourner. The Grecian woman, sadly sedentary, opened her heart entirely to Bacchus, and poured forth her loves in tears.*

---

* Women superabounded (Aristoph., *Acharn.*). And, on the other hand, they were driven to despair (Id., *Lysistr.*, v., 231), since men had entirely perished at Miletus and elsewhere. At Athens, the inexcusable indifference

She was always in company of her inseperable, indispensable, and confidant nurse, who was either a tender and foolish woman from Thracia or Phrygia, or a cunning Milesian, or a sweet female friend from Ionia. The sweetness was in going in the evening to cry together at Bacchus-Adonis', at the vespres of Syria, in which, during three entire nights, the dove sighed and groaned. People laughed at this. But they did not laugh at all, when on a certain evening, at the moment in which the fatal expedition of Sicily was decided on, a song of sorrow filled the city. It was the ladies who were crying over . . . their country? No; . . . but over the death of Adonis.*

Fear attends vain sorrow. Demons, evil spirits, bestirred themselves, going and returning. It was an epidemic. The maid was sick for it. She was told "to get married as soon as possible." But the wife was not any more tranquil. Many were so much haunted by the demons, that they were driven to despair, and strangled themselves. Their dreads, their shocks, spread the sacred sickness, the scourge of epilepsy.†

Movement, dance, the thyrsus, the noisy orgies are surely a remedy against fear. Women, who, under the guard of their nurse, hardly went in the evening to their modest Mysteries, now found themselves so bold that they went by troops to Eleusis, nay to the desert promontory; nor is this all, but they went to Delphos, to Parnassus. They wept as though each of them were a Thyades, and were delirious as Bacchantes. But, wonderful to be told! each of them was also a *Mimallone*, the warrior of Bacchus, and bore the thyrsus and the dagger.

This soft Bacchus was a god of Death. The Bacchantes took from him their name, *the servants of Pluto*. This sweet Bacchus was fond of blood, and remembered that he

---

of men, made women live among themselves, closely bound and forming as a feminine republic (Id., *Ibidem*). In all this Aristophanes is a great historian.

* ARISTOPHANES : *Lysistratus.*

† HIPPOCRATES, Littré's edition, iv., 367, viii., 467, etc.

was also Moloch. If he did not require any longer human victims, his thirst had not changed, so that his female lovers, in the rough Arcadia, lashed themselves and lacerated their bodies to offer him the blood of woman.* These impure and cruel religions spread themselves in the false Greece ; in Sicily, in Italy assuming a cynic character (as it may be seen on the vases); in Phrygia assuming a dull and foolish form ; and in Thessaly, Epirus, Thrace, and Macedonia, being commixed with barbarous magic.

There was a general foreboding that great evils were coming,—a terrible overthrow. Women had a shrinking of the heart. The sorrow of Cheronea weighed over them beforehand. And beforehand also weighed on them the dreadful end of Thebes, where Alexander in one day sold thirty thousand Greeks into slavery. Women felt and feared the danger, but nevertheless they were preparing it. It was from the dismal orgies that those evils were to spring, for which they wept, without knowing them—dissoluteness, ruin, slavery, and the barbarous victory, the living orgies, the Tyrant.

---

* PAUSANIAS : *Arcadia*, viii., 25.

CHAPTER IV.

THE INCARNATION OF SABAZIUS—CONTINUATION— MILITARY ORGIES.

THE glory of the great Gelon, *the good Tyrant*, who repelled the efforts of Carthage, had perverted ideas in Sicily and everywhere. Among the Seven Sages there were two Tyrants. The Tyrant, a chief of the party opposite to aristocracy, represented himself as the friend and benefactor of the people, their good foster-father, who would make them eat and drink, would be their Bacchus, their Ceres. To flatter him, according to these gods, the people often called him Dionysus (*Denis*) and Demetrios (from *Demeter*, Ceres).

But no dynasty of Tyrants ever long endures. They spring up and fall. It was necessary, in order to create a stable one, to have a foundation, a fixed point out of Greece. It was too hateful to look for such a support among the Persians. Philip, the cunning king of Macedonia, perceived perfectly well that the true basis of a dynasty of Tyrants ought to be half Greek and half barbarous, and that if he could group, around his small Macedonia, the rough Epirus and the wild Thrace, and especially Thessaly—the country of Centaurs—all that pseudo-Greece, which was so warlike, would be in his hand a terrible weapon against the genuine, exhausted, divided Greece. He did two very sagacious things. He freed Thessaly from its tyrants, and became the patron and chief of its wonderful cavalry. He honored Epirus by taking his queen from among its people, and thus he assured to himself the valiant tribes of Albania, their firm foot-soldiers. This is the secret of his victory, and also of his death. He perished, because he had married a woman of Epirus.

That country, the Albania of our time, of discordant contrast; that country so small, and yet reckoning fourteen peoples, is well known. An eternal storm unceasingly strikes there with thunder the Ceraunii mountains. Old volcanoes, earthquakes, violent alluvions of torrents, these things make up Epirus. There were enormous fierce dogs, but man was far more fierce. Assassinations at all times were abundant. The very women there carried weapons ; they were stern, violent, and haunted both by the old spirits of the country (in the forests of Dodona), and by the new demons of Thrace and Phrygia. They were born Bacchantes and sorceresses ; skilful in the dangerous herbs of dreams, or of poison, it was their joy, in imitation of the Medeas of Thessaly, to wind around their arms and their breasts, the beautiful, undulating adders. They used to say that they had formerly put to flight whole armies only by means of their yellings and their serpents.* Vain fables. Those innocent reptiles upon them were rather an ornament of prostitution. It is said that Hercules, with loathing and horror, saw on these barbarous lands the beginning of the Syrian and Phrygian orgies of Adonis, and of Atys-Sabazius. Those haughty women, with their thyrsus, their dagger, and their masculine pride, sank in those orgies to the level of false women or half-men, the immodest Atys, who styled themselves mutilated, the merchants of unprolific amours, of dreams, and who were trivial soothsayers. If from the holy orgies a child were born, oh, miracle ! the child was the offspring of a god !

Handlers of serpents, inspired quacks, circle-dancers of Sabazius, Bacchants, and Bachantes of Bacchus, they all held fast together. The young woman whom Philip married belonged to those who played with serpents.

---

* POLYÆN., iv., 1.

She was protected by the greatest oracles, all which at that time were subordinated to Bacchus. Philip, perhaps, knew that, and thought to make it an engine of power in his hand. He was entrapped in his own snares. The name of his queen from Epirus was Myrtalé; but she, through unseemly ambition, called herself Olympias. After the marriage, she boldly told Philip that she had conceived on the eve, that she had had the dream of Semelè, a flood of fire. The lightning had filled her bosom, and hence the whole earth. Philip little relished such a confidence. He had the apprehension that the lightning, with which she was pregnant would bring him ill-fortune. He was inquisitive to know why at night she lay alone, and, looking through a crevice, he saw near her a great serpent sleeping. He was disgusted at the spectacle. He perceived immediately that his queen was expert in the dirty rites of Sabazius.* The vast brotherhood, mixed with those of Cybelè and Bacchus, included the low bottoms of prostitution, the street-walkers and the quacks, the sellers of love, of prayers, of remedies, of abortion, and of poison.

If he had cast away this woman, he would have caused Epirus to revolt. He would have set against himself the army of Bacchants and Bacchantes. He must have believed so, when, having consulted the oracle of Delphi, he was told that he must make an offering to the god who had honored him so much, and that he would lose but one eye for the impiety of having looked through a crevice into the bed-chamber of Olympias. This answer of the oracle spread through Greece, and caused the prediction to be fulfilled. A skilful archer undertook the task.

The child, Alexander, whether bastard or not, grew up. His mother had employed every means to make people believe in the fable of his birth. She had her serpents everywhere, keeping some in vases, others in baskets,

---

* See especially MOVERS and LOBECK. I will return to this subject by and by.

from which they darted out hissing, not without terror to visitors. The boy, brought up in the midst of such come-dies, believed himself to be the son of Bacchus-Sabazius. He inclined his neck on the left, in order to imitate the gracefulness of Bacchus, the ease of the beautiful idler, as he is represented in his statues. Nevertheless, since the name Sabazius had become too synonymous with the words liar and quack, people called him Zeus-Sabazius, and later in life Alexander attributed to himself the horns of Amon.

Nobody was less Greek, nothing more opposite to the Grecian hero (Ulysses or Themistocles) than Alexander. He had the true blood of the North, was of *very white* complexion, and had another characteristic, which is never found in the South, namely, *humid eyes (hygroteta)*, eyes with glimpses of blood-red fury or drunkenness. In short, he was a perfect barbarian, full of impulse, but a toper, a passionate man, capable of great crimes and great repentance. It is known that he had at times the shame-less adventure, not heard of before among the Greeks, of killing in his drunkenness a friend with his own hand. His countenance very probably expressed too distinctly his native inhumanity ; for he seems to have been afraid of being exhibited in portrait too resembling to himself, and therefore forbade, under penalty of death, that artists should deviate from the official model of his artist, the great statuary Lysippus.

Philip forgot him, and left him entirely under his mother's care till he was thirteen years old. His educa-tion was so neglected that he did not learn even the most common exercises of Greece ; for instance, he could not swim. Philip had a son, his bastard Aridæus, a well-dis-posed and well-gifted young man. Olympias, however, secretly provided against him, by means of some bever-age, which turned his head. Philip then had to think to whom should he leave the great work of his life, his king-dom and the army which he had created with so much art

10*

and cunning.   Cool-headed as he, was, and truly superior,
he had no repugnance toward the boy, who, whatever he
was, seemed to be undaunted, and who by many was
called the son of the gods.   Philip adopted him, and put
him for four years under the tuition of a client of his
household, a man of very great genius, Aristotle ; who,
however, was so much of a Greek, and of such a reflecting
turn of mind, that he was precisely the most unfit to have
any hold on that young barbarous nature.   Besides,
Aristotle had Alexander late under his tuition, when the
latter had already been moulded by his shameless mother,
and by her lying story that he was a god, and when the vile
flatterers of Olympias surrounded him.   But the teacher
whom Alexander filially loved was not Aristotle ; it was
Leonidas, Alexander's silly foster-father, who spoke only
of Asia Minor, of India, and of the victories of Bacchus,
which the young man was to renew.   Add to all this the
concurrence of all the oracles, which foretold even the
least details of his future conquests.

Philip had reached the highest eminence of renown.
Conqueror at Cheronea, he had displayed a glorious
moderation, declining any triumph, and sending home the
prisoners.   His great work was accomplished ; he was not
only powerful, but beloved.   Many sincere men believed
that Greece could not, without him, carry on her mission,
the *Hellenization* of the East.   It was nothing to conquer it.
It was necessary to pervade it with the Greek spirit and
knowledge, to colonize and civilize, and to make such a
change desirable.   Nobody could do that better than
Philip.   Brought up in company with Epaminondas, he
was possessed, if not of his virtues, at least of his patience
and his steady mildness.   He had that in which the violent Alexander was deficient—*the conception of the time*,
of the necessary compromises, without which a conquest
would be but a scourge for the world, and create nothing
but chaos.

Philip was forty-six years old.   Around him, at the

solemn moment of his expedition, was gathering a crowd
of eminent scientific men, precisely as the Committee of
Egypt formed in our time by the *Directory* for General
Bonaparte. The soul of it was Aristotle, who declined to
go with Alexander, but who would have followed Philip,
and doubtless in company of the illustrious naturalist Theo-
phrastus. With Alexander went the school of Aristotle,
Callisthenes his nephew, Anaxarchus, and Pyrrho his
pupils, and many historians, Nearchus, the great mariner,
etc. It was perfectly easy to conjecture, after the triumphant return of Xenophon, and the success of Agesilaus,
that the war against an empire already dissolving could not
be a serious one, and that people could very easily follow
the army, study, become perfectly acquainted with the
country, and, above all, select the places where colonies
should be established. The most important of them had
been organized. A multitude of Greeks—soldiers, ma-
rines, and merchants—filled the shores of Egypt.

There was but one bristling point for Philip,—his barbarous woman of Epirus, who tried to prevent his departure, by arming against him the people of Epirus and her
son, the son of Sabazius, that dangerous young man,
fully convinced of his own divinity, and capable of doing
anything to overthrow opposition. The mother and her
son had on their side the temples. Philip, desirous to en-
courage his party, consulted the oracle of Delphi, but he
received an answer bearing a double meaning, and which
forshadowed his death : "The sacrifice is ready, the bull
is crowned with garlands."

Philip went further, and took a wife, by whom he had a
child. This hastened the catastrophe. Olympias caused
him to be assassinated, and dedicated under her own
name the dagger at Delphi. People were then enabled to
judge what they had lost, and what the new government
would be. Olympias took possession of her rival, with
her child, and caused them to be burned in a brazen
vase. Alexander, in one day, sold at auction thirty thou-

sand Greeks, the very Thebans who had raised Philip, and had made the greatness of his house.

All obstacles were removed before the son of the gods. Extreme weariness, atony, and despair produce, in this world of ours, a disease, which may be called the *Messianic epidemic.* All the superstitious elements which were in Greece stood by the young god, whose inauguration had taken place through a massacre. People saw him with lightning in his hand, an army enormous indeed, and unheard of. All the resources of wisdom had come together for the great, inevitable, and expected enterprise, which was to be accomplished by the wise, or by the fools. Its time had come, and the necessity was such that no mistake of Alexander could have made it miscarry. He made many queer mistakes, with impunity, which would have caused the ruin of another man. He fought in the most unfavorable places. He marchèd through unusual routes, and through deserts without water ; he risked his army and put it to the utmost ordeals. How was it ? People have not wished to understand it. But those who have a little experience, and the knowledge of living forces, easily conjecture that, beyond the miracle, there was some other thing than a well-trained army. There was, indeed, a God and a *spirit*, the wing of fire, and the breath of fire, that which I would call the *soul of Greece*, which always went straight forward ; seemed to be led, while it was leading ; made up for blunders, and repaired them, and which was indeed the infallibility of victory. The historians have thrown all this into the shade, as much as they could. But Alexander felt it with vexation, when ironically he said this true thing : " Could it not be said that the Greeks, in the midst of the Macedonians, are like spirits among beasts ? "

It was the peculiarity of Greece, that, for a hundred years, in the expectation of great things which were foreseen, there had been many men of equanimity, fit for all things, warriors and men of letters, philosophers,

soldiers of adventure. Men like Xenophon had already
penetrated into Asia, and acquired renown. Men like
the undaunted, cruel Clitarchus, the sophist, made themselves tyrants of a state. Such a one was the excellent
and accomplished tyrant who gave his sister for a wife to
Aristotle. But the absolute dominion of little commonwealths was not enough to satisfy them. They aimed at
higher things, at Babylon and Persepolis. They knew, as
a modern authority has said, that "one cannot work on a
large scale but in the East." In those high-minded men,
men of superior genius, there was an ambitious Greece—
waiting till at last the barrier should be put down—that
followed Alexander and served him too well. The same
signal happiness, which, in the campaign of Italy, was
the lot of Condé and Bonaparte,—everywhere taking
and gathering around themselves many excellent officers,
men beyond comparison,—was also the lot of the young
Alexander, around whom gathered themselves spontane-
ously those illustrious Greeks; and it is especially for
this circumstance that the young king became Alexander
the Great.

The Persians also had Greeks in their pay, who, however, were riotous, dissatisfied, and not very numerous,
although their number has been exaggerated as much as
it could be. Nothing was neglected to deceive the world,
and the coming generations. Many licensed historians
went along with the army. The generals themselves
wrote, lied, as much as they could ; yet Alexander did
not rely on all this. That the war was by no means such
as it has been related is evident from the fact that he had,
through all his route, the leisure of writing, at every turn,
to his friends or lieutenants in Greece, the news, which
they put in everybody's mouth.* As it is known that, in
the last century, Frederick wrote incessantly to France
and did his best to become a Frenchman, so it is certain

---

* PLUTARCH : *Alexander*, li. 93.

that Alexander seemed to be uneasy at not being altogether a Greek, and made court to the shadow of Athens. He carried *Homer* with him everywhere, and put him at night under his pillow. That which shows, nevertheless, how little he profited by Homer's poems, is that, quite contrary to the custom of the true Greeks, who all imitated Ulysses, he chose for his ideal the brutal hero of the country of the Centaurs, the impetuosity and the fury of Achilles. To imitate Achilles and the overthrow of Troy, he performed the horrible pillage of Thebes. In the most urgent moment of war, he celebrated at Ilium the games and long festivals. After taking Gaza and the chief of the city, who had opposed him a long resistance, he imitated Achilles by dragging him behind his chariot by means of a rope and his bored feet.

One fine morning this Achilles became Asiatic, and turned his back to Homer and Greece. Babylon, the great mistress in monarchical prostitutions, accomplished in one day upon Alexander those effects which it required a hundred years to produce on the Persians. Shameful and unforeseen spectacle ! The conquered found themselves to be the vanquishers. Asia, that was at that moment worn out, stained, and in the cadaverous condition of Chaldean rottenness,—old Asia obtained her master for her lover. A gilded sepulchre, the sink of love, through which the world had passed, such was the passion of Alexander the Great. Modern writers, when they see in all this an admirable political sagacity, are insane. If the Greeks had to contract a little of the Asiatic manners and thinking, this certainly was not the way to do it. Asiatic customs and ideas ought to have been controlled by the lofty Greek spirit. It would have been necessary, above all, to proceed in this business with a very slow prudence, and with wise considerations.

To lay hold of Asia through the child Bagoas, the false girls, the Good Luck, and the perversity of the magians ; to throw himself headlong in the pit and mud of uncleanness, was to show himself a barbarian by nature, delighting in impurity; it was to recall to mind his nativity, the son of a Bacchante, and of the charlatan Sabasius. His palace was crowded with soothsayers and charlatans.

He relied solely on the conquered people, and blindly, without shame or precaution, armed them. He was training thirty thousand Persians for fighting against the Greeks, or to drive them away. He wished that the latter, transformed in a moment, and becoming Persians, should *worship* him in the Eastern manner, abjuring their good sense.

It was not, as some make us believe, a childish thing, and a mere vanity. It was a perverse and calculated thing. *Adoration* was the touch-stone for the abdication of good sense and human dignity. The magians, his teachers, felt that this would be the limit of Greek obedience, and that if he were resisted, he would hate Greece, and become entirely a Persian.

When at a later period the Cæsars did the same things, the world had sunk so low, and was so much degraded, that anything was easy. But at the time of Alexander, in the presence of Greece yet alive, in that sublime light of genius and reason, the attempt to sink man into the condition of a beast was a mad crime, even beyond the foolishness of Caracalla.

Strange thing! Greek apostates were partly the cause. When in his drunken anger Alexander had assassinated Cleitus, the sophist Anaxarchus, seeing him weep, said to him, while making sport of him: "That nothing was crime in him, since he was the Law; that Jupiter had Themis, who sat near him, to serve him." Such words sank deep in Alexander's heart. From that moment he caused himself to be worshipped.

The Greeks obeyed and laughed. Only one among them did not laugh, and resisted. He disconcerted Alexander, and checked him by the sacrifice of his own life.

His name will never die. It was Callisthenes, the philosopher, and nephew of Aristotle.

Ptolemæus, later a king of Egypt, a captain and friend
of Alexander, his most serious and reliable historian,
positively says that Callisthenes *was crucified* by order of
Alexander, because he would not worship him.*

Enormous event. Plutarch, who had read Ptolemæus
and all the contemporaneous historians whom we have
lost, says that Alexander did flinch ; that Callisthenes lost
his life, but saved Greece from that extreme degree of
shame.

I have no doubt about it. This solemn action was of
an immense importance. What the deep thought of
Aristotle had just founded in the intellectual domain, by
creating in theory *the philosophy of energy*, his nephew
carried out in practical life, and from the height of his
cross he, more than Zeno, more than Cleanthes, originated
stoicism.

Rich and fruitful work, which was not only the struggle,
the heroic *defence* of the soul and of conscience, of human
reason crushed under the gods, but which was soon to
become the strong foundation of what the ancient world
has bequeathed to us of its best,—*civil law* and *jurisprudence*, which in the main points we still follow.

Wisdom is sedate. I will not describe foolishness.
The new Bacchus pushed on to India. With what real
result ? Is it really the genius of Greece which conquered its way, and penetrated into remoter Asia ? Is the
bloody chaos which we soon shall point out, the ephem
eral Greek empire, a foundation? Asia despised it, and
was filled with disgust by it, and returned eagerly to her

---

* Plutarch, who relates this fact, has under his eyes Ptolemæus, a high
authority, and the first of all authorities. Arrian, whom alone Montesquieu
follows, is the worst historian of Alexander. Arrian, many centuries after
Alexander, falsified Alexander's history, trying to put in it some good sense.
It is necessary to leave it *as it really is*, an absurd, romantic, foolish narrative.

ancient religion, a fanatic reaction, which soon created the empire of the Parthians.

The army, wiser than its commander, at last refused to go further, and behold, this powerful god was compelled to obey. The scenes which were exhibited on the return were extraordinary for madness and despair. Alexander had lost his senses, and was scarcely a man. He built a city in honor of his dog; another for the tomb of his horse. He played Bacchus, carrying the thyrsus, and crowned all his army with ivy, making Bacchantes of all those sunburnt old soldiers. From the height of his world-wide imperial throne, he taught and exemplified that which the kings of Asia hid in their seraglios. He was already an Heliogabalus, with all the infamies of Atys, and of Adonis of double sex, "the lover of Venus, and the fair beloved of Apollo." He wept over Hephæstion with the passion of a woman; he killed his physicians, burned the temple of Esculapius, and asked the oracle of Amon to make a demi-god of the dead Hephæstion. The love-feast in honor of the child Bagoas, displayed before the army, was more astonishing still—an unique scene which is not to be found in the history of the Cæsars. This example in such a man as Alexander the Great carried with it a fatality. The burden, with the weight of his glory and his immense influence, was destined to lie heavy on the future. The Cæsars were its product, and it created the military customs of armies, the morals of soldiers and of kings.

The army of Alexander clapped hands at the strange and monstrous sight, at first in mockery—and then in the wild joy of feeling the restrictions upon them loosened in the outrageous libertinism of the exhibition, and the carnival which lasted so long. All had been emancipated for all the filth of war. A spurious, unbridled Greece, formed from every people, will plunder the world. Every one through infamy will be Bacchus-Sabazius; every one, in his own sphere, will be an Alexander the Great.

His heritage was a vast one. It consisted of three things :

First. He killed hope, and human dignity. Every one felt himself a plaything of destiny, who had encountered enormous, unforeseen, casual forces, and despairing of himself, became weak and credulous. Everywhere there were tears, everywhere hands were lifted up to the sky. There was an immense commerce of slaves ; merchants followed the soldiers. Those unhappy masses of Syria, of Phrygia, and even of the upper East, brutalized Europe with their Messianic foolishness.

Second. Alexander killed human reason. The wonderful fact of his expedition made everything credible and acceptable. People did not remember any longer that Xenophon with ten thousand men, and that Agesilaus with six thousand, had crushed all the efforts of the Persians. People did not remember any longer that the miracle of Alexander had been set in order and prepared through a concurrence of the events of two hundred years. People were stupefied, and sadly bowing their head before everything which was absurd, foolish, chimerical, and which until that time they would have laughed at, they used to say : " Why not ? It is less than Alexander the Great." Intelligent men, as Pyrrho, became altogether sceptical. He had followed Alexander, he had seen the fact, and he could not believe in it ; it appeared to him to be a dream, and from that time everything seemed to him to be uncertain. The majority of mankind, on the contrary, sank into the silly belief of monstrous fables. Euhemerus flatly asserted that every god had been a king ; and the majority of men more flatly believed that every king was a god.

" Why could not a divine serpent have chosen, for his Leda, Alexander's mother ? . . . Mystery ! deep mystery ! . . . Silly human reason, hold your peace ! Undoubtedly men like Socrates had not foreseen it ! What of that ? Alexander can do without it. Suffice it that his miracles have proved his divinity."

Henceforth many kings are gods, and sons of gods. The pattern has been laid down. Any one can copy it. Augustus' mother will tell you that she has enjoyed the favors of the serpent, and that the slimy reptile has implanted the Cæsars in her womb.

Third. Imitation is the law of this world of ours. Osiris was imitated by Sesostris in his conquests; Semiramis, with few slight differences, imitated the latter. Bacchus, in his war in India, in his conquest of the earth, copied this old nonsense of the East; so did also Bacchus-Alexander, who has, in his turn, been imitated by the Cæsars, Charlemagne, Louis XIV., etc.

But, more than any other man, Alexander has been the founder of all monarchical folly, not only on account of the unmeasurable influence of his glory, but because from him began in our Europe the *royal machinery*, preserved and servilely imitated. The conception of the modern king, the court, and the etiquette have come to us taken precisely from him.

The ancient king of the East, the patriarch or sacerdotal king, had the unction and sceptre of a priest, rather than the sword. The Grecian tyrant was a popular chief, who had the sword, the might. These two kinds of authority were, for the first time, united in Alexander.* From that time the double tyranny in one man has lain, and will lie heavy upon mankind. For the modern king, in Christian times, while he carries the sword, has also the cope, the priestly character.†

It was by this that the magians so easily laid hold of Alexander. His triumphal entrance into Babylon was a curious one, as a political apotheosis, a deification of royalty.

Through a road strewn with flowers, between two long

---

* This idea, which is the animus of M. MICHELET'S work, is not accurate. In India and other countries, ages before Alexander, military leaders had usurped supreme power, and made the priests their subordinates.—ED.

† See my *History.*

rows of silver altars, on which perfumes were burning, all
of great Babylon,—with her riches and pleasures, with her
sciences and arts, with her music, with her astronomers,
women and lions, tame leopards, with her pretty, rouged
boys, the minions of Mylitta,—came to prostrate herself
before Alexander. He was so dazzled by, and so intoxicated with, this pomp, that his masters and corrupters made
of him what they desired. They made him accept the magians' purifications (so impure !). They made him accept
their solemn puerilities, and appointed for him a seraglio
of three hundred and sixty-five women, according to the
number of the days in the year.* They muffled him up in
the *cidarim*,† the diadem (of Mithras and Bacchus) anointed
with myrrh, which makes gods out of kings. They thrust
upon him a golden house, a golden throne, a golden sceptre, all the old royal curiosities, with the comedies of the
eagle, of eagle-lion, the griffin, which things the Cæsars
later put on their standards, and feudalism adopted into its
beautiful heraldic mysteries. Moreover they made him
accept a wearisome etiquette of seven tasters, of seven
nobles devoted to his person—the seven planets of the
royal sun, a haired sun ; he must wear long hair. From
this we perceive whence were derived our Roman-heads
of false hair, and the periwig of our King-sun.

---

* See DIODORUS, PLUTARCH, and the texts which have been collected by
HYDE in his book *De Regno Persarum*.

† From the Hebrew כתר, KiTaR, a diadem. The term is found in the
following passages: *Esther* i. 11; ii. 17; and vi. 8. According to the
Talmud, the *tzanich*, turban or mitre, of the Jewish high priest, was called
kitar or *cidaris*.—ED.

CHAPTER V.

THE JEW—THE SERVANT.

A TRAVELLER is arrested in his journey, about evening, in a barren region, by an overflowing torrent. There is in the midst an old bridge, but it is broken on each side. There are still two arches standing, and two or three piers, but they are inaccessible. At what time was that structure built? It would cost much labor and trouble to ascertain. One cannot even determine its very height. The unapproachable ruin, covered with wild shrubs, looks grandly solemn. Indeed, if the shades of night fell around us, that phantom would become larger, and would almost frighten us out of our senses.

The effect produced by the Jewish *Bible*, for a long period of time, has been similar to that of an isolated ruin seen from a distance. People reasoned about it at random, having neither the true perspective to examine it, nor the means of studying the approaches of such a monument, namely, the neighboring or kindred peoples who were intermingled with the Jews; the great empires to which they were transplanted, and where they lived. While all this was wanting, Judea, considered alone, deceived the eyes. She filled up all the horizon, nay, she concealed the world with her phantasmagoria of religious illusions, with the prismatic colors, or gloomy clouds of her allegorical mysticism.

. Our century did not remain an immovable contemplator of the mysterious monument. It neither worshipped nor demolished it, but completed it by rebuilding on each side the piers and the arches overthrown. The great ruin in the midst is no longer isolated. By that alone everything has been changed. There is no longer any phantasmagoria. One can now approach, view, touch, and measure it. From one bank to the other, taking in all the landscape, one sees, clear of the mist, the colossuses of Egypt and of Persia, the two masters and teachers of Judea.* Near her and round about her one sees her kinsmen, namely, the people of Syria, Phœnicia, and Carthage. From these comes the great ray of light. It was believed that those peoples had altogether disappeared. Alexander having overthrown Tyre, and Scipio Carthage, Judea remained the heiress and representative of all that was destroyed.

It is true that there never was such a terrible ruin. The remains, the fragments, the wrecks, broken over again and again, are moreover scattered on every side. A wonderful patience alone could recover them. Such a pursuit, though difficult, has however been accomplished. Men like Bochart and Selden, Munter and Movers have obstinately sought after, gathered up, and collected what they could on those peoples. They have recovered thousands of instructive texts on Carthage, which city had been so completely overthrown. The collected texts relating to the gods, manners, commerce, and genius of the Phœnicians are far more numerous. The Phœnicians were evidently identical with the Canaanites, an indigenous population of Judea, which population had lived always there among the Jews, and differed very little from them in customs and habits.†

---

* Despite the Hebrew traditions of a sojourn in Egypt, and the greater probability that the Jews descended from the Hyk-sôs fugitives into Palestine, it is noteworthy that only the name of their reputed leader (*Moses*, a child), and the father of Joshua (*Nun*, a fish, or celibate woman), appear as the name of any Israelite in the *Old Testament*. See INMAN: *Ancient Faiths Embodied in Ancient Names*, i., pp. 96, 97, 135; ii., 99, *et passim.*—ED.

† Indeed it is hardly possible to discriminate, when we consider that the same language and religion characterized the two peoples, and that they intermarried. "The children of Israel dwelt among the Canaanites, Hittites, and Amorites, and Perizzites, and Hivites, and Jebusites; and they took their daughters to be their wives, and gave their daughters to their sons, and served

How could Judea have been able to insulate herself
entirely? The country was truly nothing but a narrow
strip of hills, bounded on the East by the river Jordan,
on the West by the coast, the ports of the Philistines and
Phœnicians. Her utmost width is fifteen leagues.* On
the coast there were the large cities of the Philistines,
Gaza, Azor, Ascalon; and then the wealthy ports of the
Phœnicians, Sidon, Tyre, etc. An exuberant population
existed altogether towards the sea, that many a time
seized upon the mournful country of the mountains, but
more often despised it.

Judea, on the east of the river Jordan, possessed, outside
of herself, several tribes or commonwealths, who found in
the low valleys a little pasture-land; but the heights were
and are dreadful, and dark with lugubrious basalt.

---

their gods."—*Judges* iii. 5, 6. The amalgamation appears to have been
very complete according to the *Bible* record.

"I do not myself," says Prof. J. P. Lesley, "believe, with entire confidence, in the personal existence of the Jewish patriarchs. For you will find
in the old Hindoo mythologies the names of Abraham, Isaac, and Judah,
ranged in a similar order and connection. Brahma's son, Ikswaka, was the
great-grandfather of Yadoo. The Hebrews of Palestine were but a single
twig of that wide-spreading branch of the Shemitic tree, which had its original
seats in Central Asia, and migrating southward and westward over Persia,
Mesopotamia, Arabia, and Syria, entered Egypt under the name of Hyk-sôs.
. . . . Judging the Mosaic story from these canons, in which all agree,
we find it of an age ante-dating all precise history; we find it utterly unsup-
ported by contemporary monumental records; and we feel it to be a splendid
series of incredibilities from first to last. His birth, his miracles, his *Exodus*,
his converse with Jehovah, and his mysterious disappearance,—all stamp the
history with an indelible character of MYTH, which not a single discovery of
any branch of science has yet repaid the endeavor to efface. In less degree—
in a far less degree—but still in essentially the same mode, the legends of
the Jews of a date previous to the reign of Solomon, are utterly unhistorical;
although the stories of the *Judges* are probable enough. Nothing prevents
us from identifying the Hebrews of the Monarchy as descendants of the Hyk-
sôs race, nor from supposing that the Mosaic Records were inventions of a
later age, based on a mixture of Hyk-sôs traditions, Arabian poetry, Zoroastrian mythology, and genuine Egyptian and monumental history."—*Man's
Origin and Destiny*, pp. 144, 153.—ED.

* HIERONYMUS, *ad Dard.* 85.—MUNK, *Palestine*, p. 40.

Strabo rightly says that Judea is, on the whole, a very poor country. There.is, however, some variation from it ; vineyards, which are supported by terraces, are cultivated there, and also some patches of wheat in the many oases, which are naturally formed by the river Jordan and several brooks. In every epoch, however, the travellers, whose word may be believed, say that, on entering that country, one feels something like a great dryness and an infinite *ennui.* With the exception of the small circle of Galilee and the land of Naplous, everything is gloomy and monotonous, dull and gray with ashes.

Good sense evidently shows that there must have been very strong reasons for preferring this country to the rich Damascene Syria, to the fertile region *of the giants,* to the bewitching Ascalon, *the betrothed of Syria,* to Tyre and Sidon, the queens of the seas.

Judea seemed to offer two asylums, two natural shelters, in the two central points of her two kingdoms of Israel and Judah. On the north, the closed valley of Samaria is protected on each side. On the south, Jerusalem, which stands on a very high commanding point, can be approached only through two passes easily defended, namely, the valley of Jehoshaphat and that of Terebinth.

The Jew invited and hospitably admitted the stranger, promising to render him impartial justice ;* pledging to him an equal share of land as if he were a Jew ;† agreeing with him to admit him to his own festivals and banquets ;‡ nay, even to his prayers.§ The stranger shall be in Judea as though he were in his own country ; *the Jew loves him as he does himself.*‖

That is going too far. But who is this stranger ? He may be a fugitive entering Judea without clothing, or any means of subsistence. " *God loves him, and will give him an inheritance among his own chosen people.*"

---

* *Deuteronomy* i. 16, 24.   † *Ezekiel* xlvii. 22.
‡ *Deuteronomy* xvi. 11, 14.   § *III. (I.) Kings* viii. 41.
‖ *Leviticus* xix. 34.

A little farther one sees more clearly into this secret. The stranger may be a slave. " *The slave who takes shelter* among you shall not be given back to his master. He will dwell where he wishes, and shall find rest and security in your cities, and nobody shall make him uneasy."*

After this, we know what will happen. Under these conditions, the most gloomy, the most barren country, will never be a desert. Such policy, which wishes to procure inhabitants at any price, is all the more remarkable, because it is found among an economical, and even greedy people, as it may be seen in the books of *Kings* and in that of *Jeremiah*, etc. The Jews are altogether unacquainted with the chivalrous feelings of the Arabians,† and still more with the generous, though often imprudent grandeur of the Indo-Celtic races, which burst out in their poetry from the *Râmayana* to the *Shah Nameh*, from the *Niebelungen* to the French *songs* of Roland and of Merlin.

The Jew, from the beginning, has been a peace-loving man, a man of business. His ideal is neither the warrior, nor the workingman, nor the husbandman. Formerly a nomad, a shepherd, he returned later to his wandering life, as a pedler, as a banker, or as a broker.

The Bible strongly and simply lays down such an ideal. It is Jacob, who constituted the type and exemplar, who received the sacred name of the people, *Israel.* Jacob was a pacific man, " *who remained at home*," while his brother Esau, the Idumean, worked, or went hunting. Esau, entirely hairy, had a skin like that of a beast ; Jacob had no hair at all. Jacob a shepherd, like Abel, was blessed. Esau, a laborer like Cain, was condemned and disinherited.

---

* *Deuteronomy* xxiii. 15, 16.

† If David did not kill Saul, at the time he could have done it, it was not on account of chivalric feeling, but because the king was the *anointed* of the Lord.

II

Art and industry, as well as agriculture, are condemned
in the personification of Tubal-cain.   The builders are disparaged, mocked at, and the tower of Babel is mentioned
as the great work which they were able to perform.   The
true Jew, the patriarch, is the artful shepherd, who knows
how to increase his flock by an intelligent care of acquisi-
tion and calculating.   He is pleasing to woman, his mother
Rebecca, and he seems a very woman himself, very prudent in his submissions and adorations to his brother
Esau, whom he had so dexterously wheedled out of his
birth-right.

The beloved son of Jacob is the slave, who became a
vizier.   It is Joseph, the financier, who from being at
first a soothsayer, rose to power by interpreting dreams.*
Such a story would have been impossible in Egypt, where
the shepherd, Hyk-sôs, being considered as an impure
man, would have found every entrance closed to employ-
ments and honors,† but which is very natural in Chaldea,
where such men as Tobias, Mardocheus, and Daniel were
soothsayers, viziers, and treasurers.

The great and true glory of the Jews, which they owe
to their own miseries, is that they alone, among all the
peoples, have given utterance, in a piercing and eternal
voice, to the sigh of the slave.

Elsewhere it was a cry, hardly uttered and constrained.‡
In Judea, admirable and profound songs of grief were
sung during many centuries.   Those songs were so exquisite that men are satisfied to borrow them to express

---

* *Genesis* xl., xli. and xliv., 5, 15.

† It has been conjectured, however, that the king who made Joseph his
vizier, was himself of the hated race, which might account for his partiality.
The Egyptians detested all foreigners, perhaps from the memory of the Hyk-
sôs, who are described as Arabians, Phœnicians, Hellenes or Greeks, and
Shepherds.—ED.

‡ Virgil has scarcely dared to utter the sigh of the Italian soul, of the un-
fortunate Tityrus, who had become the slave of the soldier.   In our age the
Poles have raised their voice for a moment in a sublime despair : Krasinski,
Mickiewicz, are equal to Isaiah.

their most sincere sorrows, and personal chagrins. It is because the Jews had endured misfortune in its fulness, and under its harshest forms. At first wandering shepherds, then carried off into Egypt and becoming working-men in spite of themselves, they were employed to build up the Pyramids.* In Palestine they were husbandmen against their will. The so-called Mosaic laws show prodigious efforts made to induce them to devote themselves to the tillage of the soil. Agricultural and rural festivals were organized, but the Jews remained none the less restless and nomadic in their mind.

The miserable slave, who is essentially a hater of light, welcomes night as the hour of liberty. The *Psalms* and the chants of the prophets are, most of them, nightsongs.

He has worked at his vineyard. Night falls, and by and by all is wrapped in darkness. Stretched on his terrace, under a sparkling sky, he sleeps a few moments, and then awakes. The lions, which are in his heart, bound . . . It is a loud roaring. But before long the tears come: Ah! Ah! Ah! Lord, my God.

But God hears not. The sufferer cries out, invokes him all the more: "Arise. . . Do you sleep, O Lord? Do you wait until I die? . . . The dead will not praise thee. . ."

That which is original and extremely touching in these long alternatives is that, among his aridities, languors, and the delays of God in hearing him, the Jew reproaches himself alone. He strikes his own breast. Seated under

---

* It is hardly probable that the Hyk-sôs or Hebrews worked on the Pyramids. Hengstenberg, quoted by Lesley, states that Ramases II., or Sesostris, to guard his frontiers against the Hittites of Palestine, forced his native Hyk-sôs serfs and foreign military slaves to build a chain of forts across the Isthmus of Suez, of which the principal were Ramases and Pithom. These conscripts were called *Apura*, conj. Hebrews, as both words mean over-men or emigrants. This king worshipped the sun-god Aten or Satan, whom the Jews afterward made the Enemy of Jehovah and Prince of Devils.—ED.

the juniper tree, he says : " Take me to you, O Lord ! . . .
I am no better than my fathers were."

How different is this, not only from the indomitable
Arabian of Hedjaz (Antar), but from that of Idumea, the
nobly disputant Job, in his controversy with God. In
his violent poem it is perceived that Job, being overwhelmed at last, holds his peace and speaks not, but
does not consider himself vanquished. God, with dinning
noise speaks to him of the Leviathan, of thunder, etc.
Such arguments of the strongest against a feeble being are
no arguments at all. Job keeps his own thoughts to himself : " Thou art strong, but I am just." *

---

* The story of Job is dramatic in a high degree, and illustrates the bold
self-reliance of the Arabian Emir or Sheik, such as Job is represented. He
acted as the Hebrew *zachans* or patriarchs. In his controversy with his three
friends, Job had asserted that his champion or next of kin would deliver him
and stand up in his behalf; and even now, though he was black and putrid
with disease, he would yet see God, and judgment would overtake those who
now condemned him (xix., 21–29). In the latter part of the poem, Job and
the Deity are brought into conference, and the steadfast chieftain " holds fast
his integrity," as he had declared that he would (xlii., 1–6).

" Then Job answered the Lord, and said :
' I know that thou canst do all things,
And that thy decrees no one can resist.
How should I disapprove of thine inscrutable wisdom ?
I have been speaking of what I did not understand ;
Things too marvellous, that I did not comprehend.
Hear me, I beseech—I will speak :
Let me ask questions and explain them to me,
—I heard of thee by the hearing of the ear,
But now mine eye hath seen thee—
Wherefore do I abhor myself,
And turn myself about in dust and ashes ? '
" Then Jehovah said unto Job :
' Let him who disputes with the Almighty stand to it ;
He who censures God let him awe him.'
" Then Job replied to Jehovah and said :
' Behold, I am a poor creature, what shall I answer ?
I will lay my hand upon my mouth.' "

The discussion ended by the vindication of the patriarch, the Lord himself
taking the part of his champion.—ED.

The thoughts of the Jew are quite different. He en-joys not the expansion of the wilderness as does the free Arabian, who breathes at his leisure and whose life is high and proud, things of which Job bears witness to himself. The greatest misery of the slave is that he per-ceives that he wallows in those vices, which slavery in-volves with it, and that his will grows corrupt in them. Thus, there is neither mildness nor innocence in his lamentations. They are not like the song of the nightin-gale, but one may hear in them the inauspicious cries of some night-bird, or the *bewailing* of a heart, which in its prostration still feels itself impure. But pride has had the best of it. "God will be my justice! God does not impute my transgressions to me. Blessed be he until the break of day, and from morning to evening."

Meanwhile the darkness is becoming clear. A black carob-tree appears on the horizon under a luminous gray sky. The day is near. "If tears flow from my eyes in the evening, gladness will come in the morning."

It is daylight at last. The Dead Sea sparkles! . . . And the red image of the sun, even before he goes beyond the barren summit of the gloomy hills, stains with blood the dismal waves. . . . Thus the Liberator, the cham-pion, IAO or Jehovah is near coming! Such a conception of an avenging, destroying God, is the intense passion of the slave. He broods over it; and it is his precious treasure. The undefined Iao of Chaldea, who, according to MOVERS, was only a breath of life; the gloomy Iao of Phœnicia, who was a voice of death, a voice of sorrow, in Judea is the soul of the desert. Look toward the South. Everything ends there; life ceases there; no visible form—neither of animals, nor of vegetables. As a compensation of all this, a burning breath (which recalls the Egyptian Typhon), an invisible power makes itself felt. One sees nothing, and yet one cannot face it. This invisible power said to Moses: "If thou dost see me, let it be at the back. . . . Otherwise thou art a dead man."

The Jews incessantly leave this terrible, savage God, and always return to him. " Is this a wonder ? a miracle ? " Not at all. This God, notwithstanding his irksome laws, is, however, the Jewish liberty, the liberty of hating, and cursing the gods of powerful peoples. In order to understand this passion for such a repulsive deity, the faithful and obstinate returns to him, it is necessary to consider that the Jews, over whom the torrent of Asia passed again and again, were the playthings and the victims of all those other gods. The Midianites, with their black god, encamped, like devouring locusts, among the Jews, and ate up everything. The giants, as the Philistines were called by the Jews,* made them bondmen of their goddess Astarté, of her outrageous orgies, in which even Samson and David figured as actors.† Nor is this all, but in the middle of Judea, door by door, the old tribes of Canaan remained as a perpetual temptation to the Jews, whom the Canaanites united with in the lascivious dances of the Heifer or of the Calf.

This was a worship of deep enervation. The serf, allured into it at night, found himself on the morrow worn out and more a slave than before. Then he would return with shame and pious zeal to his male God, to his austere Jehovah, who alone was to him a wall, an invisible wall of fire against the sweet pressure of those deities of death, that surrounded him on every side.

All this remained obscure, until, in the last century, Astruc, a keen critic, threw a glimpse of genius on the Bible. He saw the duality, the struggle of the Jewish soul. In the *Bible,* which had been always considered

* Raphaim, a designation of the aboriginal races east of the Jordan, and of the country of Palestine. It must relate to other peculiarities than a colossal body, for one of the archangels, or Amshaspands, was styled Rapha-el.

† The Hebrew word does not bear this out. Samson "made sport" in the Temple of Dagon, the Kèto or Hoa of Asia; and David, though he established the worship of Iao in Palestine, as the national divinity, nowhere is mentioned as taking part in the worship of the Syrian goddess. But his grandchildren did.—Ed.

a simple book, he saw two *Bibles;* and his view has since been adopted by all critics. Two religions—two different worships, exhibit themselves side by side in the *Bible.* The agricultural religion of ELOHÈ, or of the ELOHIM, was practiced by the majority, and easily mixed itself with the Cananean worship of the Heifer or the Calf. An austere minority,* out of hatred for the oppressive idol, made efforts to be faithful to the invisible Jehovah, the ark and adytum of whose temple, however, was decorated with the awkward figures of terror—two cherubs on winged bulls. This God, who in the most extreme misfortunes, or in panics, was very easily taken for the iron bull (Moloch), remained none the less the soul of the proud purity which upheld and saved the people, giving them unity.†

The prophets of Judea are true martyrs, tortured by the contrasts of a violent situation. They are the popular representatives of the true Jewish spirit against the kings, who were too Syrian. The prophets struggle likewise against the people, against the barbarous tendencies of the two worships of Elohim and Jehovah, which divide them. The great concern of the prophets, between these two opposite gods, is to purify the first, to separate him from the orgies—the fanaticism of the nocturnal worship of Baal—and to humanize the second, to thrust aside from

---

* It is evident that the worship of the Elohim or Caheinan deities was maintained among the plebs of Palestine, who were a non-Shemitic peasantry, while the religion of Iao or Jehovah was adhered to by the aristocratic.—ED.

† Nations, without coming to an understanding, were advancing toward the idea of the *Unity of God.* From the year 1000 B.C. to the year 500 B.C. this unity was manifested everywhere and in the same manner, a negative and destructive one, through the eclipse and the death of the gods. The Greek Olympus, in its high sphere, pale and withered, spiritualized itself, and became the *Nous* of Anaxagoras, or from below was blended and mixed in the impure vat of Bacchus. The great struggle ceased in Persia. Ahriman, enervated, inclined to be absorbed by Ormuzd. All the Baals of Babylon were buried in the bosom of Anahid or Mylitta. Those of Syria, as a judgment, appear to have been burned in Jehovah. The impure unity belonged to Babel. In Judea there was the unity of hatred.

his worship the brazier of Moloch. In doing this the prophets are noble, the true benefactors of mankind, venerable guardians of the people against those worships, which they repelled in a desperate struggle, often by the sacrifice of their own life.

"Sons of my barn-floor and of my mill-stone! It is you whom I have crushed, that are my sons!"

This sublime sentence of Isaiah, which sums up the prophets, has produced strange consequences. The heavy, redoubled blows, the shower of griefs and outrages, have neither tired out, nor broken down the surprising elasticity of the *Eternal Patient*. Beaten down, he rises up again. Disappeared, he is found again. Against the cruel, very real and very certain present, he considers chimera and the impossible as a more certain blessing.

He hopes against hope, and the more the storm increases, the more he thinks that the hand of God is near to show itself. He would groan to be saved by his own foresight. He longs for the hazard of Grace; he wishes to be saved by a throw of the dice. These tendencies, depending on chance, deeply corrupt the judgment of the slave, *make him hate Reason and despair of action.*

It was the expectation of the Messiah which troubled and tortured the Jewish people from their remotest antiquity. This is admirably shown in the book of the *Judges.* Each of the seven captivities ended through a miracle, the hazard against Wisdom. The very proud as well as very humble principle of this curious history, is that the people of God, a perpetual miracle, must have a constantly extraordinary fate, beyond any human foresight.

God, in order that he might manifest his glory, singled out, in the midst of the chosen people, *the weak rather than the strong*, the *little rather than the great*, the younger against the elder. He preferred Joseph to the haughty Judah; Jacob, cunning and mild like a woman, to the valiant Ishmael and the strong Esau. The little David, through God, kills the giant Goliath. In the same manner, God loved and chose for himself, and adopted a small people, the only one chosen. The other families of mankind were cut away.

We must follow the ulterior consequence of this principle. God loves and willingly singles out the *smallest in merit*, he who is of but little worth, who wishes nothing, and does nothing. He says, and incessantly repeats, that the chosen people are *worthless*. He chooses the *idler* Abel in preference of the *worker* Cain. Abel, who makes no effort, who brings no merit which requires a reward, and so compels the hand of God, pleases him, and is blessed by him.

But what follows is stronger still. He, who not only has no merit, but *has dishonored* and outraged the divine law, and who cannot be chosen and blessed, except through an astonishing miracle of mercy and goodness, will be precisely the very man who will glorify most the free power of God. He is chosen rather than the just man. Jacob, who cheats his brother, and deceives his own father, is *chosen*. Levi, cursed by Jacob for treason and murder, is *the father of the sacerdotal tribe*. Judah, who sold Joseph, and who shamelessly bought the impure embraces of Tamar,* Judah is the *chief of the people*, who are called by his name.

Is all this a positive preference for evil and sin? Not at all. It is a system, a strict application of a principle, according to which, he who owes nothing to God, if he be chosen, *exhibits* all the more gloriously the *gratuitous mercy*, the omnipotence of God.

Some will say: "Are not the Jews a people under a law which requires Justice?" Yes, but this very Law,

---

* *Genesis* xxxviii., "When Judah saw her, he took her to be a *priestess* (Hebrew *Kadesha*, a consecrated woman) because she had covered her face." A woman of this class was considered holy and pure, and not as a prostitute. —Ed.

11*

given exclusively to a *favorite* people, to a people whom Moses himself declared *worthless*, this Law is established on a basis foreign to Justice—a basis of *unjust* preference.

The Law itself, loaded and overloaded with minute ordinances, and with an immense formalism foreign to conscience, tends to lull the latter asleep. So much the more so, that, in performing those rites and all those vain prescriptions, one feels himself to be dispensed from doing right. The ground of the Jew is this: "I am the happy one, whose Justice is God himself." Why? "I am of *the chosen people*, the son of the divine favor."

But, after all, why *chosen?* Through what merit have Abraham and Jacob deserved that God should make with them an eternal covenant? Without any merit. *They pleased God.*

Thus this Jewish antiquity gives already the theory of Grace in all its nudity. And the Jewish history close by shows the natural result of that theory, the repeated sins and relapses, vainly lamented, and, in the midst of those tears, the secret assurance of this proud doctrine, which is summed up in this: "Any transgression will be forgiven me; I am the son of the house."

Let Moses speak gruffly; let Isaiah beat them with his thunderbolts! All these manly appearances will not prevent this doctrine from being the doctrine of passion, of the *feminine* fancy—of the caprice of woman, who wishes to give no other reason for her love but love; who by choosing the *worthless* thinks herself to be a queen, and who says: "As thou art nothing, thou shalt glorify so much the more my favor, my goodness, my grace."

Such a theory is the desolating of the just, the discouraging of endeavor—is the shutting of the door for ever *to a great will.*

God's justice, they say, exceeds all our acts of justice, all the little ideas that the heart of man has about what is just. Then God can punish the innocent. When he punishes the guilty, he is compelled to do it ; he cannot do otherwise. But when he crushes the innocent, the innocent son of the guilty, oh ! how great then he is ! how much more of a God then he is !

It was only at the time of the Captivity, when such terrible events shook all existence, every idea, and all the old groundwork, that two prisoners, two prophets, Jeremiah and Ezekiel, rooting out from their bleeding hearts those detestable principles, with a great and noble effort proclaimed at last *the Right.*

The unfortunate Jeremiah, who had given the Jews a very reasonable advice, but whom the Jews called a traitor, when he was enfranchised by the general of the king of Babylon, availed himself of his liberty only to go back to Jerusalem, and to weep upon her stones. It was there that he had this beautiful thought, this anti-Jewish, anti-Mosaic idea, above the ancient Law. "The Lord says : I have destroyed, but I will rebuild. They will then no longer say : *Our fathers ate the sour grapes, and our teeth are set on edge.* Each man will have the toothache, according to what he himself has eaten, and he shall die only on account of his own sins. I will make a new covenant. I will write the Law no more on stones, but within the heart and bosom of man. Man shall no more set himself as a teacher, and say to his neighbor : *Know God ;* because every one then shall know me, the most humble as well as the greatest shall know me."

Ezekiel is still more admirable on the point of personal responsibility, *of the salvation of each through his own works.* He wards off any equivocation, takes up the argument thrice, and dwells on it with a vigor, a slowness, and a gravity worthy of the Roman jurists. It is evident that he is aware of the importance of the sacred stone, which he lays firmly and seals with lime and cement. The Jewish prophet and the wise man of Greece here agree and for once unite. The chapter in which Ezekiel sets forth God as a just judge, as Justice, is precisely in the spirit of the *Eutyphron* of Socrates: "The divine is divine in so far as it is just."

The Jews, when transported to Chaldea, or sojourning in Egypt, experienced no great misfortune in their exile. *They made a fortune.* From a small people, exhausted, drained off, and ruined, they became, in those great empires, what they have been since, namely, rich and numerous tribes, carrying on commerce everywhere; and the commerce of money entering through the back door, but entering nevertheless the palaces of kings, who appreciated their merit, their humble way, and their versatility. They became the general *medium* of commercial transactions.*

The Jewish people, without abandoning the Mosaic institute, or the faith of the prophets, adopted also another faith—the faith in gain, in money. In their great over-throws they said to themselves that riches were the only guarantee. "Riches are to the rich man a city, a fortress, as a wall by which he is surrounded" (*Prov.* xviii. 2). But what riches? The easiest to keep or to save is gold. Indeed, is that so? Something better, the *invisible* riches, gold invested in sure hands. If the Phœnicians, as it is said, invented alphabetic writing, the Jews invented the *promissory note.*

This is a natural result of slave-life—an uneasy life—like that of a hare between two furrows. The Jews soon found out, also, the politics of the slave, which never failed at a court, *to give, to give secretly.* "A gift in secret allayeth anger" (*Prov.* xxi. 14). Servility, the unlimited worship of kings, now characterized them: "My son, fear thou Jehovah and the king" (*Prov.* xxiv. 21). "The wrath of a king is as messengers of death. In the light of the king's countenance is life, and his favor is as a cloud of the latter rain" (*Prov.* xvi. 14, 15). "Exhibit not thyself in the presence of the king, and stand not in the

---

* This would seem to demonstrate their generic identity with the Phœnicians, who did precisely the same thing.—ED.

place of the great " (*Prov.* xxv. 6). A great number of
similar maxims teach an extreme prudence, a perfect obedience, even a genuine admiration of monarchical power.
The Jews will be loved by kings. There are no better
slaves, more docile and more intelligent. Often they
believe that the king is from God, but *as a. scourge*
(*Prov.* xxviii.), and they honor even *this scourge*, being
stayed by no humiliation, because, by keeping their own
law, they believe that they do not debase themselves
inwardly. Such a distinction is in practice a delicate and
difficult one ; to be a saint behind the scene, and at the
same time in front the pliable instrument of all the
tyrannies of the world.

The beautiful Jewish encyclopædia, which people call
the *Bible*, is in all its parts strongly marked with this
spirit of business, of skill, and of thrift, which characterized the Jews when they had become familiar and active
with the affairs of great empires, by means of the bank,
and intrigue—a pious, humble, prudent intrigue, which
declined to play great parts. Its books were composed
or rather written over again, and put in order from ancient
fragments or records, perhaps ; and were then reviewed,
adopted and fixed permanently by the *Great Synagogue*
that Esdras kept long assembled. In those books many
antique features have been preserved. Many things, also,
which the priests might have thrown away for the sake
of decorum, have likewise been kept up in those books
with a tenacity purely Jewish.

What strikes us the most is a true, lively, but grave and
moderate genius of narrative kept within bounds. Joseph
and Jacob—the cunning man—delight and inspire the
narrator. But his favorite hero is David, an Arabian-Jew,
shrewd, valiant, impure, descended from Ruth the Moabitess (one of the tribe that was begotten through the
incest of Lot), "the chief of the ruined people who fly
into the desert." This cunning politician, more priest
than the priests themselves, charmed and edified the peo-

ple by dancing before the ark, by singing and playing the fool.*

All this is wonderfully artful, strong, even savoring of the free-thinker. That which is wrong in it, is the pleasure with which the narrator seems to relish the general picture, relating over and over again the sensuality and revenge. He takes delight in describing some impossible revenges. The reader cannot believe a word of the frightful massacres which the Jews had made in the country of Chanaan, of the pretended extermination of tribes, which were still extant in subsequent periods. Their numerous servitudes show conclusively that the Jews differed widely from the warlike Arabians, and could not have achieved those bloody glories. Such narratives are mere bragging, a revenge in words for the many evils endured. Similar narratives are found in the monkish chronicles of the age of Charles the Bald, in the *Friar of Saint-Galb*. This good-natured friar, shut in his cell, wrote only of death and havoc. In his pages blood flowed like water. One of his convent heroes was so strong that with his lance he ran through seven warriors at once, and carried them all as on a spit. This reminds the reader of the wonderful stories of Joshua.

Yet, that which saddens, that which may dry up the soul, are not so much those improbable massacres, the gross sensualities, as the general aridity. With the exception of some parts in *Genesis*, in the *Judges*, and in the books of *Kings*, the spirit of the *Bible* is harsh and dry. There is sometimes a flame, but it is the flame of a bush which blazes for a moment, glitters, burns, and frightens, but neither warms nor illumines.

The aridity is radical both in the form and in the subject-matter.† All the progress of the Jews ends in deep sterility.

---

* As was done at the processions of Bacchus or Baal.—ED.

† Nothing has cost me so much labor as this chapter. I love the Jews. I have not let slip any occasion to call to mind their martyrs, their family

On one side there were the Pharisees, a set of men more estimable than it is generally believed, who were zealous of the Law, and who, according to Jeremiah and Ezekiel, seemed to have a natural bias toward the fruitful doctrines of the Greek and Roman uprightness, but they stopped in the narrow formalism of the Mosaic prescriptions. *

On the other hand there was the mystical party, more independent of the Law ; this party appeared to gravitate toward love and Grace, but not finding in them the waves of the heart, sank in the strange eccentricity of a worship of grammar, the adoration of the language, and the religion of the alphabet.

The Hebrew language, essentially fragmentary and ellip-

---

virtues, the admirable abilities which they have displayed in our time. How could a man remain unconcerned about the destiny of this people, authors of the Christian world, and so much persecuted and maltreated by the Christians ? As soon as one wishes to be severe toward them, he regrets it, and says : " The vices of the Jewish people are those which we have produced in them ; their virtues are their own." Let us then respect the patient people, whom, for so many centuries the world has smitten so hard, and who, in our days, have suffered so much in Russia. Let us respect the faithful people whose antique worship preserves the type from which humanity departed, and to which we are going back, *the family pontificate*, the type toward which the future bends. Let us respect the lively energy, which from the Oriental stock has raised up so many unforeseen talents, so many *savants* and proficients in every art. And yet how can one hold his peace ? It is through the ancient books of the Jews that slavery is authorized everywhere and sanctified. In the South of the United States of America, the slave-holders cited texts of the Bible to justify their prodigious crime. In Europe the Holy Alliance swore on the Jewish and Christian books. The Jews, all over the earth, have been the best slaves, and the prop of their tyrants also. Why ? Because they, more than any other set of men, had the secret liberty of that religious feeling which makes bondage and outrage an endurable burden. Moreover, they had the industrial turn of mind which makes the best of a tyrant, and converts slavery into the field of speculation. The Jewish race bids fair to have great destinies in future, because it is one of the acclimatable races of the world, as has been remarked by Mr. Bertillon, in his valuable book on this great subject of *acclimatation*.

* Does not the name Pharisee suggest that of Parsee, the votary of the religion of the *Avesta*, a religion which evidently permeated the Mosaic polity in historical times?

tical, has the most rebellious idiom. It excludes deduction. The most cruel sentence of Jehovah on the prophets, was that of imposing on them an impossible language. "I am a stutterer," says Moses to him. All the
prophets are so. All of them make terrible and desperate
efforts to speak. Those efforts sometimes are sublime.
Darts of fire leap up. . . . The lightnings, the night
which follows them, penetrate the prophets themselves
with sacred horror. This language seems to them to be
either divine or God himself. The scribes call God the
Word.

Is it the Word of Ormuzd brought back from Persia ?
Anybody would almost believe it to be so. Wrongfully.

What Persia calls the *Word* is the emission of life, the
divine manifestation of light and being, identical to the
tree of life (Haöma), to the universal river, which proceeds
from it and flows at its foot.

The rich life of trees, fruits, flowing rivers, which had
made Asia a paradise, is foreign to the Jews. The tree is
accursed. The Word is no longer life, love, and generation. It is the command, *the saying of God.* There are
no more preludes. The being, that till that time came
into the world through the progressive ways of impregna-
tion and incubation, in their idea, is born all at once,
alone, full-grown, and such as he will always remain. He
springs up from nothing, is struck with terror, and falls on
his knees. He is the effect of a masterstroke of divine
policy—an arbitrary, accidental fact of that divine terrible
will.

But what will, what saying, what name ? Here is the
rub, the great uneasiness of man. The universal mystery
is to know of what syllables, of what letters the *name* of
God is composed. A dreadful power is in it, and as soon
as one can pronounce that name, one partakes of that
very power. Let the profane who betray the secret be
accursed ! The seventy authors of the *Septuagint* wish
him who reveals it to be stoned.

The name of God enlarges. From three letters (to express and embrace the divine perfections) it increases to twelve, to forty-two. The alphabet is divine. Each letter is a force of God. It is by the means of the alphabet that he has created. Man himself, through the use of certain letters, could create, could heal. The thirty-two *ways of the almighty Wisdom* comprise also the numbers (which are letters still), and some *forms of grammar.*

Infancy of decrepitude! . . . Piety is made to consist wholly in childish practices. The scribes called themselves *numberers*, because they spent their lives in counting the words and letters which are contained in the sacred books.*

In dotage all things unite. This magic of the alphabet, this queer superstition of letters, blended itself in a strange manner, with a unitarian mysticism in which man thought himself to be lost in God. Like things, however, are seen among Christians. The barren schoolmen, in their empty brains, fancy to rave of love. Saint Augustin, Saint Bernard, in imitation of the Jewish Rabbi, dare to imagine that God will descend into their hard hearts, into their searching minds disputing on a pin's point and aiming at a spark, and that he will consummate with them a spiritual marriage. They dare propose such a strange union, a nuptial bed made of needles and flints, to the great Soul, the Mother of worlds. They pretend, the insolents! to possess this eternal lover! they sing the song of love on their shrill psaltery.

And what a song! They go too far indeed! Such a pathological case will astonish posterity. They are so far from nature, their minds are so much led astray, that both Jews and Christians choose a song of passionateness, the song of the morbid, shameless voluptuousness of Syria, to celebrate a marriage with God, a thing so frightful as to make angels turn pale!

* FRANCK: *Kabale,* p. 69.

It is indeed a devilish and demoniacal spectacle to see those Rabbis, those doctors, those bishops, those Fathers, repeat over and over again such impudicities, squeezing and wresting them, and say solemnly, but with a frightfully-grimacing mouth, those words which are whispered on the pillow, the most secret avowals of a girl lost in the rage of love, and who can no longer refrain herself.

CHAPTER VI.

THE WORLD-WOMAN.

THE *Song of Songs* is unquestionably the most popular part of the most popular book—the *Bible.* Wordly-minded men and unbelievers, as well as believers, have admired and read it over and over again, as the high expression of oriental love, or, simply of love.

It is evidently an incoherent collection of love-songs, but arranged in such a manner as to give some idea of unity to the whole.

What is astonishing is that the Jews, who had no song of joy, should, for the celebration of their Passover, have adopted this song, which, in its principal features, is by no means a Jewish song. There is in it such a flight of imagination, such a charm, such peculiar liberty, that it jars and contrasts with the gloomy *Bible* of the Jews, which in general is dry and constrained. In this song, on the contrary, there is an unbounded effusion and openness, not indeed of the heart and love, but of passion and desire. It is a song of Syria.

The Shulamite * is of Syria. The Jewish woman is more restrained. Her lover would surely not have compared her with " the wild Arabian mare of Pharaoh. † " It is not of her that he, in trembling admiration, would have said, " that she was more terrible than an army in array of battle."

The Jews have, through the means of harshest laws, restrained woman, imputing to her the *Fall*, and always

---

* This term is the feminine of *Solomon*

† i. e., Hebrew, כוסה, *Susa*, a mare.—ED.

fearing her as impure* and suspicious, and so much so as
to give to a father the following strange advice : " Never
smile to your daughter."†

The *Song of Songs* would, surely, have never issued
from a Jewish source.   The marriage-ceremony among the
Jews was severe, for the bought woman, led away by the
man who placed a ring in her ear (or in her nose)‡ underwent a very hard judgment (too publicly) on her virginity.   The Jewish woman, so charming and so affecting
through her humility, § does not exist in the presence of
the law ; she is not numbered in the census of the people.

The Shulamite in the *Song of Songs* is rather a girl of
Syria, armed with seven spirits, in order to invade,
trouble, tempt, unnerve man, and make of him a weak
boy.   This is the meaning of the *Song of Songs*, and it
strongly stands out as soon as the reader throws aside
the awkward additions by which it has been obscured.

The Jews, having had the very strange idea of singing

---

* *Leviticus* xii. 5.   † *Ecclesiasticus, or Wisdom of Jesus,* vii. 24.

‡ Even in our time, the Eastern woman carries often a ring at her nose as
she would say : " I am obedient, subdued, and I will go whither people wish
me to go." (All travellers are agreed upon this. See SAVARY I., 298 ;
LEFEVRE I., 38, etc.)   There was little difference between the married
woman and the captive, who had a ring put on his nose or lip. (RAWLINSON :
Assyria, Vol. i., plate 297.)   In the book of *Genesis* (ch. xxxiv. 47) the
servant of Abraham places a ring on the nose of Rebecca, and Saint Jerome
translates ridiculously : " I put the earring upon her face." (See CAHEN'S
Bible.)   The ring which disfigures the face and excludes the kiss, humiliates
the woman very much, renders her more passive, a subdued female who sub-
mits herself to pleasure.   The reciprocity of it disappears.   As to circumcised
persons, who are less sensible than the uncircumcised ones (see *Egypt's Plague*
by the Surgeon SAVARESI), pleasure is slow and indefinite, single in the very
conjugal act, as a long mystic dream, in which one sees only one's thoughts.
When the lover in the *Song of Songs* says to his beloved that "her nose is
haughty like the tower of Lebanon," he means to say that she is a virgin,
has not received the ring at her nose, and is not yet subdued to conjugal
humility.

§ Among the Jews, a man says in the morning : " I thank Thee, O Lord,
for not having made me a woman."   The Jewish woman says : " I thank
Thee, O Lord God, for having made me as Thou hast wished to make me."

such an erotic song at their holyday, believed that they
sanctified it by supposing at first that it was a song of a
legitimate *marriage.* They next supposed that it was a
song for royal nuptials, that which purifies anything.
Then they supposed it to be the song of the blessed nuptials of the *holy King Solomon.* Hence some of its grotesque ornaments, as for instance the fifty strong men
around the bed, etc., and then luxury and gold. Oh!
holy metal! At the moment in which the beloved girl
resists no longer, yields all herself, her lover who admires
and adores her, says, insipidly : " The joints of thy thighs
are like jewels, the work of the hands of a cunning
workman " (vii. 1).

These are miserable additions, but which can easily be
thrown aside. Freed of them the *Song of Songs* remains
admirable for its local beauty, altogether Syrian, burning
with physical passion, though not very edifying, but full
of a morbid spirit and of a kind of fever, as an autumnal
wind, deadly and delightful.

The story is not obscure, as people have tried to make
it. Indeed it is too clear.

It is spring-time, the moment in which a festival was
celebrated in Syria, Greece, and everywhere in order to
open the casks and taste the wine of the last vintage.*
It is the moment in which the red blood of Adonis flowed
at Byblos with the sands of the torrent, itself a torrent of
love, of desperate pleasure, of tears. A beautiful young
man, an emir's son, I think, in his very prime of life,
white, delicate, has come to the cellars which are excavated
in the mountain, near the city, in order to open and taste
the new wine. On his way thither he sees a beautiful girl,
a dark one, whom the Eastern sun has richly colored, and
who guards her vineyard thereabout. He invites her to
go with him, to enter and to taste. She is very ignorant.
This pretty young man with so sweet a voice appears to

her a girl, a small sister. She obeys, follows him, and I know not what he makes her drink, but she goes out of the cellar enraptured. She says: "Once more! kiss me with kisses of thy mouth! To touch thee* is better than the wine thou hast made me drink! Oh, what a fragrant odor comes out of thee! I will run after thee because of the fragrance of thy unguents!"

The admiration of the innocent girl is occasioned by the very white breast of the young man, "ivory variegated with sapphire."† She compares herself with him and blushes; she excuses herself for not being white: "If I am dusky the sun has scorched me. My mother's sons, who are angry with me, made me keeper of the vineyard. . . . And behold, mine own vineyard I have not kept."

I see her sad and pleading smile. No complaining. But I imagine that her little heart is uneasy. If her brothers are her masters, it is because she is an orphan. Will she not be ill-treated? I fear it. She also fears it. She looks as though she is feeling in her heart that now her lover is to protect her. She presses close to him and will not quit him. "Tell me, thou whom my soul loveth so much, where feedest thou?" In her simplicity she believes that he leads his flock himself. "Tell me where dost thou recline at noon?" And as he holds his peace, she, in order to render him jealous, adds, with a pretty threat: "That I may not mistake, and go as one straying toward the tents of thy companions." But she cannot get a word out of him about that. He flatters her, caresses her, and promises her beautiful necklaces.

---

* To touch *thy breast* [דדים didim]. "Thy breast is more pleasant than wine." Nobody has understood that. It is necessary to imagine that the scene is in the country of Adonis, where the boy and the young man are more womanish than woman. In soft and warm regions woman is the true male (for instance, at Lima, etc. See ULLOA). In such a warm climate, the beautiful and strong girl of the fields sees this fine creature of a superior rank as an object of voluptuousness.

† "I felt pity for Bajazet, I described to her *his charms.*—RACINE.

She is a poor girl. He is rich, and evidently he is afraid that she attaches herself to him. Is he of age to get married? Would he not rather forget? Nothing is known about all this.

"This is a very common story." Yes, but the sequel is by no means a common one. A charming and terrible power reveals itself in this girl. She is enraptured, transformed by love and passion. The seven spirits are in her, as they were in Sarah, in the book of *Tobit*, and in the Magdalen, who, by a single word, created a world. The power of this girl consists in her actual weakness, in following desperately her passion, in concealing nothing, in saying: "I am dying of love," in saying what no woman ever said. From that time the short poem, like the winged trumpet of demons, hurries on and carries everything before it.

The loving young man comes to her over and over again in spite of himself. It is in vain that he escapes and eludes. Nay, for a moment (the ingrate), he laughs at the expense of the poor girl, and boasts of his good fortune with his friends.* But he boasts in vain. He is subdued. The wonder is that in seven nights she is really grown up in an extraordinary manner. She is noble and haughty, she is a queen; he is struck with astonishment; he is almost afraid of her. She has become so imposing

---

* He really speaks of her with an outrageous thoughtlessness, and already with the insolence of satiety. "Eat and drink, my friends! I have harvested completely. I plucked my myrrh with my balsam. . . . I have drunk my wine with my milk. I have eaten so well my honey that I have eaten also the honeycomb." Ignorant! But everything remains yet; there is still what is more delicious. . . . Nevertheless it is in vain that he speaks, it is in vain that he plays the proud. He is attracted by an invisible power, which brings him back. He goes where she is, over and over again at night, and wishes that nobody may awake him. He is touched, he trembles, when, after some vain caresses, she on a sudden becomes gloomy. "Don't look at me so! thou art terrible as a bannered host. This made me fly from thee. . . . It seems to me that thou comest from the desert, from the dens of lions, the mountain of panthers!" "My sister! my friend! one of thy sweet glances, the smallest of thy hair is enough to wound my heart."

and beautiful. In one word, she is the mistress of his house.

Everybody knows this song by heart, and remembers the beautiful scene in which it is stated that she is lying sick, oh! so very sick and fainting away, while her friends attend her—in that stormy and terrible night in which she, quite ready and having used perfumes, is waiting for him, hears him, thinks that he touches her, starts. . . . O! misfortune! he went away! She goes round about the dark city, meets with soldiers, is beaten and wounded. But her lover is soft-hearted, he is moved, comes back, brings with him jewels, shoes, and beautiful robes. There he is dazzled with her beauty, he laughs no longer, and bends his knee before her.*

This moment carries everything before it. "Let us set off," she says; "let us go out into the country, and lodge in the villages! Oh! what a happiness to see on the morning the blossoms of the vineyard, and of the fruits! There will I give thee my love!"

The evening has come. They are in the retirement of the country. She lovingly says: "The mandrakes give a smell," rendering women prolific. This tender hint

---

* Lying still, languishing, having lost her garments on that cruel night, or not being able to endure them because of the overwhelming heat of the evening, she is waiting, she is in readiness for him. He is struck with compassion, tenderness, and admiration. He counts her charms, and describes his treasure as a miser does his gold. Although she is so confiding, and so submissive, she is none the less worthy, and she inspires every kind of respect. He puts on her naked foot elegant and rich shoes. She walks, and behold she is the daughter of a prince! "O my beautiful one! How noble thou art! Thou art the queen of love! Thy flowing locks are like the dark purple which consecrates the forehead of kings! Thy head upon thee is like Carmel! Thy nose like the tower which from a summit of Lebanon looks toward, and defies Damascus! Thy throat is the full bunch of our rich grapes of Judea! Thy stature resembles a palm tree. . . . Oh! yes, I will climb the palm, and I will gather my fruits, and thy breast will be my vintage." This word falls on her heart like a spark. She throws her arms round his neck and exclaims: "O! the sweet word! It is like the delicious wine which one tastes and relishes over and over again between his lips and teeth. . . . Let us go then." (The sequel is to be seen in my text.)

is not lost, as far as we can guess. On the morrow when
he saw her quite another creature, perhaps already a
mother, and transformed by an indescribable solemn grace,
he says proudly, with an Oriental emphasis : " Who is this
soft and voluptuous one, coming up out of the wilderness,
leaning upon her beloved ? "

All this is very natural, it is the manifestation of the
blood in the South; it is the very climate of love. I confess,
however, that one cannot read this song without feeling
his head heavy. I prefer the pure love of Rama, of Sita,
the scene in which the holy mountain, as spotless as its
snows, poured over them a shower of flowers ! . . . In
this song there is too much of perfumes, of sharp and strong
aromatics, and of drugged wines. I know not whether
the Shulamite has, like Esther, passed "six months in the
oil and six months in the myrrh ;" but the perfumed oil
which swims in the cup of love makes one hesitate to
drink. From verse to verse we meet with the word
" myrrh," the perfume for embalming. In this song there
is of it at least as much as would suffice to embalm three
dead persons. There is also the spikenard, the dark Indian
root of valerian, which has so powerful an effect on the
nerves. There is likewise the cinnamon and numberless
other aromatics of all kinds, from the insipid odor of the
lily to the bitter and burning aloes, which puts forth its
flower every ten years.*

But is not love in itself intoxicating enough without
having recourse to those odd drugs, so apt to confound
the senses and pervert voluptuousness itself ? They both
smell each other, and do not distinguish themselves from
their perfumes. " I will run after thee, because of the
fragrance of thy unguents," she says; and he languishingly

---

* In four pages, the word myrrh is employed seven times; there occurs
seventeen times the word frankincense and other perfumes, many of which
are not very agreeable, as aloes, etc. In short, in this song there is a complete assortment of perfumes.

12

enumerates one after another the exquisite odors, the emanations that come to him from his beloved one.

All this is unwholesome, morbid. One turns mad at all this, and behold! this ignorant girl, who yesterday was a virgin, has, all at once, some diabolical ideas in the presence of the young man asleep. Is that her fault, or that of her race ? Innocently impure, in her veins runs some of the blood of Lot and of Myrrha. " Oh that thou wert as a brother of mine!" etc. She looks as if she were groaning because she could not sin much more. Moreover, as a *last motive*, she many a time employs an astonishing request, boldly mentions the holiest remembrances. (There is the room in which my mother. . . . There is the tree under which thy mother. . . . etc.)* This is the greatest impudicity and it smells of the sepulchre.

These words, uttered on the morrow of the last night, are the *completion*. They are followed by the decisive formula which puts an end to everything, and which might be interpreted thus : " For ever and ever."

" Place me as a signet ring upon thy heart. Love is strong as death. . . ." That is to say : love is *irrevocable*. He takes her, embraces her and she becomes his wife. He wished he had all the world, to give it to her. At least, he gives her all he has, wishes to have nothing but with her.†

She is delicate, but she is very shrewd. She thinks of her family. " We have a small sister, and she has no

---

* This is even worse than Ham showing the drunkenness of Noah. There is in it something of the old genius of the Magians, and of the impiety of Babel. The principal passage has reference to the morning which follows the seven-night, in which he enjoyed with her, in his own house in the solitary country. His love is quite assuaged. But she turns like a panther : "that thou wert as a brother of mine who sucked the breasts of my mother," etc. " I would lead thee," etc. " Thou wouldst instruct me ; under this apple-tree," etc. " There thy mother was deflowered " (viii. 1, 2, 5).

† Nobody has understood this. But many have found out something better than the text. Mr. Dargaud says, in commenting upon this text with a charming delicacy, which this coarse text has not : " Man will give his life for love, and believe at the same time that he has given nothing."

breasts. What shall we do for our sister in the day that she shall be spoken for?" She remembers well the two sisters, Leah and Rachel, wives of Jacob. When the second wife is to come, as it happens in the East, she herself prefers to give her, to take the little girl who will be docile to her, to make the happiness of the small sister, toward whom she is rather a mother than a sister. Her husband smiles, understands, and under an Oriental, delicate form, promises all that she wishes.

To what a degree then she is the mistress, the spouse, and sure of her own situation! "I feel to be as strong as a wall, which would protect a city. My breasts are swollen, and come up, as a tower, when I have found my peace in thee."

Meanwhile some noise is heard. His young friends have discovered where he is, they come to search for him, they call on him. But she can dismiss him now. All is accomplished. He may go and amuse himself: "Go my young hart upon mountain of spices. . . . Flee and be like a gazelle!"

The explanation which I am giving is taken not in the clouds of the vague imagination, but in the text itself, followed closely, sentence after sentence, and brought back to its true local character : *Syrian voluptuousness* and now and then *Jewish rudeness.* It is to Solomon himself, to his vast experience of woman that I have asked the interpretation of the *Song of Songs.* Here I mean for Solomon the books attributed to him, *Proverbs, Ecclesiastes*, etc. These books, sometimes harsh toward woman, especially the Syrian woman, describe none the less with force her mystery which may be rendered in this sentence : Magic of the *seven demons.*

And this holds good not only in the woman of pleasure, the Delilahs, the Magdalens, and in those women of intrigue and audacity, the Herodiases, the Jezebels, but also in the very virgin, the young Sarah of Tobias.

Seven devils in this innocent one. All of them are in

love, jealous, domineering by turns. They all, from Astoreth to Belial, from Adonis to Balphegor, bustle about and fight for her.

The seven gods of Syria—fish, serpents, doves, or enchanted trees—"have been born by the god Desire." It is this god who endows the woman of the *Song of Songs.* When she comes out blushing from the cellar and says: "Once more!" a luminous circlet is round her head. Is it the Arabian flash of the lightning of Jericho, of the girl with dark eyes? Is it the expiring softness of the weeping women of Byblos? Is it the strange, voluptuous enigma, which the eastern Jewish woman shows yet, and which one would fain divine?

All this is in it, but there is still more, namely, that which will be temptation itself—the humble avowal of woman, which, while it degrades her, makes her so strong. The bewildered enchantress of Theocritus and of Virgil, who melts away as wax before the fire, and who, through a desperate effort, calls back an absent one loved too much, has more of nobleness in her and agitates one less than the sick woman in the *Song of Songs*, who faints away among her friends and plainly says: "I am dying of love."

She unites in herself the two characters of that woman, who, of all women, is to accomplish the *Fall :* She partakes of the Angel and of the Brute. She is a queen, and a slave, subdued and desirous to obey. It is through this that she reigns, that she is irresistible.

She has the force of binding up. Solomon, who had so much experienced it, says this in a marvellous way: "She is like the nets of the hunter. She is like the snares of the angler." * There are three things that are not to be satisfied, and a fourth one which never says (*enough*): "The world of the dead, the fire, and the barren womb; the earth which is not satisfied with water." †

---

* *Ecclesiastes* vii. 27.　　　† *Proverbs* xxx. 16.

That which in the *Song of Songs* produces astonishment is, that at the moment in which the woman there spoken of seems abandoned to nature, and in which the mild Syrian female appears to be led astray in a dream, the perfect lucidity of the Jewish woman subsists, and timidly reveals itself. Though young, how she knows already the course of the Oriental life, and the shortness of love!

This does perfectly agree with what the *Proverbs of Solomon* say elsewhere of the cautious, clever spirit of the mistress of the house, of her aptitude to business. She increases the fortune of her husband, makes and bids her servants make tissues, which she sells. With the labor of her hands she acquires, she buys a vineyard; she becomes a land-owner and dresses herself in purple. But she does all this without injuring the interest of her husband—a simple easy man, magistrate of the city, whom she directs in his judgments.

Solomon, who had seven hundred wives, and, as it is said, was terribly enslaved by them, did not forgive them. "I have found," says he, "that woman is more bitter than death." He advises the husband to do what undoubtedly he himself did, * namely: when she is unbearable and quarrelsome, to go to dwell in a corner of the house-top.†

---

* It seems that whilst the Wise man was studying the Universe, from the cedar to the hyssop, his queens, wanton Syrian women, or Arabians with burning blood, like the queen of Sheba, changed the gods, built temples—in a word, imposed on this great king the shame of the worship of Baal, which sets man at the foot of the woman. What is related about Aristotle in love, in a story of the Middle Ages (Aristotle, subdued by a fair woman, who rides on him and makes an ass of that wise man), is a mere trifle in comparison with the peculiar rite of Syria, which has been preserved among the Druses. Woman, any woman, and of whatever age, seated majestically in the temple, exacted from man, prostrated before her as an avowal of his nothingness, an obscene, humiliating homage to the power which people call feeble, and which, however, shares in the indefatigableness of nature.—"It is the very women of Syria who have introduced this rite."—SACY, *Asiatic Journal*, 1827, x., 341.

† *Proverbs* xxv. 24.

The Jew, according to the advice of the wise king, goes more frequently to dwell in a corner of his house-top, far, very far from his wife, and there he occupies himself in making accounts, or in counting the words and the letters of the *Bible.* In his uneasy, trembling life, he is afraid of fecundity and follows the advice of the *Ecclesiastes:* " I wish thee to have few children." In the book of *Wisdom*, in order to reassure his conscience altogether, it is said : "that even the eunuch may be blessed by God." ·

To all this must be added the weakening of the character, a fact general at that time. In the innumerable misfortunes, and unforeseen, continual revolutions, which happened after Alexander, the heart and strength fell off. No men were left in the world. Each people lost the vigor of manhood.

Vico has uttered this profound sentence : " In the ancient languages, he who says *vanquished* says *woman.*" Sesostris, in having his victories engraved, gives to the vanquished man the sex of the spouse. The captive, like the bride in the East, had a ring in his lip, on his nose, and in his ear, in order that he might be led. Entire populations were thus dragged away, herds of children and women. From hand to hand, from master to master, they handed, with their gods of Asia, their voluptuous and gloomy rites.

At this agitated time, there appeared a thing quite new and of infinite importance—*the Novel.*

The history of the Jews, even their grave history, has the mark of romantic groundwork—the arbitrary miracle, in which God takes delight to choose the commonest man, even the unworthy one, as a *Saviour*, liberator, avenger of the people. At the time of the captivity the banking business, or the intrigue of the court, the sudden fortunes, hurled the imaginations into the field of the unforeseen. It was at that time that appeared the very beautiful historical novels of Joseph, Ruth, Tobit, Esther,

Daniel, and many others.* They are always interwoven with two ideas : It is the *good exiled man*, who, through the explanation of dreams and his financial skill, becomes a minister or favorite—or the *woman loved of God*, who makes a great match, acquires glory, allures the enemy, and (astounding thing, contrary to the Mosaic ideas) is the *Saviour of the people.* According to Moses, woman was impure and dangerous, and had brought on the *Fall.* But it is just the unforeseen influence that the novel takes hold of.† God makes of woman a snare, makes use of her seduction, and through her operates the *Fall* of him whom he has condemned.

Love is a lottery, Grace is a lottery. That is the essence of the novel. It is the contrary of history, not only because it subordinates great collective interests to an individual destiny, but because it likes not the ways of that difficult preparation which produces what happens in history. It moreover takes delight in showing us the cast of dice which hazard sometimes brings in, and in flattering us with the idea that what is impossible becomes sometimes possible. By means of this hope, of pleasure, of interest, it gains over the reader, spoiled from the beginning, and who reads on with such an eagerness as to overlook the want of talent in the plot, and even the want of tact. The chimerical spirit finds itself interested in the adventure, and wishes that it may have a fair issue.

These Jewish novels, even the most admirable of them, Ruth, which is so finely planned and *unexceptionally* lascivious, are sensual.‡ They abound with feelings of devotion

---

* The anacronisms in them are monstrous, as, for instance, if one should place at the same epoch S. Louis and Louis XIV. See DE WETTE, etc.

† Sir, what is a novel? Madam, a novel is what you have at this moment in your mind. For, as you care neither for your country, nor for science, nor even for religion, you brood over what Sterne calls a *hobby-horse*, and what I call a pretty little *doll.* Our novels are dull and insipid. Why? Because we have not great poetry.

‡ It is a skilful imitation of ancient times. The language does not show

and submission, and they breathe the deepest feeling of
fear, fear of God and fear of the king, but they do not disguise at all the cunning by which woman is dexterously
pushed forward, and the best made of her.   Judith frankly
says that the high priest sent her to the tent of Holo-
fernes.*   In the novel of *Esther* it is stated by what
means the shrewd Mordocai engratiated himself with
the eunuchs, in order to introduce his niece and secure for
her the preference.

Esther, a beautiful novel, is profoundly historical, and
of immense instruction.   It is not only at Susa and Babylon that captivity leads the beautiful and impressive girl.
She will enter everywhere.   Esther, through a thousand
adventures of slavery, travels also in the West, and with
her, her thousand sisters.   If Asiatic men sought out and
stole Grecian women, those splendid girls of the Peloponnesus, with deep bosom, who had powerful voices,
were good singers, and amused them—the Western men,
on the contrary, wished to have Syrian women, the Greco-
Phœnician of Cyprus,† of Ionia, of the Cyclades, of those
dove-nests formerly established by Astarté.   These had
not run on the Taygetus, danced, wrestled, and taken those
faultless forms, which the art has made eternal.   They, in
requital of that, appeared to have more of womanish
nature, and they were soft and loving from their birth.
Easily trained to all lascivious arts, they made pleasure a
religion and sexual rites a duty.   The intelligent slave-
merchant—an Ephesian or a Cappadocian—and the Roman Knights, who at a later day conducted this commerce, gave the preference to those girls of the East who
had voluptuous blood.   They bought Jewish women who

anything very ancient (DE WETTE). It must have been written against Esdras,
who was driving away foreign women.

* Saint Jerome is not scrupulous at all.   He adroitly cuts off this verse.

† See in Lamartine's *Voyage* the marvellous description of Miss Mala-
gamba, a Grecian of Cyprus, with Syrian blood in her.   Farther off, see in
the same author the *female* of Jericho, with charming, eager, and terrible eyes.

were modest and restrained; in reality, however, they were, if we must believe the prophet Ezekiel, of such a prodigious ardor as to astonish Syria. Possessed of the gloomy spirit which sleeps beneath the Dead Sea, they besought to be enjoyed.*

Those dreamers carried with them their ceremonies of impudicity, their purifications, their fears and remorses, their desires, and fetiches. Slavery, a powerful vehicle to scatter abroad woman and gods, led everywhere the deities of Syria. And it was because they were slaves that they became the rulers of the world.

The Syrian woman, pursuing her destiny from one seraglio to another, and from one paramour to another (the seven devils helping her) ascended often very high. He who had had her when she was a little one, had despised and sold her over again, saw her one day seated at the side of a tetrarch, or of a Roman prince, under a name which disguised her.† Bearing a Roman name, and a Jewish soul, and smacking always of Esther, she acted through a morbid charm—the voluptuous and funeral odors of Adonises, the perfume of a god in the grave—and that magic of grief which made the Roman say: "Oh! how much I like thee in thy tears." ‡

Many and many women, called by Greek names, came from the Phœnician temples scattered in the islands, and may have been Orientals. Does not the same origin pertain to the Delias, the Lesbias of Catullus, Tibullus, and Propertius? Those women were from the Cyclades, and their lovers describe them as passionately fond of them, and very religious.

They were brought up carefully by avaricious owners, who derived profit by them, and they were far more accomplished and learned than the fashionable ladies of our own time. They were not at the disposal of every passer-by. They were hired for a prescribed time. They followed

---

* *Ezekiel* xvi. 33. † Drusilla, Procla, and others.
‡ Martial.

12*

obediently such a great personage, or such temporary
owner, occasionally in hard journeys, and even in the wars
among the barbarians, as the Lycoris of Virgil. We perceive that this beautiful one, who inspired Gallus with so
much love and so much despair, had a refined mind,
capable of feeling the tender farewell of the muse.*

"When I set off, Delia consulted all the gods."† These
were surely the gods of Chaldea, Egypt, and Syria, the
gods of the East. The women I speak of were very superstitious. The weariness of their situation, the dislike of
themselves made them wish and search for purifications.
They willingly fled from their hard profession to obtain a
liberty in I know not what chapel. The dearest liberty
to them was to shed tears.

Holy chapel! At the smoky glimmering of old oils,
with which the Chaldean and the Jew nourished their
lamps, Delia, under the blackened vault, was not alone in
praying. The noble and haughty matron, disguised, and
in plain head-dress, is near to the humble girl. The hired
beauty, and the great, powerful dame (who knows who
she is ? Perhaps Cæsar's wife) joined together will change
the world.

At Rome, customs mocked at laws. By law the woman
there was poor ; but in reality she was very rich, had influence, and ruled everything. Tullia, Volumnia, Cornelia,
Agrippina show to us enough to make us believe that

---

* "A few things to my Gallus, but *which Lycoris herself may read!*"—
How much this tenth eclogue is pure and a thousand times lovelier (if we must
say the truth) than the *Song of Songs!* Lycoris would surely not have needed
to use the impure stimulus, the sharp *cantharis* of Lot and Myrrh. What I
say of Lycoris holds good also of the Delia of Propertius, and of Tibullus.
In those charming little poems of melancholy love, one forgets altogether that
they are addressed to unfortunate women who could not dispose of themselves.
Some admirable sentences call to mind the sweetest household affections.
"What happiness ! She is everything ! At home I am nothing !"—And
again : "To embrace her tenderly ! To listen, in her company, to the wild
winds roaring at night !" An humble wish, but so touching and so full of
tenderness and innocence.

† PROPERTIUS.

they were queens as well as the Marozias, the Vannozzas of the Middle Ages.

Twice they undermined Rome. While Rome was striking hard on Carthage, and was thrusting back the East, they were undoing its victory, and were by night introducing in the asleep city the Eastern orgies (*Bacchus Sabazius*), and placing in it the horse of Troy.

Now let us see the second blow. The orgies had been exhausted. But the gods of death, all the gods of Egypt, arrived. The funeral Egypt, enemy to the sea, embarked for Rome, carrying with Isis, its mixed, new god—Serapis with the sacred canopus. This Osiris from below—this Pluto—he alone swallowed and buried thirty gods ! He healed, killed, and buried. Anubis, his jackal, the barking corpse-eater, came with him : the *bambino* Horus in his mother's arms, and the wan Harpocrates, who followed with a halting step, were with him. The strange procession came down from the ship with torches, flames, and lamps. Amusing and dreary spectacle ! All this happened under Sylla. He was on the point of putting down all these gods of death in his tablets of proscription. But those gods were stronger than he. The women were not afraid, and protected them. Cæsar, as a friend of Isis-Cleopatra, kept them up, and Antony did the same. They both did so for their own misfortune. Tiberius proscribed them, but in vain. If Rome adopted all the gods, why not likewise take in Death himself, the god whose love and worship increases and flourishes more and more ?

Egypt is still too living. Humanity will go further into the gloomy kingdom than even Egypt itself. We shall find there dead men and ghosts even more dead than those we have just considered.

CHAPTER VII.

THE STRUGGLE BETWEEN WOMAN AND THE STOIC : LAW AND GRACE.

THE haughty genius of Rome seemed to have been ordained to continue the Greek work of protecting the world
from being swallowed up by the gods of Asia, who came—
cruel or weeping—to bury the human soul. Whether
Moloch assailed it with his iron horns, or Adonis interred it
in the myrrh of the eternal wedding, the East was the grave.

Immense and enormous struggle. In the history of the
world there is nothing like the Punic wars. It is not there
an Alexander who rushes through an overturned empire.
The Punic wars are not the obscure wars of Cæsar in wild
forests, where he kills a hundred nations. Here everything is done in broad daylight. Hannibal and his army
were indeed quite another thing than all this. It was a
great day that on which the *Unnamed* God of Carthage,
with the terrible machine of an army *without a name*, and
with a strong genius of war, the strongest that ever was,
rushed on Italy ; great was the day on which the East and
Africa came into Italy through the Alps. It was then
that the world knew that which Italy—the fruitful mother
—had in her bosom. Italy did what Greece could never
do, by raising two millions of soldiers—a rural mass,
deeply thick. An honest, docile mass, indomitably resigned and indefatigable to die. Rome, in those days,
taught the whole world how to die. And in the long run,
it was the monster that died. Infinite thanks are due to
thee, great Italy ! all this will last for ever.

> Salve, magna parens frugum, Saturnia tellus !
> Magna virûm ! *

---

* VIRGIL, Geor. II., 173–74.
> Hail, sweet Saturnian soil ! of fruitful grain
> Great Parent, greater of illustrious men.
>   DRYDEN : *Georgics ii.,* 241–42.

The old Italian *genius* possessed a great science which is worth many philosophies, the science of the hearth and the tombs. The married household gods, guardians of the family; the great gods *Consentes*, married two by two—who, happier than men, are born and die on the same day—are an agreeable and venerable spectacle among the ancient Italians. The Etruscan and Italian tombs do not overwhelm us as the cemeteries of Egypt. They exalt our minds; they console. They speak from man to man; they teach us the course of time, the great ages of the world, the regular return of things.* Deep sense of history possessed only by this people, and which vivifies death and makes graves flourish. *In the urn was a perpetual spring.*

The respect of boundaries, of property, of the ground sacred by labor or by tombs, was admirably preparing this people to become, under the inspiration of Greece, the universal teacher of municipal laws. No other people was so strongly attached to the rights of the past, even to the imaginary ones. The infinite patience of the plebeian who fought so many centuries for the commonwealth, which however was so stern as always to thrust him back, cannot be accounted for but by the infinite meekness of the Italian husbandman. No mutiny but that on the Aventine hill—a peaceful *secession.* The result of it was a great one. Three things proceeded from it: the Roman *fasces*, by which Carthage was crushed; the conquest of the world, and the organization of the most magnificent empire which the sun has ever beheld; finally an immense work, unalterable in many parts, *the colossal body of the Civil Law.*

I know what some say: "The Romans made war"— as well as other nations. "Rome had slaves"—as well as other nations. "The Roman proconsuls abused their power"—as it always happens. Was Verres worse than

---

* See my *Roman History* and especially *Vico.*

Hastings, whom the English acquitted? Was he worse
than the first Spanish governors, who depopulated America? Or was he worse than the Christians, who have
made the year 1864 remarkable by the death of three
peoples? *

Did Rome make the decline? No, she inherited it.   It
was an ended world which fell in her hands.   Men too
frequently forget the depopulation, the chaos, the military revels, which humanity had undergone since Alexander the Great.   The orgy centered and expired at
Rome; but it must by no means be called Roman,
because, when it was almost a shadow, even in the
midst of Rome, it was the debauchery of Asia, of the
East.

Rome admitted all the gods, maintained all the laws of
the vanquished, reserving for herself the right of appeal.
She rendered homage to their genius.   There is nothing
which so much honors those sovereign magistrates as the
boundless deference manifested by them towards the Grecian genius, acknowledging in it the authority of light,
and confessing that they were indebted to it for everything.

"You are going to Athens," Cicero writes to Atticus.
"Revere the gods!"

The Greeks themselves have never spoken of Greece as
Lucretius did in several lines, so solemn, so touching,
and in such a deep strain.   Virgil, the sacred genius
of Italy, when he speaks of Greece, humbly descends
from his tripod, lays down the laurels from his head,
makes himself a disciple, an *offspring* of Hesiod, and
follows him.   Beautiful, amiable, touching tenderness!
He did not know how much the master was inferior
to him.

Rome herself was thrice on her knees before Greece, on
account of language, philosophy, and the inspiration of
the law itself.

* Poland, Denmark, and Circassia.

Every Roman had a Grecian preceptor, and learned the
language of Homer thoroughly, even to the neglect of his
own. They spoke Greek at Rome, even on those lively
occasions in which the heart itself was prompted to speak,
in the paroxysm of love,* under the stroke of death.
When Cæsar was struck, he *cried out in Greek* (*hellen-
isti*).†

The Romans asked of the Greeks the rule of life. In all
the schools of Rome the Grecian philosophy sat as a queen.
And I am not speaking about theoretical ideas, and speculation. I speak of action, of customs, of deportment.
The Greek philosopher, in every Roman household, was
the adviser, of whom they asked strength and light in the
perplexed moments of life. The heroes of resistance, the
Thraseas, had *their philosopher* to attend them at their
death. The emperors themselves had their Greek attend·
ant, who restrained and soothed them. Augustus would
have been but Octavius, except for his Greek adviser.

In this noble antiquity there is nothing greater and
nobler than the simplicity of Rome, who, although all-
powerful and mistress of the world, asks help of Greece,
of that ruined old Greece, already almost a desert, of
Athens, which was comparatively a solitude. Rome,
overwhelmed by her own grandeur, addressed herself to
the poverty and moderation of Greece. " The Greeks
were gifted by the muse with genius, speech, *and a soul
above desire.*†

But how did Greece herself still live ? After the terrible conflict with the armies of Alexander, Greece was
broken down, crushed, and desolated. What did remain to poor Greece, when the Romans themselves carried away her gods, perhaps a million of statues ; when
every altar was empty, and the heroes that decorated
her squares, her streets, and her porticos were captives in
Italy ?

---

* JUVENAL.   † PLUTARCH.   ‡ HORACE.

It is in this that we must admire the might of the Hellenic gods. In them was found the basis on which Greece upheld Rome and humanity. Greece leaned upon Hercules.

There was at Athens a portico, called the Cynosarges, sacred to him. It was there that, after the death of Socrates, Antisthenes fixed himself. He had been a disciple of Socrates, and alone pursued the revenge of his master and punished his accusers. In the decline which followed the Thirty Tyrants, he undertook the valiant enterprise of placing before the eyes of the people the ideal of liberty. Hercules was eminently free, for, being able to have everything, he would have nothing. With the skin of a lion, and a club of olive-tree, he was king even more than Eurystheus himself. He was the model of Antisthenes and of Diogenes, his disciple. Diogenes was by no means the fool some writers have represented him. He did what Solon had done before him—like the Hebrew prophets. During a century he preached by his deeds, acting the comedy of Hercules. His exaggeration was the result of a purpose: " The teachers of a choir," he used to say, " force the tune that they may bring up to it their pupils." The *key*, the *tension*, in the general slackness, is the philosophy of Hercules.* Thus the bow and the lyre had been strained in the hand of Apollo. There is a monument from which it is seen that Hercules while still young, in his enthusiasm for the beautiful and the sublime, takes the lyre and vies with Apollo himself. This *tension* is but harmony and mildness. Diogenes gave the solemn example of it. Although he was a slave, when charged by his master to bring up a child, he made of him an admirable man, through the most gentle education.

The great myth of the *Twelve Labors of Hercules*

---

* In all this I follow the Greek texts so well interpreted by RAVAISSON (*Aristotle,* 11), VACHEROT (*Introduction to the Philosophy of Alexandria,* 1), and DENIS (*History of Ideas,* 1).

was the idea of the new philosophy, *the glorification of labor*.

"The good god is Nature. Nature is reason, which *toils and fashions* the world."

" Labor is the sovereign good."

The workingman, *the slave, is rehabilitated.* Hercules is a slave to Eurystheus. Diogenes, sold by hazard, wishes to show that even in the midst of slavery, one may keep himself free. He declined to be ransomed. Some men who had been born slaves, as Menippes, Monimus, etc., were admitted at the Stoa, or Porch of Hercules, and they did the honor of it.

Was all this a play ? One might have thought so. But through terrible circumstances, through the dreadful blows of fate, the barbarous military orgies, and the incarnation of the Tyrant, the Stoic was under the necessity of evincing that he was THE STRONG. The *Passion* of Callisthenes, crucified by the cruel madman at whose foot was the universe, for having stood up for honor and reason, this solemn event placed the school on the battle-field in the presence of death and torments.

From the cross of Callisthenes was heard the sentence of *the Prometheus*, " O Justice, O my mother!"—and the last sentence of Socrates (in the *Eutiphron*) : " There is nothing holy but the Just." All this made up the doctrines of the Porch. Zeno and Chrysippus taught that *Justice is holiness.* "*Themis* is not enthroned beside Jupiter, as it is said. She is Jupiter himself, god of gods and sovereign good."

" Good creates happiness. The wise man alone is happy. The just is happy in death, in grief, on the rack." Are these vain sentences ? No. Action corresponded with them. The inward soul found a sublime *alibi*. A Stoic, when he was crushed and pounded, said to the tyrant who put him in the mortar : " Beat, crush, and pound. . . . You cannot reach my soul."

The great part of resistance played by the Stoics at the

beginning of the Empire, presents them under a too peculiar aspect. What Horace calls *the ferocious spirit of Cato* obscures for us his *stoicism*, makes us believe it to be narrower than it is, and partly conceals its grandeur. It is generally unknown that stoicism, besides its fundamental principle of *Justice*, from which originates Duty, admits also another principle, namely, *Love*, which is implied in true Justice. It is, however, to be observed that this is not a tardy mitigation of the time of Cicero, or Marcus Aurelius. Five hundred years before Marcus Aurelius, at the time of Alexander the Great, Zeno, who was the first Stoic, in his explanation of the universal commonwealth of the world, had said already : " Love is the god that saves the city."* He is speaking of that love which is also called mutual friendship and human brotherhood. At the very first appeared then, distinctly, this sacred Trinity : *The liberty* of the soul,—the *equal* liberty (and which is extended even to the slave)—*Love* (of all for all), the great fraternal unity.

It is easy, it would seem, that a happy man shold *love* and fraternize. But it is a beautiful, a great thing, to see a wretched man—in the midst of hard, monotonous, barren labors, which dry up the soul—still love and fraternize. Zeno had the good fortune of finding such a miracle in his disciple Cleonthes, who at night toiled, drawing water out of wells to irrigate gardens, and in the daytime meditated and philosophized. Zeno, delighted with him, called him the *second Hercules*. Cleonthes was gifted with the very soul, tender and good, of the hero. He laid down the great unalterable formula : " Love begins with the mother and the father. From the family it extends to the village, to the commonwealth, to the people, and it becomes the holy love of the world. From that time man,

---

* DENIS (*History of Ideas*) points out, with just reason, the error (voluntary ?) of those who try to make people believe that these great ideas of the primitive Stoicism did not appear but in the Christian era.

on the account only of being a man. is no longer a stranger to another man." 300 B.C.

They did not stop here, by stating the principle only ; they carried its spirit into many practical questions which concern the province of Jurisprudence. From Paulus Emilius to Labeon, a Stoic lawyer, the Greeks, especially those of the Porch, prepared at the same time men and ideas. The right of equity softens and modifies the antique barbarity. That was the concern of the Prætor. But who is the Prætor ? The pupil of a Grecian philosopher, most frequently of a Stoic.*

What stopped the work of the Greek philosophers, and the Greek Wisdom ? What made barren the experience of the Roman statesman and jurist ? In a word, what prevented the restoration of the Empire ? Assuredly, it was the vices of the supreme power, but especially the weariness, the incredible weariness of the world at this epoch. The end of the *Thirty years War*, the exhaustion of Europe after Wallenstein and Tilly, the long devastations of the hireling soldiers of that time, give but a feeble idea of the conditions of the ancient peoples after the *three hundred years*, during which the successors of Alexander, Phyrrus, Agathocles, and the *hireling soldiers* of Carthage spread death and ruin everywhere. Above all, add to all this Marius and Sylla, the ferocious struggle of Italy herself, divided among soldiers—divided without profit ; for any improvement ceased. The wilderness began then, even at the gates of Rome. " Even in the ancient cities an inhabitant rarely is to be seen going here and there." †

The Fathers of the Church deceive us strangely, wishing to make us believe that the times of the heathen orgy continued through the Empire. It was concentrated in Rome with the excess of vices and that of riches. Any-

---

* See MEISTER, ORTLOFF, and especially LAFERRIÈRE, 1860.

† " Rarus et antiquis habitator in urbibus errat." (LUCAN.)

where else everything was dismal and poor.   Greece was
deserted, and the East had grown old.   Except Alexandria and Antioch, new cities of some activity, there was
everywhere a great silence, a great calmness, or rather a
torpor, somnolency, paralysis.

There was another cause of weariness, which the Fathers conceal from us.   During three or four centuries several different gods had appeared, and passed away, suc-
ceeding each other like shadows.   The beautiful Grecian
gods, Apollo and Minerva (about 400–300 before Christ)
had made room for Bacchus, who swallowed up them all,
even Jupiter himself.   Bacchus, transformed into an Eastern God as Adonis-Sabazius, lost all his character.   His
mysteries were mixed and incorporated with those of
Phrygia and Egypt, Atys, Isis, etc.   Worthless displays !
Mithras, the inefficacious reviver, marched behind them.

There were three epochs of gods after the effete Jupiter.   The Fathers revive all those gods to make us believe
that the new god, who vanquished them, had to fight hand
to hand the fury of the antique orgies—the true Bacchus,
with the horns of a bull, and the roaring lions of Cybelès.
But all those gods had been buried.   Jupiter and Bacchus
had long been cold statues * in the Pantheon at Rome, and
had no longer any power ; and they, unconcerned, could
contemplate at leisure the struggle between Mithras and
Jesus.

There was a power, which undermined that worn out
world.   What power ?   Strange as it may appear, it was
the progress of humanity and equity—the vast and generous equity of Right—that gave a hold to the deadly
enemies of reason, to the gloomy destroyers of Right, and
the Empire.

Every nation step by step came to Rome.   Rome was
the common country.   When Italy had taken down the
barrier, when *the good tyrant Cæsar*, and *the good tyrant*

---

* This is admirably stated in QUINET'S works.

Marc Antony, both lovers of Cleopatra, opened the door to the East, all mankind repaired thither and presented themselves. They were all admitted little by little. For, after all, they were men. The indulgence of the new Bacchus (Cæsar) who, in imitation of his god,* *went about without belt*, agrees on this point entirely with his enemy —the Stoic—and with the unbounded humanity of the doctrines of the Porch. Rome looked upon, and admired her new sons. She saw black Romans, from Libya ; yellow Romans from Syria, and green-eyed Romans from the marshes of Friesland. The most incoherent mixtures were made of men half-made up, of barbarians (bears or seals ?) with the corpses and skeletons of the impure East, the residuum of empires, the tomb of tombs and *caput mortum*. And it happened, as in any mixture, that the wholesome sap was absorbed, and vitiated by the old rottenness.

Alas ! rottenness and death were in the slave ; the vices of the free and his own. Raised up by the Stoic, the Roman Jurist and Law, replaced near the free, can the slave remove from himself the traces of his long misery ? Mark, that he is not the innocent laborer, the negro of America. The ancient slave was the match of his master in culture, malice, and perversity. Almost always it was the humble, graceful son of the East who came like a child-woman, and by means of love and intrigue made his Asiatic gods circulate in every palace of Rome.

The agreeable Tyro is to Cicero more than a slave. He is his friend, the most obsequious of his friends, and yet at the same time the most powerful one, and the master of his master. Does any one likewise believe that Lycoris, the poetical, the Lycoris of Virgil, could really be a slave ? Those beautiful ones, as soon as they were getting old, redeemed themselves and remained rich. In their return

---

* VIRGIL : " Daphnis et Armenias curru subjungere tigres," etc. (Fierce tigers Daphnis taught the yoke to bear.—DRYDEN, *Past.* V., 43.) The ancient commentators apply this passage to Julius Cæsar.

to Asia or Greece, they, honorable ladies then, and free
to love whom and what they liked best, loved dreams,
fables, the gods of the East.

Scarcely different is the spirit of the true Roman Lady,
the free Roman woman, the independent wife of a shadow
of a husband, or the widow, a reigning, absolute mother of
a child.   If she is not a guardian, she does really perform
what belongs to guardianship, having the custody of her
son, and administering his property.   Horace and Seneca
inform us about that.   Nor is this all.   Precocius excesses, which are more deadly to men than women, concentrated at Rome, as well as in Greece, the family
property in the hands of the woman.   Both, the Law,
generous and humane, and Nature, more and more powerful, contributed to bring about this result.   The heart
speaks, and always to the advantage of the daughter.   If
the charming formula of the Northern laws* had not yet
been written in the Roman statutes, the spirit lived through
them all.   " My sweet child, a severe right withheld from
thee my property.   But I, dear child, I make thee equal
to thy brothers," etc.

The France of the Revolution felt precisely this same
outburst of the heart, when, on a sudden and without preparation, humanizing the civil law, she made of the French
woman the richest woman in the world.   The result was
the same.   By giving her property without giving her
education, by making her rich without enlightening her,
without placing her on a level with the culture of the age
she lived in, the Law put in her hands the weapon for
destroying the Law.   The obstinate return of errors
and misfortunes has never been more striking.   To-day
as at that time, then as to-day, the Revolution only succeeded, to end by stifling itself.   Paula and Metella, provided with immense fortune, either as a dowry or heritage,
had built for Serapis, for Mithras, for Jesus, chapels

---

* MARCULF.

and temples, like those which in our own time crowd our cities—temples and chapels which were then as they are now the strongholds and citadels of counter-revolution.

Strange sight! To whom does the Law entrust these enormous forces? To the feeble person, to the sickly hand, to the fanciful and troubled heart, which is so easily preyed upon by imposition of all kinds. Who will save women from themselves? Paula, in her vast abode, was afraid. Those rich enfranchised women, the Chloes and Phœbes of Saint Paul, Mary of Magdala, who has become so famous, trembled, haunted as they were by unknown Spirits. On the morrow of the ancient orgies, when everything had grown pale, and decayed, they hastened to the gloomy Chaldean (astrologer, or *savant*) who had succeeded the magians, and who consulted the sky and the stars to foretell destinies. Even the meagre and dirty Jew, who, in *the field of Mars*, lay down in a *basquet*, was consulted by the uneasy woman. Great changes were at hand; she was sure of that, she felt that; she had them in herself, for they were struggling in her bosom. What were they? Terrible things, scarcely uttered, and only hinted at. . . . . First of all, the end of the world, the universal death, a supreme catastrophe, which, carrying away at once our lives and our stains—an immense loathing—would free us from ourselves.

She however had grown pale. . . . . She would die and she would not. She was ready to ask for favor. . . . The man had got hold of her now. He made her hope (buy?) a great secret. "The world, in dying, does not die. An epoch passes away and another comes. Egypt and Etruria had no other mystery at the bottom of their tombs. The *revolutions* of things, the chorus of *the hours of the world*, in their eternal round, in each thousand years, bring back the sunset and the dawn. A living dawn is at hand, and it will begin again everything. The dawn is already beginning to light up the sky, the mystery is on the point of being accomplished, and the cradle is ready. . . . Let us wait for the Divine Child. . . . ."

"Begin, O little boy,
To single out thy mother with a smile !"*

Expiring Italy raised herself in her poet Virgil to make that vow, and tried to hope. Her poet, with long hair like that of a woman, her poet, an unhappy Sibyl, whose sighs were stifled, could on this occasion speak, and prophesy. His masters, the cruel statesmen, hoped that his sacred voice was just uniting the world on the cradle of a son of Augustus.

The *revolution* of ages, the universal expectation, had to bring in a child, a little god-saviour. The *lost*, or Proserpina, the *child* Bacchus exposed on the sea, the gentle Adonaï, wounded and risen,—these three young *deities* had enchanted the world. Atys had enraptured it by the touching show in which the recovered child gushed forth from a tree full of sighs. All this was very ingenious and charming, but at the same time it was worn out. In the halls of the emperors, it had not yet been determined whether the Messiahs were to be made anew, or to be proscribed. The mother of Augustus failed in the attempt, and every body laughed at her serpent, a servile imitation of the incarnation of Alexander. Mæcenas judged it better not to try this expedient any longer, nor endure those contrivances, but to proscribe the Saviours, as dangerous to the Empire. Though endowed with so much mind, he was however not aware that any royalty is a Messiahnism. That individual, whose vast soul contains and exceeds the soul of a people, is necessarily an *Avatar*, an incarnation.

The last popular form had been Atys, a true image of the exhaustion of the world. After the fruitful and Priapic orgies, the powerless *furor* burst forth in this mutilated Atys, a girl-boy, and weak in both sexes. No

---

* " Incipe, parve puer, risu cognoscere matrem."—VIRGIL.

more robust men. Atys mourning over himself, mourns over humanity itself.* Nature appeared to have been herself contaminated with the sterility of man. The wan sun did not warm any longer. The tree dried up and the grass turned yellow.

But though people cannot create any longer, they can remember, they can speak, and repeat words. What remains of life, is especially the voice, the echo. The god-word outlives the gods. Nothing was left of the Commonwealth. But the *School* subsisted. The new Saviour was the *teacher.* A gentle teacher with a low voice, who put the damper to render fainter the high tunes of the past, who introduced no change, and excited to no effort in order to know something new. The ancient teachers, Apollo and Orpheus, sang. Pythagoras taught by silence. Silence is too eloquent. There is no sweet- ness like that of those vague words muttered about night- fall to the woman, or to the child that wishes to sleep, and cannot. One cannot really tell whether the voice, which is uttered at that time, proceeds from without or from within. Is it a self out of one's self, the soul beloved, or own-self? The charm is too great to wish to dispel it. We hold fast to it ; we lazily fear to awake and to be too lucid, to resume the life of effort and of reason. " Above all, no more reason ! Let conscience be asleep ! Complete passivity ! Let the soul be nothing but an instrument !" This is just what was inculcated by Philo, the contemporary of Jesus, and, as he has already been called, his brother as to his doctrine. He expressed very well the lazy somnolency of this passive epoch, when the world lay down under the fatality of the Eternal Empire.

As to the pedantic discussions added to it by the Rabbis on the coming Messiah, who was to put an end to all things ; as to their rigmarole about the *Logos, Wisdom,* " the Son of man coming on the clouds,"† they had no

---

* CATULLUS.   † DANIEL.

13

influence whatever on the spirits.   The crowd held more tenaciously to the tradition of Syria, the incarnation of the Dove, and to the Jewish tradition of the Holy Ghost descending into a barren mother, causing her to bring forth a great Nazarene.

These Biblical miracles, read over again and again on the festival days, made woman very pensive, when she mused on them in the evening.   From the East, the golden star was seeing her, was following her, and darting its twinkling rays.   The Saviours of Asia were the *Sons of the star.*   Who has not sometimes seen it falling, and leaving here below a luminous trail, as a flow of heavenly life ? . . .   Its warm radiance makes the cheeks burn. . . . And even less than all this is necessary ; the Spirit, of which Elijah speaks, the softest *breath of air* is enough : " At first it was a storm, and it was not He.   Then a strong wind came on, but it was not He.   At last passed close by a tepid, soft wind. . . . It was He."

CHAPTER VIII.

TRIUMPH OF WOMAN.

IT is very logical that Christianity, conceived and born by the Virgin Mary, has produced, as its latest outcome, the Immaculate Conception. Mary contains it and includes it; the mother of Mary and their female ancestors also contain and include it. A long feminine incubation, a continual bringing forth, produced this creation, which, as it has been truly said, owes nothing to man, having been brought about solely by woman.

Up to the year 369, *woman was a priest* in the Greek, or Eastern Church, which is the mother church. There has never been a more legitimate priesthood. She is the true Christian priest. Who can, better than she does, explain, make feel, and worship that which she herself has made ? It was in those first centuries, and through this charm, that the ancient idolatry was overthrown. No marble divinity could stand up when the living grace officiated at the altar.

Mary was put aside, but only in order to return more powerful. She reigns at last. The Christians have made to her the avowal that she is the whole of Christianity. Saint Dominic declares that he has seen heaven, nay, more than heaven, in her bosom. He saw in it the three worlds, purgatory, hell, and paradise.

The schoolmen were simply ridiculous, when they, wishing to be delirious in a wise manner, spoiled the *foolishness of the cross*—the feminine element, grace--by an impossible alloy of manly reason and justice.

How is it that they did not perceive that at every step they made out of the path of grace in order to make a masculine person of Jesus, they strayed out of the field of religion, and were but dialecticians and jurists? Saint Thomas, who wore out his life in this impossible enterprise (a triangle without any angle), repented of his fault on his death-bed, gave himself up to grace, and in his last moments he wished the *song of songs* only to be read to him.

The lonely woman saw rising from her bosom her genius, her angel, and her young soul, a speaking soul which teaches in being born, and which tells to its mother all that she was already acquainted with. This soul, which was her son, was also her soft reflection, undistinguished from herself, but by being loved the more. When he was twelve years old, and already grown handsomer, he was quite her mother, and yet her master, her lesson, her little doctor. She placed him before herself and knelt down at his feet.

Ah! behold him grown up, a beautiful and stately adolescent, with long hair which seems that of his mother, and with a sad and serious look. Is he her son? Does she know it yet? She likes much better that he be anything else,—a charming and austere doctor, a little feared, but so gentle! Oh! what voluptuousness it is to be taught, to obey, and in all this to be only timid, but not afraid! This is more, or this is less than love! The lover in the *song of songs* seems to know that, when she utters the subtle and deep sentence: "Thou shalt teach me."

This is like the effect of a fair moon, when with its rays is blended a weak reflection of the setting sun. Many persons, from the very first, saw in all this an illusion, as though all this were nothing more than the soul of Mary contemplating itself, speaking to itself, teaching and loving itself, and creating itself, outside itself in order to be able to love itself. All this gave to tender-hearted people the advantage of allowing them to believe that the son of Mary had not suffered, and that his Passion had been an illusion likewise. The *Docetæ* believed so, thinking that

God, having compassion, had not permitted his son to be tortured, but had given up to the fierceness of death only a shadow. This question is a very curious one, but nothing can elucidate it, and it will always be discussed and uncertain for ever.

If somebody insists upon, and wishes, as my friend Ernest Renan, to state that Jesus lived and suffered, the essential point to sustain this assertion, and to consolidate what STRAUSS has vaporized, is to replace him on his mother, to give him again her warm blood, and her tepid milk, and to look at him in the arms of the dreaming woman of Judea. One is astonished in seeing that the skilful galvanizer, while with a caressing and fine hand he is making up the child again, denies him his mother. But without Mary,* no Jesus.

The first Fathers of the Church, Origen, Epiphanius, Gregory of Nyssa, have by no means refused the *Gospel of Mary* written by James, the son of Joseph.† They call it *the first of all gospels*, and it is indeed the natural introduction to them all. Why does the Roman Catholic, or Western Church, so characteristically in her faith and preserving record of so many miracles, why does she put this small book among the apocryphal ? The ancient churches of the East accepted it without any objection, and had it translated into the Syriac, Arabian, and other languages. Our wise men of the sixteenth century have distinctly

---

* RENAN owes much to her. And his charming book, which perhaps will give to what is dying the respite asked by HEZEKIAH, does discuss in vain, because his book believes and makes others believe. It is useless for RENAN to say that he doubts; the reader is touched. Whence does such a charm come ? From RENAN's genius ? . . . . From the power of the recollections of infancy and of the household ? Yes, from all this, and also from something else. He has something more than his books in his stirred up journey. People see him now, and the future generations will always see him, between life and death, between the angel and the holy. . . . The wilderness decks itself with flowers it never had before, the fig-tree becomes green again, the water murmurs, and the birds of the parable warble.

† *The first Gospel of James.* PHILO JUDÆUS, *Codex apocryphus Novi Testamenti.* Lipsiæ, 1832.

stated that it was the groundwork of all—"*the true pre-face to Mark.*" It is an innocent and amusing book, and not extravagantly doctrinal; it is not full of Gnosticism, like the *Gospel according to Saint John.*

Postel says that it is a pearl. And it is a pearl indeed for everybody that wishes to have a living Jesus, who, without his mother as the basis of his existence, seems to be a transparent shadow.

The Jewish novels are greatly important. *Esther*, a well combined and very expressive novel, gives the key of the history of customs. From the remotest part of the East, from the inmost recesses of the seraglio, it illustrates everything. The novel on Mary (if one wishes to call it so, according to the Latin Church) is not less instructive. In reading it, one feels that there is in it the eternal Mary, who was in the Jewish soul.

I have stated before, that the peculiarity of the Jewish people is, that behind the masculine forms of the *Law* and its stony tables, the stern countenance of the frightful, bull-faced Cherubim, there are among that people feminine sighs, vows of the *gratuitous salvation*, and the expectation of deliverance through the unforeseen Grace from above.

Peoples, no more than crystals, are ever to be classified according to their external form, but according to their nucleus. Here, under a rough outside, under angles and points, you will find at the bottom the feminine element, *Grace*. It is Mary disguised with the beard of Aaron.

The East was worn out. The Jews made illusion. But, they themselves, as it may be seen in their *Nehemiah*, were eaten up by usury at Jerusalem which was in ruin. The military plundering incursions made on them by Ptolemeus I., in favor of Egypt, the unclean inhumanity of Epiphanes, who contaminated everything, blunted many a soul, and, morally speaking, the Macchabees did not raise them up. The government of the Idumeans, confirmed and upheld by Rome, the eternal Rome—sealed the Jews forever under the tombstone. In the infirm minds, the *Legion* of demons stirred and acted vigorously. There were possessed persons everywhere. Even this was an attraction. Many Jews from Egypt and from the East, as well as many other people who were not Jews, flocked to Jerusalem. The pride and the haughtiness of the *Temple* were repulsive. The Pharisees, the party that stood for the *Law*, the country, Jewish liberty—a sincere party, but a violent one—offered to those, whom they wished to convert, nothing but harshness and aridity. One liked better to hear, in the small synagogues, the condescending, indulgent Rabbis, who were popular both for the exemption from the Law and for their satires on the haughty doctors. Hillel, a predecessor of Jesus, was such a Rabbi as has been described. John the Baptist, a kinsman of Jesus, was such another.* The lessons of these teachers were, by no means, new ones. They said what the prophets, especially Isaiah, had said wonderfully well : "The heart is all." "Eh ! what have I to do with your sacrifices ? " etc. This is identical with what is said in the sixty-first chapter of the *Râmayana.*

The precept "of loving one's neighbor as himself," precept of Confucius and the Stoics, had been, in a very peculiar manner, given to the Jews in the *Leviticus.* Even toward a stranger, whose ideas and ceremonies were so repugnant to Jewish feelings, the Jew was commanded "to love him *as himself.*"† The precept " of rendering good for evil " is everywhere, especially in *Manou* VI. 92.

The popular teacher *appears* to lead, while he really follows the people. He is, wittingly or unwittingly, the echo of the popular mind. The Jewish people found the yoke of the Pharisees to be heavy, for they made the

---

* Jesus himself, it is said, is cited in the *Talmud*, as was also his brother, James the Just, or *Yakob ha Tzadok.* But this distinction between the Rabbis or Scribes, and the Pharisees, appears fanciful.—ED.

† *Leviticus* xix. 37.

Mosaic virtues a condition for salvation, and imposed
works—works in both senses, the work of the Law and
the works of Charity.   The Rabbi neither commanded nor
required anything, but he said :   " Love and believe. . . .
All your sins are forgiven you."

" But what to love ? what to believe ? "   About that
there was not a precise formula.   To love the teacher, and
to believe on the teacher ? *   To take his very person, a
living creed, for a symbol and a creed ?   This is the very
accurate meaning of all that Saint Paul has written and
which has been marvellously well stated in this sentence.
" Jesus taught nothing but himself."†

Every Rabbi gave himself for an object-lesson.   If any
had put the question to these crowds of women and simple-
minded persons: " What do you believe ? "   Each of them
would have answered, " I believe on Hillel, the teacher.
I believe on Paul, or I believe on Jesus."

Personality is a singular mystery.   Genius and beauty
have often much less to do with it than some inexplicable

---

* Could he teach otherwise the crowds whom he addressed ?   With difficulty.
The rough minds of the inhabitants of Judea, and the uneducated people of
Galilee would have been shut out and deaf to fine moral inferences.   It is a
mockery to confound their short-witted *sophia*, which moves only on aphor-
isms, and cannot analyze nor infer, with the Greek *logos*, which is *undulating*,
deductive, and of a *boundless scope*.   In Hebrew, even the most elementary
distinctions are impossible.   Our modern Hebraists, more precise than the
Rabbis, and who know the Hebraic language thoroughly, say that it is an obscure and indistinct language, and so much so, that in it the words *crime* or
injustice cannot be distinguished from the words *misfortune, punishment,
suffering*.   This is an obstacle for the translator at each step ; it creates for
him a very great difficulty of becoming himself so much of a barbarian as to
preserve to such words their immoral obscurity.   The Jews did not accept,
but at a very late period, the tenet of immortality, which, among many other
peoples, was the foundation and support of morals.   (See the excellent
pamphlet of Isidore Cahen on this subject, and what he says at the beginning
of the book of *Job* in the *Bible* translated by his father.)

† This sentence is from RENAN.—HAVET, in an admirable article, which
is according to my heart's wishes, has judged of this literary masterpiece of
Renan with a young, eloquent, and sympathetic ingenuousness, which does by
no means exclude a very solid criticism.

aura or emanation of the individual. Nothing like personality gives an energetic impulse to the great current of
fanaticism. The Polish Messiah, a truly holy man, who
in our own time attracted after him the greatest minds,
possessed such a charm. A Russian Messiah in our days,
although he was a nullity, possessed it likewise; and he
had the startling success of being followed, in his own
spite, by ten millions of serfs.

In the remarkable dispute in 1863, to which the book
of Renan contributed so much, I regret two things: First.
That the disputants held too closely to history, and spoke
little about doctrine.* But doctrine is the main point.
It is the doctrine that makes the doctor. Second. I regret
that the disputants, holding fast to biography, put aside
the little popular gospels, which, homely as they are,
make us acquainted with the real condition of that age,
more than the official gospels. I will not fill up the gaps
of that discussion; it is not my business. I only observe
how very strangely the *primitive gospel* characterizes the
world of women, by adding to the narrative appropriate
words about the *nativity* and *the life* of *the carpenter.*

Three women begin the whole: Anna, mother of the
Virgin;—Elizabeth, her kinswoman, the mother of Saint
John the Baptist;—and another Anna, a prophetess, and
the wife of the high priest.†

The foregoing incidents evidently took place around
the temple, and under the direction of the priests. The
families in question were dependent on them. The
women believed that the fulness of time had come, and

---

* PATRICE LARROQUE, a worthy and austere wise man, has vigorously filled
up the gap, with a courageous boldness and seriousness which cannot be admired too much.—PEYRAT has exhausted the biographical question, making
it plain with a firm and impartial logic, in a book which ought, in a definitive
manner, to put an end to this great criticism.

† There is no evidence in the text that Anna was the wife or widow of a
priest; but simply that she was a woman who abode at or near the temple,
perhaps as consecrated. But the first two chapters of the Gospel of Luke,
and the stories of Anna, mother of the Virgin, are hardly trustworthy.—ED.

that a wonderful personage would proceed from them; they were in a feverish state of mind because of their dream, had almost become pregnant by their dream, and ardently wished to give birth to something. The priests, on their part, seeing that everything was ready, hoped and desired that nothing of the sort would occur, except through them.

The Messianic condition, to be an aged person, and barren up to that time, was precisely verified in the two cousins, Anna and Elizabeth. Was their barrenness procured, or designed, according to the cunning prudence taught in the book of the *Ecclesiastes?* The ministers of the temple put Zacharias and Anna, his wife, to shame for their sterility; and then Anna became the mother of Mary.

The little Mary, a rich heiress, given to the temple, remained in it from the time she was three years old until she was twelve. The priests, being unable to keep her among their sons, and near the son of the high priest, for whom she was intended, compelled Joseph, who was one of the carpenters of the temple and a man devoted to them, to take her with him. Joseph was the father of several boys and girls. His wife died, his sons married, except Juda, his eldest son, and James, his grandson, whom the good little Mary consoled, adopted, and brought up.

Mary, whom the priests did not lose sight of, worked for the temple. Her task was one of confidence, namely, that of weaving the purple (very dear stuff), for the great vail of the Holy of Holies.* Here is a pleasing description of her life as a working woman. She prayed in the morn-

---

* The weaving of curtains appears to have been a pursuit at all temples, and the *Kadeshuth* or consecrated women performed the work. When Manasseh placed the *Ashera*, or image of Astarté or Venus-Urania, in the temple, there were houses of *Kadeshim, Galii*, or consecrated persons there, "where the women wove hangings for the grove or *Ashera*." In many temples young girls were chosen for the purpose, and dismissed at the conclusion of their tas : —ED.

ing, in the pure hours ; she prayed in the evening, in the mysterious hours. She worked from nine to three o'clock, and in those hours it was warm ; she scarcely ate in the evening. One seems to be reading the life of a little devotee of Flandres. Those pious working-women, in the darkness of their cellars,* poured out their overflowing heart in small songs of infancy, called the songs of *lolo.* The poor girl of Judea, who sang less, and watched over everything, at intervals "shone forth as a dazzling snow, which the eye could hardly look at."

One may conjecture her thoughts. It was now six months that her aged cousin Elizabeth, who had never had a child, was pregnant. With a prophet ? With a forerunner ? One might well suppose that. At that time everybody spoke of nothing but miracles, of Messiahs, and of incarnation. The air was impregnated and heavy with this subject.

At the burning hour, when her work ceased, during the long hours of the afternoon, those sickly hours in which Cassianus says, that the friars pine away, of what did this young woman dream ? She was already sixteen. What did she see ? The heavenly dove ? The divine lightning ? Or did she see in the evening the angel, who brought her nourishment ? All this is pure and affecting in the little *Gospels,* which in some parts bear the *characteristic of the people* more than the official ones, and exhibit more of nature and more of heart.

They tell us distinctly that Joseph and Mary were not united in wedlock. They thrust away the idea of adultery. This was a wise foresight, which would have made the legend less dangerous, by hindering the indecent jests, the facetious Christmas songs, which during all the Middle Ages made marriage contemptible.

The fate, the fruitful extent of this religion of woman would have been quite different, if the official *Gospels,* in-

---

* Damp, and therefore dark apartments, were necessary for this work, to enable the threads to be of sufficient fineness.—ED.

stead of weaning Jesus harshly and abruptly, had given
him the milk of nature.   He would have been more of a
man.   What beautiful and useful fables might have been
imagined upon that subject!   It would then have been
necessary to have heart, *goodness*, and affection.   And all
this is wanting in the *Gospels*.   There is *love* in them, but
that is quite another thing.   *Love* is not *goodness;* it is
often a dry, and sometimes a violent and passionate ardor.

Nothing is more likely than the journey to Egypt, as
Munk has well remarked.   Egypt is very near Palestine,
and people went there by sea continually.   Philo,* the
Egyptian Jew, professed the doctrine of Jesus and of Paul,
under a more philosopical form.

Moses, as is expressly said, received his education at
the Egyptian court.   Hence the precocious understanding
of Jesus, who, when he was twelve years old questioned
the doctors and made them hold their peace (as Daniel
when a boy had made the judges dumb).   The mother
of Jesus, who had encouraged him at first, began now to
be afraid, and would stop him.   Poor mother ! . . . And
why speak harshly to her ?

---

* Philo Judæus who was born a short time before Jesus, and who died a
short time after him, under Claudius, exhibits in a clear manner the chaos of
those foolish sciences, which in the brains of the Jews mixed up the doctrines
of Plato and Moses with the revelations of Ezekiel and Daniel.   On the very
obscure epoch of the Messianic precedents, between Daniel, Jesus son of
Sirach, Philo, etc., MICHEL NICOLAS, one of the ablest critics of our
days, has thrown such light as the subject allowed.   His is a robust mind,
cautiously bold, which scorns false splendor, aims at the bottom of any
subject, and reaches its depth.   In his article on L. MÉNARS he has in a
wonderful manner laid down this great principle : " The heart creates faith.
Greece created her gods before the gods themselves had given her an existence."   The great question of sacerdotal genius, in which the poor BEN-
JAMIN CONSTANT maintained the truth against ECKSTEIN with so little en-
couragement, has been now decided with the ever increasing light of science
by MICHEL NICOLAS. (*Essays*, p. 76.)   He says that if the Greeks had not
escaped from theocracy, HERODOTUS would have been a VINCENT of BEAU-
VAIS ; PLATO a DUNS SCOT ; that Homer would have written a work like
Fiert-à-bras, and the *Prometheus* of ÆSCHYLUS would have been like the
Mysteries of the Passion. MICHEL NICOLAS : *Essays*, p. 76.

Henceforth it was the crowd that was Jesus' mother and sister. He was followed by his mother's sister, Mary, the wife of Cleophas. He was also followed by other ladies whom he charmed and consoled. They were very interesting women, some of them the wives of magistrates, and, alas! connected willingly or unwillingly with a thousand unjust and cruel things. They flung themselves at this young Rabbi's feet, and gave themselves up to his soft doctrine, which washed off and wiped out all this. They followed him; they could not quit him, and they ministered to him. He was followed even more eagerly by many unhappy women, weary of their unchaste life, and their sins, who had no repose and whose disordered life made them seem to be *possessed of the demon.* Such a one was the unfortunate Mary of Magdala, who has been called a courtesan, and who (as likewise those women I am about to mention) must have been, as is often the case, an enfranchised woman, ransomed and retired from such a cruel infamous life. The warm outpouring of her heart and of her gratitude, the perfumes with which she embalmed her teacher while he was still living, and which she wiped out with her hair, is a very beautiful and passionate story, forming the most perfect contrast to the coldness with which the Virgin is treated in the *Gospels.**

This, however, is a logical sequel of the Jewish tradition, in which preferences are given less to those who are just and irreproachable, than to those who, having sinned much, and standing in more utter need of pardon, make Grace shine much more.

Magdalene, according to Saint John, was the sole wit-

---

* It will be seen from this attributing of several incidents to one person, that the legends from which MICHELET derived this story, treat Mary of Magdala in Galilee, the courtesan at the house of Simon the Pharisee (*Luke* vii. 37-50), and Mary, the sister of Martha, whom Jesus loved, who "chose that good part," and anointed the head of Jesus at Bethany, at the house of Simon the leper, as the same person. The *Gospels* are not quite clear on the matter.—ED.

ness of Jesus' resurrection. She alone saw it with her heart's eyes. The world has believed her word.

Violent doubters are very liable to become quickly credulous. Men, self-styled *positive*, by a sudden change which happens very often, are wistful visionaries. Paul, a Jew from Tarsus and a tent-maker, a haughty and vehement man, showed, in his commercial travels, the great zeal of a Pharisee.* He had the misfortune to take part in the stoning of Saint Stephen. The young martyr's figure, in all its touching meekness, remained, doubtless, impressed on him and never left him. A storm, a fall, a flash of lightning, accidents which are so common, upset him. The more impetuous zealot he had been for the Law, the more ardent, hasty and imperious he was under Grace.

Such a man belongs to women. And indeed the *Acts of the Apostles* and the *Epistles* exhibit him always with them. They seem to let him never go out of their sight. Thekla follows him as a sister, and performs for him the humble duties of Martha, if not those of Mary.

In all this history the personality of this impetuous man is a curious one on account of its variations. His peculiar struggle is against the Greek mind, and, as he boldly states it, against Reason.† In his *manifesto* to the Greeks,‡ he acts precisely as David did when he danced before the Ark, boasting of his folly, and proclaiming himself a fool for Jesus sake, "because the foolishness of God is wiser than men."§ And all this is said in a hasty, eloquent, very naïve manner, showing all the heart,

---

* Living away from Judea, Paul could not be as acceptable to the residents of that province. Besides, Tarsus was in constant communication with Greece, Alexandria and Pontus; so that he had abundant opportunity to be indoctrinated in the Mithraic doctrines as well as the Mystic and Platonic learning. Indeed, he shows as much in the *Epistles*, which on all doubtful points, are more reliable than the *Acts of the Apostles.*—ED.

† Not quite correct. It was the *logos* or *sophia* of the Grecian philosophers, that he thus abjured.—ED.

‡ *Epistles to the Corinthians*, I., II.   § I. *Corinthians*, i. 25.

and the very real difficulties of an honest and pure man in a society of ardent and passionate women.

At Macedonia, whence he writes, he is between two women. Lydia, at whose house he dwells, and *the Pallid*, Chloë, at whose house the small congregation met. This nickname, *the Pallid*, seems to be that of a retired, enfranchised woman, and doubtless a rich woman too, as Mary of Magdala was. At the beginning, while he gives advice about continence, he boasts to be above all that.* Wrongfully. Later he confesses that he has " *a thorn in his flesh;* that the messenger of Satan buffets him, lest he should be exalted above measure."† This is a moving avowal, which one would least have expected. It is to be regretted that we know not who were those charming and dangerous persons, that had such power over him as to put an obstacle to his so great burst of purity.

Nothing is known about this Lydia. She seems to be of Syria, the country of seductions. She was a tradeswoman, and, doubtless, a prudent one like the woman who, in the *Proverbs of Solomon*, so well superintended housekeeping, enriched her home, made and sold tissues, etc. Lydia sold purple, a costly article of merchandise, bought by the Romans, especially by Magistrates, Prætors, and Procurators. Such a tradeswoman was a lady, and perhaps of the first rank.

The continuation is a peculiar one. He says, that in the midst of those temptations he *besought the Lord* thrice, *that it might depart from him.* "But he has said unto me : *My grace is sufficient for thee. My strength is made perfect in weakness.* Most gladly therefore *will I*

---

* I. *Corinthians*, vii. 7, 8.

† II. *Corinthians*, xii. 8. He seems to have undergone a kind of *ecstasis*, which he regarded as equivalent to the disclosures to the Epopt at the Mysteries. "I come to visions and revelations of the Lord. I knew a man in Christ about fourteen years ago, whether in body I cannot tell, or whether out of body I cannot tell, caught up to the third heaven . . . . into paradise, and he heard things arcane." It is in this connection that he speaks of the thorn in the flesh, and in no relation to seductive women.—ED.

rather glory in my infirmities, that the power of Christ
may rest upon me." Such ideas have a dangerous import,
which, without doubt, people did not consider at those
times of primitive purity. The mystics have interpreted
them thus : "By sin, one rises. In sinning we glorify
God." These are the proper expressions of Molinos.

Paul himself, however, was, as I believe, indignant
against his fluctuations. One seems to feel his indignation
in the vehement words which he addresses to woman to
humiliate her, harshly exhorting her to silence, to submission ; reminding her that the image of God is in man,
and that she has been created for him ; that she may
not pray except vailed, and that her long hair has been
bestowed on her for this purpose,* etc.

Such vehement outbursts would make us believe that
woman will be kept far off from the altar. But the contrary happened. *She was a priest,* officiated, and was
consecrated during four hundred years.

Paul even contradicted himself. Arriving at Corinth, he
perceived quite well that the Grecian woman, with her
noble beauty, her subtle and eloquent speech, was his
great auxiliary. Phœbe, *the Brilliant,* the name of another
enfranchised woman, was already the active minister, the
factotum of the church of Corinth. She was a deaconess
at first. The former companions of Paul, Barnabas and
Thekla, were no longer with him. Phœbe was now everything. She gave him lodgings. She wrote for him † under

---

* I. *Corinthians,* xi. 3-15.

† This has been suppressed in the Latin translation of the *Bible.* It has
been suppressed also in the Greek original of the *Didot* edition (1842) which
is dedicated to AFFRE.—The original Greek says : Εγραφη δια φοίβης. The
ancient French translator of the Reformed Church honestly and literally
translated that Phœbe *wrote* from the dictation of Saint Paul. If the Greek
word meant only that he sent the letter by Phœbe (as Jowett of Oxford
thinks), it would be a useless repetition. Paul had spoken before of the expedition of Phœbe, had recommended her, etc.*

---

* Nevertheless, other Epistles have the same preposition, and several persons are so indicated. M. Michelet is probably in error.—ED.

his dictation. The reason of it is not known. Was he sick? And what did she write? The most vehement writing of Saint Paul.

Here is expressly stated what one might have conjectured, that such a hasty, lively, but incoherent eloquence, which goes by fits and starts, and is so often in violation of logic and reason, is not written. A Jew of Asia Minor, a country where languages were mixed up, a travelling tradesman and merchant of Cilicia, the Babel of freebooters whom Pompey crushed, must have spoken a Greek very much mixed with Hebraisms and with Greco-Syriac dialects. But the ardor, the boldness, the vehement spirit which hurried him on, scarcely stopped at that. He spoke, he thundered, he overwhelmed. The Greeks around him, with their rapid hand, and the ladies so zealous, picked up what they could from his talk, and wrote off-hand. Very often they were compelled to translate, and they performed the task without scrupulousness (for they were animated by the same ardor), but not without danger; because Paul's ideas, thought in Hebrew and uttered in bad Greek, at the risk of their sense and inspiration, could hardly be settled in tolerable Greek language, except by serious changes, mutilations, and suppressions which are quite well perceptible in the shocks and jolts, as of a race at full speed on a very uneven ground.

A complex and collective work, the *Epistle to the Romans*—the Marseilles Hymn of the Gospel of Grace, the utter setting at naught of the law—seems indeed to have been composed by the whole church of Corinth. Saint Paul contributed the glimpse of genius, and Phœbe her skillful pen. Erastus, the public treasurer of the port through which at that time passed all the commerce of Greece—Erastus, the important person, whose greeting Saint Paul sends to the Emperor's household, may have had a great influence on the contents of that epistle.

A profound revolution was taking place in the Empire. The Emperor almost everywhere had substituted for the

20

Prætor, who was the man for the State, his own *Procu-rator*, his agent, a steward of his household, of his own interests—whether he were a Roman or not—and often one of his freedmen. Erastus, whose name is a Greek one, and who was the friend of Saint Paul, may have been an enfranchised man. This representative of personal government, of favor and of Grace, raised as he had recently been to dignity by Claudius or Nero, was fatally, as well as Saint Paul, an enemy to *the Law* and a born adversary of the *Jurist*.

The whole Epistle is contained in this sentence : The Law alone made sin : the law being dead, sin is dead.* This is a sentence with many meanings. The word *Law*, among the Jews, signifies *the Mosaic Law ;* in the Empire, *the Roman Law ;* and according to the Greek idea, *the law of conscience* and natural equity.

But now, by having broken to pieces the tablets of stone, and the tables of brass, and having struck out the prohibition of evil, is it by any means certain that evil has disappeared from the world, and eternal justice has also been struck out ?

Justice, that was a queen in Æschylus and Socrates, in Zeno and Labeo, has became again a servant ; or rather Justice has been destroyed by love and faith, by the divine intoxication and the orgies of Grace.

It will be seen with what power the administrative revolution, and the religious revolution agreed well together ; and to what a degree the agent of good favor, the delegate of Cæsar must have been in secret understanding with Phœbe, and with the Apostle of the East. Their manifesto to Rome, to the city of Authority, means precisely this: "Death to Authority."

Phœbe did not trust to anybody for carrying this Epistle to the *palace of Nero*, to the friends of Narcissus. This is expressly stated in it.

* *Epistle to the Romans*, vii. 8. The same sophism appears also in the *First Epistle to the Corinthians*, xv. 56, 57.

I say Nero and not Claudius, because the latter had expelled the Jews from Rome. In his reign it was hardly possible to send to Rome the embassy of a sect which at that time was considered to be entirely Jewish.

Phœbe did not go unarmed. She carried with her two keys which would open the household of the Emperor with great facility.

The real masters of the Imperial household were the priest-prostitutes of both sexes, *the Galli and Nautch-girls, the Narcissuses and Pallakies*, peculiar to the worship of Cybelé, Venus-Ery-cina and the Syrian goddess. These debauched wretches constituted a world of people apart by themselves, and were for this very reason wholly devoted to the promoting of the ideas of the East. All the gods were there as well as the little arcane worships, the mysteries of every kind, expiations, purifications, a thick vapor of vice and remorse, of panic and of odious dreams. The flagellants of Atys surely were there, and perhaps already the unclean Taurobolia,* washing of blood. What power could equal that of Phœbe arriving there with the simple sentence, which dismisses and makes all those things useless? "Good news! . . . Sin is dead! . . ."

The other key powerful to open was this. Jesus, the Teacher, had said: "Render unto Cæsar the things which are Cæsar's, and unto God the things that are God's."† Paul, the disciple, had said: "Let every soul be subject to the higher powers. Whosoever resists the power, resists the ordinance of God." "Pay ye tribute also to princes, for they are God's ministers, attending continually upon this very thing."‡ Peter had frankly said: "Be subject to your masters, even to the froward ones."§

---

* The Taurobolia or baptism of blood was one of the Mithraic ceremonies which spread over all Western Europe and into Northern Africa.—ED.

† *Gospel according to Matthew*, xvii. 21.

‡ *Epistle to the Romans*, xiii.

§ *First Catholic Epistle of Peter*, ii. 18–20.

The question is to obey not only *de facto* and in deeds, but also with the soul. The question is not to obey by making the Jewish reserve : " Through the transgressions of the people, their princes become many,"* and they are the scourge of God. No reserve. One must subdue one's self and obey in conscience ; serve willingly, and love—love Tiberius, love Nero. This is a new slavery, hollowed out under slavery; this is a great and ingenious deepening of all the ancient servitudes, and which, in the Middle Ages and afterward, operated to transform all princes into zealous Christians.

The great fact of the moment, the personal government of Cæsar, free from the idea of magistracy ; of Cæsar, ruler of the Law, and *become the Law itself* in the person of his procurator, received from the new tenet a marvellous sanction. Must not Cæsar have welcomed this voice from the East, this Messiah who enjoined that man should obey from his inmost heart ? Nero, on his accession to the throne, although still docile to his Roman teachers, was already in an underhanded way surrounded by enfranchised persons, who had been governing till that time ; persons of any kind, who amused his artistical imagination, some of them being poets and declaimers, others charlatans and ministers of some god. Nero, on account of his vast disorderly imagination, was a natural prey for them. His head was full and bursting. He revolved in his mind enormous things and in a thousand different ways. Ought he to be the Cæsar of Rome and the Jurists, or the supreme artist, the emperor of poetry ? or rather the restorer of the genius of the East, a Mithras and a Messiah ? He himself did not yet know.

He would be loved. Brought up by Seneca, a generous Stoic, who dined with his own slaves, Nero had embraced the cause of the enfranchised. He contemplated an immense Utopia—the abolition of taxes. This would have

---

* *Proverbs of Solomon*, xxviii. 2.

been the realization of the Stoic ideal, as stated by Zeno :
" Love is the safety of the commonwealth ! "

But, oh ! how vague and obscure this word " *Love* " is !
Love without Justice, love of caprice and favoritism may
become a hell, the scourge of the commonwealth, and *by
no means its safety*.

One of the greatest struggles which ever took place on
earth is that which we may conjecture, and which doubtless took place at this very moment in the Palace of Nero,
and perhaps under his very eyes ; I mean the struggle
between *Woman and the Stoic*.

It has been already remarked that *Woman* in the first
four centuries of the Christian Era (till the year 369) was
a *priest*, the true Christian priest. It was her special
prerogative to protect that faith, which issued forth from
Woman.

But, oh ! how different the part of the two adversaries
is ! The Stoic reascends by the universal propensity of
the world. And Woman goes down on it at her own ease.
The Stoic commands *effort*, enjoins *work* to the exhausted
and worn-out world, which teaching of his made him
hated. . . . And oh ! how easily Phœbe could answer
in a scornful manner : " The lily does neither work nor
spin, and yet it is better *dressed* than Cæsar."

Jurists or Stoics, magistrates, philosophers, all, in asking
of the world to be watchful, to live yet, were asking an
enormous, unbearable thing, while the world, sickly as it
was, settled itself down so well to go asleep ! How much
better it liked the voice of the nurse, alluring to sleep, the
sweet and voluptuous voice of woman, that said : " How
sweet it is to die ! "

To die, to be free from the bonds of the body—what a
happy prospect ! (*Who will deliver me from the ties of
this body ?*)* The body means work, the care of taxes,
the burden of the law. The body is the militia, the war-

---

* *Epistle to the Romans*, vii. 24.

fare against barbarians, the exile to the frozen Rhine, the defence of the Roman frontiers.

On this point the Jurist was strong. He thought to stop the Christian woman, and to perplex her. But she answered with a smile: "What! To thrust back our Northern brothers, who come to seek salvation? It would be much better to invite them, to open them our doors, to overthrow from their foundation the walls of our cities. . . ."

But the Empire, but our laws, our arts?—

What are the arts good for?—

But our sacred country, the City, this vast harmony of wisdom and peace?—

There is no peace here below. There is no City but the heavenly one.

Down, thou vain Wisdom! Reason, cast down thy eyes! make an apology both of you before the *Foolishness* of God. . . . Justice and the Civil Law, thou art the enemy. I know thee, O proud one; thou haughty mother of human virtues, come down from thy prætorium. . . . The sinner already sits higher than thy false just persons. His sin is the field where Grace triumphs.

Oh! what mockery Phœbe could make, and what contempt she must have had of the Julian law, which was an official glorification of marriage!* What! to bind yet one's self by vow, to generate beings for a world, which must die to-morrow, to perpetuate this mean thing—the body—which God wishes to abolish! Immortal thanks are due to him that the desert is becoming a fact and it enlarges itself. In many provinces, the Empire is already expurgated. Let some other scourge be applied, and all

---

* People quoted a terrible sentence of Jesus against marriage. Salome said to Jesus: "How long will people die?"—"How long will you bring forth?"—"Ah," she answered, "I have done well in not having children!" —"Salome, Salome! eat of anything," said he, "but do not eat the bitter herb."—CLEMENT of Alexandria, *Stromata* III., 345.

will be released. Husbands, fly from your wives. . . . .
Let everybody go away and live isolated. "So much the
more speedily will the world come to an end, and the City
of God be filled up." *

Death is the supreme argument, and to it there is no
reply. Phœbe preaches her cause on the sepulchre of a
hundred nations, whose gods, cold already in the Pantheon, and with empty eyes, were, in the apparent struggle, easy fighters for this priestess of death. If they had
been able to answer, they would perhaps have said, that
the new faith, triumphing through Woman, followed, in
spite of Paul himself, the way of the old. Paul had wished
her to be vailed, silent, and dependent. I see her at the
altar preaching and prophesying, teaching man, telling
him of God—nay, making a god for him. A powerful and
charming contrivance, quite natural after all, which the
ancient worships had not abused. The gloomy Iphigenia,
the foaming Sibyl, had less charms than terror. The
Vestal, obedient and silent, was a statue. The priestess of
the new faith was a living woman, she spoke and officiated;
raised above the people, she blessed them and prayed for
them; she was their voice to the throne of Jesus.

As long as the goddesses of art, production of the
Greek chisel, were not overthrown, people, during four
centuries, opposed to their dead beauty, life itself, the
visible Wisdom, the pontificate of Woman.† The silent

---

* 1 *Augustine.*

† Like any other priest [presbyter], woman was solemnly consecrated, and
received the Holy Ghost by the laying on of hands. (*Council of Chalcedonia,*
the fourth Œcumenical.) The Council of Laodicea, in the year 366 or 369,
forbade her to be a priestess. (Chapter XII. Collection of *Denys the Little,*
Mayence, 1525. LABBE and MANSI have omitted this council.) The Council of Carthage, in 391, forbade her to catechize, to baptize, or even to study,
except with her husband. Till that time she used to preside, to preach, to
confer orders, to officiate. ATTON remarks that she at that time was worthy
of doing all that "for the instruction she had received in the heathen times."
It is easily conceived what must have been the power of woman in those high
functions which made her almost divine, while she was about thirty years old,
and still beautiful, eloquent and dexterous, as women are in Greece and in

Ceres could not struggle much when the new Ceres enchanted the ancient *agapæ*, and administered the sacred bread. Pallas, the austere virgin, must have yielded altogether when Magdalene made the altar dramatic and wetted it with her tears.

What did she say to the dying world? . . . " Let us die together ! " A tender sentence of a sister, which was very sure to be listened to ! What would, however, become of the world, if everybody remained always suspended on this sentence, not able any longer either to live on or to die altogether ?

---

the East ! Enthroned at the altar, admired and the beloved of everybody, she possessed a true power and, surely, the most complete of all. The gloomy TERTULLIAN was indignant against her. The fierce ATHANASIUS, over-excited about Egyptian monachism, feared the too sensible effect of the moment in which she consecrated and made the marriage of heaven and earth, and in which all communicated with her and received the Sacrament from her gentle hand. If she consecrated, he wished her to do it with closed doors and for herself alone. But often she had not the strength thus to shut herself up altogether. The door was not shut very strongly; the zealots, who were without, took her by surprise at the decisive moment, when she was in a touching trouble of modesty and holiness. Then ATHANASIUS in a new fury forbade her to allow herself to be taken by surprise, and he forbade her also to wash herself, hoping thus to make her repulsive. By a more refined, more exalted scrupulousness, the sect of the Callydicians feared that the love of Jesus might too much agitate the *priestess*, and that she might wander in the dreams of the spiritual marriage ; and therefore, among them she was a *priestess, but only of Mary*. In the West, women, much more ignorant, never exercised the priesthood, but only the deaconship, or the material cares of the Church. In the fifth century three Western councils and two popes decidedly removed woman from the ministration of holy things.

CHAPTER IX.

PERIOD OF UNIVERSAL WEAKNESS—THE CRUSHING OF
THE MIDDLE AGES.

LET us suppose that on a fine morning the observatory
and the Academy of Sciences, which are our popes, inform
us that on such a month, and on such a day, the earth
will pass across a comet of igneous aerolites, a shower of
iron and of fire. Great stupor. At first people will
doubt. But the event is certain, calculated, demonstrated.
All activity, all pleasure, all work stops. People cross
their arms. The event, however, delays ; the astronomer
has mistaken the year. No matter. No work begins
again. The languor of the people is the same. Everybody had settled himself down for that.

Death ! there is nothing more dear than death to him
who has no longer any part in active life. In the early
Christian times, the expectation of death simplified
everything. A silence, a strange calm of all human passions took place. Law-suits ceased. Mine and thine became indifferent. People hardly contended over that
which might perish to-morrow.* Everything was com-

* People willingly got rid of their slaves, under the belief that the judgment was so near at hand, and that everything was soon to come to an end.
Christianity had, by no means, abolished slavery. The text of Saint Paul
(*Galatians* iii. 28), which WALTON and many others have quoted, has
nothing to do with it. DESPOIS has conclusively shown this in his articles
of impregnable strength, and to which no answer has been made. (*Avenir*, 2,
16, 23, Decem. 1855.) BOSSUET, on this point, agrees with DESPOIS:
" To condemn slavery is to condemn the Holy Ghost." (*Warning to Protestants.*) DESPOIS has also, in support of his reasoning, the teaching of the
Ecclesiastical seminaries of our own days, which teaching " condemns the
negro who escapes from his master." (BOUVIER, *Bish. of Mans*, 6th edition, VI., 22-25.) The Koran, on the contrary, declares free the slave who
embraces Islamism. It says : " He who enfranchises a man, frees himself
from the penances of this life, and from eternal punishment."

mon between brothers and sisters. Sex was forgotten. The very wife was no more than a sister. The hearth was cold and its fires extinguished.

Death was hoped for. Oh! that it would come speedily! Ignatius says: "I am hungry of it, I am thirsty for it."

Nature was the curse. Nature was damnation. In the fourth chapter of *Genesis*, it is stated that "it repented the Lord that he had made man on the earth."

To leave nature soon, "to depart as soon as possible," says Tertullian, "is the true object of man."* Saint Cyprian made vows for plague and famine.† He who has children, says Tertullian, must pray to God "to the end that they may depart from this impious world." This is just what Saint Hilarius did for his daughter, and his prayer was answered. Afterward he prayed for the eternal departure of his wife, and he received this grace also.‡

But how continue life, its duties, its actions, which are necessary even if it has to last one day? How obtain some indispensable action from this great sluggish people? And yet, if they cannot be brought to act, the world infallibly must come to an end. At least, if somebody could devise for such sick persons a passion, or even a vice! They could then be saved. But what can be done? What can be drawn out from the distressing perfection of those pale lovers of death, who smile and give thanks when they are struck?

We see nowadays in India the feeblest men, who are beaten with impunity; we see timid women, old women who are at their last gasp, throw themselves under the wheels of the car of Jagernat, which slowly runs over them, and yet such horrible torture does not draw out of them a sigh. They are unable to do the least action. Nothing is more usual, especially at the outset of great

---

* *Adversus Gentes*, v. 2.　　† *Ad Dem.*　　‡ FORTUNATUS.

religious epidemics, than this hunger after death, this facility of undergoing martyrdom, this joy of deliverance.   On this point the most despicable, the humblest man has yet this happiness of pride, namely, that of destroying, of trampling under foot order and Law, and of being a Law to himself.

The example was contagious.   A few Christians perished.*   But immense masses that did not imitate their martyrdom, imitated their refusal to bear the burden of civil life, and especially the military service.†   The latter, hard as it is in itself, was harder still on account of the immense journeys of the legions—from the river Seine to the Euphrates—and hardest of all things on account of the work of masons and mechanics, which the legions had to do, and the wretchedness of their pay, made less by the increase of price of everything.   Tacitus has described all this in a masterly way.   What did the soldier do ?   He made war against the Empire itself, he created a Cæsar, who augmented the pay, but it soon again became insufficient.   At last, disheartened, he abandoned the Rhine and the Danube to take care of themselves, if they could, and threw away his sword, saying : " I am a Christian."

Then the barbarians passed over.   They were disorderly multitudes—of whom Marius and Tiberius in their day had made great slaughter—and confused masses of women, children, oxen, chariots, than which nothing was easier to arrest.   And to stop them was also the wisest thing. Whatever Tacitus in his *Germania* (which is nothing but a novel) may have said ; whatever our extravagant *Teutomaniacs* may have added to what he said, the barbarians carried into the Empire only disorder and ruin.   The best the Romans could do was to make a choice of them, to

---

* DODWELL: *Fewness of Martyrs.*   RUINART himself acknowledges that the number of martyrs has been exaggerated.

† The text is precise : " All they that take the sword shall perish with the sword." (Matthew xxvi. 52.) TERTULLIAN expressly enjoins the soldier to desert. LACTANTIUS forbids even the sea-service and commerce.

scatter them among the provinces, and thus to make them Romans. But to open the barriers, and foolishly to fraternize with them, to admit them by tribes, was the same as to accept chaos. The tall, insipid-looking young fellows were very, very far from being able to understand the Roman life. They broke everything, and turned everything topsy-turvy. And then, those men who appeared very strong were too effeminate, and they melted as snow at the heat of the South, at vices and excesses. Of their corruption, there remained only a mire, into which the Empire stuck fast, every day falling lower and lower, instead of being regenerated.

The few Italians and Greeks who yet remained, Celtica and Spain, the hard, indestructible races of Lyguria and Dalmatia, maintained to the Empire, even in its depopulation, some resources more real indeed. Was there no genius in the nation, which at that time gave to the world Tacitus, Juvenal, and Marcus-Aurelius; Gaius, and Ulpian teachers of jurisprudence, and the oracle of it, the great Papinianus? It could then have been held for certain that if, on the one hand, the world was falling off since Aristotle and Hippocrates, it was raising itself on the other hand by *Equity* and the *comprehension of Justice.*

The vulgar belief "that the Empire was dying without remedy" had its origin in the idea which rashly confounds the life of nations with that of an individual. Nothing, however, is more different. Nations have in their constitutive elements a principle of renovation, which the individual has not. But in order to live again, one must believe in life; in order to conquer, one must believe in victory. What can we do with persons who have been struck at heart? " What is left to you ? " " Myself," answered Medea. If *self* remain, that is all. But if it does not remain? if it is shaken and sickly? To believe that one is dying, and to say so, is to have died already.

The great colonies of Trajan, which were so strong and so durable—one of them of six millions of souls existing still in Roumania and Transylvania—appeared to consolidate the Empire. But neither the great military chief, nor the greatest of jurists were sufficient for the conditions of the minds. The Eastern enervation was daily gaining ground, as well as its effeminate gods, the feverish malady of Syria and Phrygia. The Cæsars were compelled to imitate their rivals, the kings of Parthia, who were *Sun-kings*, as the ancient *Phra* of Egypt, the *Nabis* of Babel, and the *Mithrases* of Iran. The Greeks of Bactriana, and the unconquerable Mithridates, the immortal Mithra of the kingdom of Pontus Euxinus, had borne that title.

Such a thing seemed foolishness at first. But Nero was thinking on it, and it was this that undoubtedly made him cruel toward the Christians, and their Anti-Christ.* The childish Elagabalus, the little pontiff of Syria, tried it, and lost himself. Both of them were very unclean, effeminates and grotesque Adonises, and wonderfully ridiculous. Their foolishness, however, was imitated by the wise and brave Aurelian when the highest necessities compelled him. He was victorious in twenty battles, and proclaimed himself an *incarnation of the Sun-god.*

Every dying god had declared himself a *Sun*, Serapis, Atys, Adonis, and Bacchus; everything came to an end that way. The Empire, in its decrepitude, looked toward the sun for a little warmth. And for a moment people thought to make Mithras—*the invincible Sun*—the god of the armies, the worship of the Roman legions.†

Mithras had derived great renown from Mithridates, the last enemy of Rome, and from the mysterious empire which Pompey destroyed, namely, from the association of pirates, who for a while were masters of the whole Mediterranean. This association was a Mithraic one, the secret of which has never been wholly unfolded.

---

* See RÉVILLE *on the Apocalypse.*

† See the texts collected in PRELLER's *Romish Mythology,* 1858.

What we know precisely about it is, that among those desperadoes, Mithras was worshipped as *energy*, the solar and human energy. Their initiation to the military service of Mithras was performed in caves. The god was represented to be born in gloomy caves, as a young and strong man, dazzling with splendor, throwing down and killing a bull. The pirates very ingeniously adopted, for the ordinary representation of Mithras, a beautiful Greek statue of a virgin (it is Victory) killing the enormous beast. But they put on her head the Phrygian cap, made of her a young Atys, who, however, was not mutilated, but, on the contrary, had an unfailing arm, and struck down the bull at one blow.

The degrees of the initiation were as follows : *Soldiers, Lions, Scouts of the Sun,* to run over the world sword in hand. A sword and a crown were offered to the novice, and he took only the sword, saying : "Mithras is my crown ; I will be a king of energy."

That had a very great success in the legions. It was believed that the blood of the bull, issuing forth red and warm from it, and falling upon the enervated individual, poured forth on him its strength and even its amorous valor. *Mithraism* for a while was the genuine religion of the Empire. Constantine himself hesitated to have a hand in it.

Its effect did not last long. Mithras himself, struck as he was, far from healing others, languished and decayed. Though he was the *Sun*, though he was *Victory*, he also, like many others, became a penitent god.

In order to understand well the nothingness of this epoch, and to value its fall, it is enough to consider the pale literature of that time, which is like the breath of one who dies, an unmeaning mess of fables and vague words ; a deep poverty and extreme impotency. Everything was languid, soft, old—and, what is worse, bombastic, swollen with air and wind, and strangely exaggerated.

There is nothing in any language to be compared with

those strange letters, in which Saint Jerome, while advis‑
ing a Christian virgin to embrace religious celibacy,
related his temptations, the fury of his own old desires.
As a compensation for this, there is nothing so cold and
tame as the narrations of martyrs, which are indeed feeble
productions for so glowing a subject. But the best of all
that literature is the universal and popular hand-book,
the insipid *Shepherd of Hermas*, a libretto of the small
mysteries into which the novices were admitted, and
which Ireneus, Clement, Athanasius, Jerome, Eusebius,
and many others quoted and admired during two or three
centuries. That book was in vogue as long as women
were *priests*, probably because it exhibits many parts for
young and old women, in which they could at leisure dis‑
play their apostolic graces.

It was a sad production, too like those pale eggs
which the male has not fecundated. And yet, who will
believe it? it was not woman's fault. Her softness and
her gracefulness, her charming faults are absent. Lo!
what it is to believe that people can do without love,
without child, without maternity, that which is a powerful
initiation! The idea of the child scarcely appears in
the Jewish monuments, except the pride of succession,
and appears not at all in the Christian monuments. Jesus
seems to be a child and he is not. He preaches. His
mother dares not interpose. As for her, he is fruit‑
less, neither suckled nor brought up. What follows
of all this? Woman is sad and dry, an ungraceful and
pitiful-looking being. The impotency of man is un‑
doubtedly lamentable. But an impotent, atrophied woman
is *a dry fruit*. Her impotency is worse than death, it is
desolation!

Look likewise at the silly appearance, the idiotish face
of those Northern people who go to this school. They
are Ostrogoths and Visigoths, who have become a by‑
word for decrepit foolishness. Look at them on the
benches of the old school of Hermas, reciting *"musa,*

a muse." Behind them comes another, Attila, a cruel teacher, with his iron rod.

It is to be observed that the kings of the Goths have still the countenance of men in comparison with the sons of Dagobert who came afterward. The same is to be said of their *chronicles* in comparison with those of Frédégaire, who, however, was better than the Carlovingian friars, for the latter were dumb beasts who could scarcely lisp and bleat out words.

In the terrible voyage of Kane to the polar seas, nothing strikes the reader so much as to see Newfoundland dogs or Esquimaus "that were very wise and strong-minded" becoming mad through the excruciating severity of the cold. The same sadness, the same dismay seizes me, if I may make use of such expressions, at seeing in the Christian legends that the lion, the dog, and the birds, formerly so wise, have become imbecile. The beasts are silly. The animal which in India was the friend of Rama, and which in Persia had its celestial, winged genius,* is a ridiculous penitent with Saint Antony, Saint Macarius, etc. The lion becomes a lay brother of the hermit, and carries his baggage. The hyena listens to his preaching and promises to steal no more.

Illusive legends. In the Christian mind, the animal is suspicious, the beast seems to be a mask. The *velus*, an inauspicious name, which the Jews give to animals, are dumb devils. And nature becomes demoniac. The tree, with its gloomy foliage, is full of terror and snares. Is it not the tree, that guilty one, to which the serpent twisted itself in order to seduce, to deceive Eve, and to ruin mankind? If it be not the serpent now on the tree,

---

* *The City of Beasts,* their grandeur and their decline, is a beautiful subject. Eugenius Noël, a writer of a very charming mind, has found out such a title, and he alone can write a book on it. It contains an immense part of human affairs. It is evident by the *Avesta* that mankind has lived only through the alliance of the dog against the lion. The dread of the lion brings people together. Where he does not exist people live isolated. The lion made society.

it is the bird, it is the nightingale (a demon of melody) which sings still on it to trouble and to lead human hearts astray. Through those enchanted trees the magic of the desert was performed; the cloud gathered, and the rain poured down; hence, flowers and fruits, and all the temptations of man. Down! O fatal trees! Let the plain be spread, rugged, naked, and desolate! The earth has made love for a long time; let it now do penance.*

Thus began here below that strange phenomenon—the hatred of creation, and persecution, the exile of God the Father. The Word alone reigned. Until the year 1200 there was not an altar, there was not a church dedicated to the Father, there was not even a symbol which called him to mind. It was not the fault of man that (oh! enormous thing!) God was not banished *from nature*, from the great church, of which he is the life, the soul that is unceasingly born of him.

Father! It is a dear, sacred word, the love of the ancient world. The household had in it its firm support, its noble *genius;* the home had in it its solidity. Everything wavered in the Middle Ages. The husband, was he the husband? the father, was he the father? I do not know. The ideal and mystic family, which was shaped according to the legend, has its authority elsewhere. There was no head of the family. *There was no father*

---

* The *three peoples of the Book*, the Jewish people, and their two offshoots, the Christian and the Mohammedan (studying the Word and neglecting life, rich in sentences and poor in works), have forgotten the Earth, *the Mother Earth.* Oh! what an impiety! Look at the nakedness of the old *Greco-Byzantine* world. Look at the desert of Castile, rugged, salt, unpleasant. Look at all the canals of India neglected by the English. Persia, once the Paradise of God, what is she now? A Mohammedan sepulchre. From Judea to Tunis and Morocco, and on the other hand from Athens to Genoa, all those bald summits which look from on high into the Mediterranean have lost their forests, their crown of cultivation. And will those forests adorn those summits again? Never. If the ancient gods, and the active and strong peoples, in whose time those shores were blossoming, should to-day rise from their graves, they would say: "O *gloomy peoples of the Book*, of grammars, of words, and of vain subtleties, what have ye made of Nature?"

21

in the ancient meaning of the word. A third person now
assumed this name, which formerly meant a creator, a
generator. The father said to him: " My Father! "
What is he then in his own house ?

Let us put aside the idea of adultery, which, however,
recurs everywhere in the Middle Ages. Let us suppose
that the family is respected, pure, and holy. The fact is
always sad. It is the scorn of the man, it is the dispar-
agement of the husband. As to him, his wife is a virgin.
For her soul is elsewhere, and while she gives all, she
gives nothing. Her ideal is another. If you see that she
has become a mother, it is because she has conceived of
the Spirit. The son belongs to her. And to her husband ? No. Behold then the household made at the
image of the external society. The mother and her son
constituted one people, the husband an inferior people.
He was the serf, the beast. The crushing of the world was
here reproduced in the very shelter where the unhappy
man would have wished to revive his wretched heart.

Who is that child that grows up apace and flourishes
with a precocious gracefulness under the complaisant eye
of his mother? The woman's husband himself is proud of
him, and prefers him to all other boys. And yet how he
differs from him ! One feels that too strongly at intervals.
Oh! bitter fluctuation ! Oh ! incurable sadness ! He
will be uncertain whether he may love him or not. In the
meanwhile he loves him. But he has no feeling of security. There is no complete and true joy for him. He has
lost his smile, and he will never recover it on earth.

In the *Primitive Gospel* (*Protoevangelium*), a book quoted by the first Fathers, the touching figure of Joseph has
been set down, namely, his compassionate goodness, as
well as his deep chagrin and his tears.

The Gospel of the Carpenter is much more explicit. It
is a serious and artless book, which people have done
their best to destroy. It has been recovered in an Arabian translation. But it is not an Arabian book, for it has

none of the silly flowers of Arabian literature. It is a Greek or a Hebrew book. This poor little book has, with a prophetic vigor, pictured in Joseph and in Jesus the whole situation of the thousand years that followed— the cruel plague of the family.

Joseph has, from the beginning, been worthy of admiration for his behavior toward the orphan girl, harshly rejected by the priests of the Temple, who sent her away, while she was compromised and poor. Joseph, scarcely engaged and simply betrothed, opened his arms to her and saved her. He was none the less sad, however, and he remained so through his life. On his death-bed, it went still worse with him. His soul, weakened by chagrins, troubled itself and despaired. He cried over his destiny, cursed his birth-day, believed that his mother conceived him in a day of bad desire, according to the idea of the Psalmist, and at last he said : "Woe to my body ! and woe to my soul ! I feel that my soul is far from God !" What a bitter cry ! He has had neither earth nor heaven. He has lived near *her*, with *her*, and without *her*. And, at the end of such a gloomy life, he saw " *the lions of hell.*" He was afraid of Jesus himself on account of the bad thoughts which he had entertained about Jesus's mother. But he was wrong in this. Jesus had a compassionate heart, and his tears flew copiously to calm and reassure him, driving away from him the terrors of death. " Be not afraid, nothing of thee will die ! Thy very body will remain, it will not be dissolved, and it will be intact till the great *Feast of a thousand years.*"

Thus, from the earliest Christian times, was described in a wonderful manner what was to come, and to be repeated everywhere. That which, however, was not foreseen was that, in this hell, the victims of marriage would embitter their griefs by making sport of each other. The cruel songs of the Christmas-carols follow them through the whole of the Middle Ages. They must laugh at those songs, and sing them, and be merry. To be sad is al-

lowed to nobody. And it is the saddest married man
who sings, that he may avoid being the laughing-stock of
the party. That follows him everywhere. Wherever he
turns himself, either at the evening songs, the Mysteries
which are performed at the doors of churches, or the
Mysteries figured in stone, the same legend follows him
always and everywhere. To the songs of the Christmas-
carols succeeds the novel, which like a sweetish diluting
makes the legend worldly. A whole literature spreads
and stirs up the poison, pouring it in the wound, giving
to the heart nothing but the sharp cut of doubt on the
dearest thing . . . love !

There will be at least always subsisting the love of the
child to the mother. " In this worship, is not the child
the beloved object ? " He, who thinks so, is wrong.

Even among the Jews the family relation was hard-
hearted. " Withhold not correction from thy child."
" Beat him constantly." * " Never smile to thy daughter,
and keep her body pure." † What a strange and shocking commandment ! It will be handed to the casuists so
much the better. And they will take hold of it, and make
shameful commentaries. One of these commentaries
prohibits the mother to look at her son !

What is, then, this child ? Flesh, incarnated sin. The
more beautiful the child, the more abundant the blending
of lilies and roses on its cheek and brow, the more it
represents love, the moment of love, in which Nature—
the condemned one—spoke. Alas ! on her knees, in her
arms, over her breast what does she hold, but Sin ? . . .
Thus, how sad and timid she is ? Will she dare love ?
Yes and no. . . . If she should love too much ? . . .
Where must her love stop ? Oh ! cruel doctrines, which
breaking the links of home, and making love a bitter
thing, freeze even maternal affection.

* *Proverbs of Solomon* xiii. 24; xxxiii. 13; xxix. 15; and *Ecclesiasticus* xxx.
1, 9, 10.
† *Ecclesiasticus* vii. 26.

" Therefore, no love but in God.   God loved so much the world. . . . He can require all, since he has given all, his Son !"   Enormous sacrifice through which the *Gospel* appeared as infinite Forgiveness, and showed sin dead, justice impossible, hell vanquished and extinguished.   How is it, then, that still subsists the barbarous old idea, *Predestination*, which teaches that there are people condemned before their birth, and created for hell-fire ?   This disheartening idea hovers vaguely here and there over the *Old Testament ;* but it stands out in bold presence in the *Gospels*, as if in red lightning on a dark background.*   In the writings of Saint Paul it becomes a man in the vigor of his youth, and in the works of Saint Augustin, a hangman.

Oh ! how terrible Love is !   On the door of hell, according to Dante, there is the following inscription : " Love made me."   The fury and ferocity of Augustin has its foundation in Love.   He, with his African nature, in his ardor toward God, blamed and condemned the Greek Fathers, who entertained doubts about an everlasting hell, and dared believe that the blessed, in looking at the reprobate, could feel pity.†

---

* " Unto you it has been given to know the mysteries of the kingdom of heaven. To them it has not been given." (*Matthew.* See also *John* xii. 40.)   But why speak by parables ?   " That seeing they may see, and not perceive ; and hearing they may hear, and not understand" (*Mark* iv. 12 ; *Luke* viii. 10) ; and Mark adds : " Lest at any time they should be converted, and their sins should be forgiven them." (*Mark* iv. 12.)   What is stranger still is that according to the old Jewish spirit *"God tempts man."* (Lead us not into temptation.)   I wish I were mistaken.   Perhaps I have not understood well !   Is there anything more cruel than this to the heart ?

† The terrible barrenness of the Middle Ages has passed judgment on these doctrines.   It seems as though they had been wasted by fire.   How many centuries in vain !   A patient erudition finds out this and that.   But, truly, how can we desist from blushing at it ?   What ! so few things in a thousand years !   A thousand years ! a thousand years ! I say, and for a society of so many peoples and so many kingdoms !   How they go slowly till 1200 ! . . . And after 1200 their condition is more lamentable, for they can neither live nor die.   During six hundred years, with so many resources, they cannot create or institute anything which is not hatred and police supervision.   In 1200 the Orders of Mendicants, their burning charity, and the worship of Mary.

And who is the reprobate? Why, everybody. It is evident in Saint Augustin that in this doctrine of Love, the loved is undiscoverable, the chosen is rare, almost impossible. . . . Good gracious! What in the Law could have been harsher than this? Give back to me Justice. With her I might have had at least some extenuating circumstances. But I have none under the dispensation of Grace. My lot is fixed beforehand. Oh! release me from Love!

. . . .

"If you have sometimes travelled among mountains, you may perhaps have observed the same spectacle which I once met with.

"From among a confused heap of rocks piled together, amid a landscape diversified with trees and verdure, towered a gigantic peak. That object, black, bare, and solitary, was but too evidently thrown up from the deep bowels of the earth. It was enlivened by no verdure; no season changed its aspect; the very birds would hardly venture to alight on it, as though they feared to singe their wings by touching the mass which had been projected from the earth's central fire. That gloomy evidence of the throes of the interior world seemed still to muse over the scene, regardless of surrounding objects, without ever rousing from its savage melancholy.

"What were then the subterraneous revolutions of the earth, what incalculable powers combated in its bosom, for that mass, disturbing mountains, piercing through rocks, shattering beds of marble, to burst forth to the surface! What convulsions, what agony forced from the entrails of the globe that prodigious groan!

"I sat down, and from my eyes tears of anguish, slow

And all this was a new kind of police, (heaven help us) the police of the Inquisition. About the year 1500 the crusade of Ignatius, knighthood, and yet penalty, a net of infinite intrigues. In our days, Saint Vincent de Paul, a philanthropic devotee. But the Public and the State have seen in it nothing but *police* still.

and painful, began to flow. Nature had but too well reminded me of history. That chaos of mountain-heaps oppressed me with the same weight which had crushed the heart of man throughout the Middle Ages, and in that desolate peak, which from her inmost bowels the earth had hurled towards heaven, I saw pictured the despair and the cry of the human race.

" That Justice should have borne for a thousand years that mountain of dogma upon her heart, and, crushed beneath its weight, have counted the hours, the days, the years—so many long years—is, for him who knows it, a source of eternal tears.

" My very heart bled in contemplating the long resignation, the meekness, the patience, and the efforts of humanity to love that world of hate and malediction under which it was crushed.

" When man, resigning liberty and justice, as something useless, entrusted himself blindly to the hands of Grace, and saw it becoming concentrated on an imperceptible point—that is to say, the privileged, the elect—and saw all other beings, whether on earth or under the earth, lost for eternity, you would suppose there arose everywhere a howl of blasphemy ! No, only a groan.

" And these affecting words : ' If thou wilt that I be damned, thy will be done, O Lord ! '

" Then, peaceful, submissive, and resigned, they folded themselves in the shroud of damnation.

" And yet, what a constant temptation to despair and doubt ! How bondage here below was, with all its miseries, the beginning, the foretaste of eternal damnation ! First a life of suffering ; next, for consolation, hell ! Damned beforehand ! Then, wherefore those comedies of Judgment represented in the church-porches ! Is it not barbarous to keep in uncertainty, in dreadful anxiety, ever suspended over the abyss, him, who, before his birth, is adjudged to the bottomless pit, is due to it, and belongs to it ?

"Before his birth !—the infant, the innocent, created expressly for hell ! Nay, did I say the innocent ? This is the horror of the system ; there is innocence no more. I know not, but I boldly and unhesitatingly affirm this to be the insoluble knot at which the human soul had stopped short, and patience was staggered.

"The infant damned ! This is a deep, frightful wound to the maternal heart ! In exploring its depths, we find there much more than the terrors of death.

"Thence was it, believe me, that the first sigh arose of protestation ? No ! And yet, unknown to the timid heart of woman, whence it escaped, there was a terrible *But* in that humble, low, agonizing groan.

"So low, but so heart-rending ! The man who heard it at night slept no more on that nigbt, nor for many a night after. And in the morning, before daylight, he went to his furrow, and there found many things were changed. He found the valley and the field of labor lower, much lower—deep, like a sepulchre ; and the two towers in the horizon more lofty—more gloomy and heavy ; gloomy the church-steeple, and dismal the feudal donjon. And then he began to comprehend the sounds of the two bells. The church-bell murmured *Ever ;* that of the donjon, *Never.* But, at the same time, a mighty voice spoke louder in his heart. That voice said, *One day.* And that was the voice of God !

"*One day* Justice shall return ! Leave those idle bells ; let them prate to the wind. Be not alarmed with thy doubt. *That doubt is already faith.* Believe, and hope ! Right, though postponed, shall have its advent ; it will come to sit in judgment on the dogma and on the world. And *that day* of Judgment will be called the Revolution." *

---

* MICHELET : *History of the French Revolution.* 1st vol. *Introduction,* p. xli. (January 31, 1847.) Prof. C. COCKS' translation. London, 1848.

CONCLUSION.

I had wished that this sacred book, which really contains nothing that is originally mine, but is the utterance of the soul of mankind, might not exhibit a single word of criticism, but that all in it might be words of blessing.

And yet in the last chapters the spirit of criticism seized us again. It is not our fault. And, indeed, how to speak of modern thought, of its happy agreement with the remotest antiquity, without explaining the long delays, the halt of sterility which we underwent in the Middle Ages?

We undergo it still. To speak the truth, the delay, the stop occurs again too often. At intervals we lag. In spite of the immense powers we have, we seem out of breath at every step. Why? The reason is evident: we drag after us a dead thing, which is so much the more heavier. If it were our own skin we could manage to get rid of it, as the serpent does. Many shake themselves vigorously. But the evil is at the bottom.

It is in our friends as well as in our enemies. Each of us is bound inwardly by a million of threads—remembrances, habits, education, affections. Great men are bound as well as others. Even the imagination which thinks to be free and a queen has its interior servitudes, by fluttering about from *Equity* to *Grace*. The very lively and so strongly concentrated sensibility of artists feels so much the less the evils of men. Dante appears to have known nothing of the great Albijenses terror, of the eclipse of a world, of the appalling fact which in the year 1300 opened the way to the worship of Satan. He raises his standard, not in the eternal Gospel (the high conception of this epoch), but in the past, in Saint Thomas. Shakespere, the king of magicians, wanders from heaven to hell. But the earth? his own epoch? Behind the arras he feels only Polonius, but not the black mole which prepares *Thirty years' war* and the death of ten millions of men. Rousseau heedlessly hurls a century of reaction by a sentence of his *Emilius.*

Some geniuses in our time (who, I think, will not blush to find themselves ranged in such high society) believe that they are able to reconcile the irreconcilable. Either through compassion, kind heart, or through old habits, they keep a shred of the past. The tender remembrance of their mothers, the thoughts of the cradle, and, perhaps, the floating image of some good old preceptor, all these things stand before their eyes and conceal from them the world, the immensity of evils indefinitely prolonged, the *Spielbergs*, and the *Siberias*—I mean to say the moral *Siberias*, the barrenness, the progressive coolness which is going on at this very moment.

It is necessary to wheel about, and eagerly, frankly, to turn our back to the Middle Ages, to that morbid past, which, even when it does not act, exercises a terrible influence through the contagion of death. We need neither to fight nor to criticise, but to forget.

Let us forget and go on!

Let us advance toward the sciences of life, the museum, the schools, the college of France.

Let us advance toward the sciences of history and humanity, and toward the languages of the East. Let us consult the archaic *genius* in its harmony with so many recent travels. There we shall take the *human sense.*

I entreat you, let us be *men*, and let us be exalted by the new and unprecedented grandeur of mankind.

Thirty sciences, which had been belated, have just made their appearance, and with such a new vision, such a power of methods, that undoubtedly the number will be doubled to-morrow.

Thirty centuries have been added to antiquity, and with them numberless monuments, languages, religions, and worlds, which reappear to judge this world of ours.

An immense light, with crossed rays, terribly powerful

(even more than electric light), while crushing the past in all its scientific nonsense, has shown, instead, the victorious harmony of the two sisters, Science and Conscience. Every shadow has disappeared. Eternal Justice, identical in all epochs, and standing on its solid foundation of nature and history, sheds its beams.

This is the subject of this book. It is great and easy. The things for making it up had been so well prepared that the most unskilful hand has been sufficient to write it, but mankind is the real author.

The vow which a great prophet used to make in the sixteenth century is an accomplished fact now. *Here is the deep Faith.* Who could shake it, and from what part could come the attack? Science and Conscience have embraced each other.

Somebody is striving at something, or seems to be doing so. He gropes along in open day. He is a counterfeit blind man, who will have a stick when the road is even and very wonderfully illumined.

Here is the whole mankind in perfect harmony. What do you wish more? What interest have you in doubting?

A torrent of light, the river of Right and Reason flows down from India to the year one thousand seven hundred and eighty-nine. The remotest antiquity is thyself. And thy race is the year one thousand seven hundred and eighty-nine. The Middle Ages are the stranger.

Justice is not the foundling of yesterday, but the mistress and the heiress that wishes to return home—she is the true lady of the house. Who was before her? She can say: "I did spring up in the dawn at the glimmerings of the *Vedas.* In the morning of Persia I was the pure energy in the heroism of work. I was the Greek genius, and emancipation by the might of a word: 'Themis is Jove.' *God is Justice itself.* Hence Rome proceeds as well as the law which thou dost follow yet."

"I should like . . . I perceive well that . . . ." But it is necessary to will completely.

To come to a close, I say only three words, but practical ones, which ought to pass from father to son : Purification, Concentration, Greatness.

Let us be honest and pure from mixture with the old. Let us not halt from one world to another.

Let us beware in two senses—let us be strong against the chaos of the world, and of opinions—and let us be strong at home through the unity of the heart.

The fireside is the stone which upholds the commonwealth. Without home everything perishes. To the vain systems which would break it down, the answer is a terrible one: " The child will not live." Men will be fewer, and the citizen an impossibility.

People cry out : "Fraternity !" But they scarcely know what it is. It requires a security of morals as well as of character, and a pure austerity of which our century has little idea.

If the fireside must be enlarged, it must be done first of all by making sit down at it the whole heroic humanity, the great church of Justice, which, among so many people and ages, has been perpetuated to this time.

The fireside will then become again what it formerly was, *the altar.* It is enlightened by a reflex of the universal soul of the worlds, which is but Rectitude and Justice, impartial and unchangeable Love.

It is the firm fireside that this book would make, or at least begin for you. It proposes to give you in the fireside what it so often gave myself during this long work, which kept me up by day and awoke me by night—a great alleviation of suffering, a solemn and holy joy, the deep peace of light.

ALPHABETICAL INDEX.

COMPRISING ALL THE NAMES OF

DEITIES, HEROES, PERSONS, REGIONS, CITIES, MOUNTAINS,
RIVERS, ETC., MENTIONED IN THIS WORK.

22

www.ingramcontent.com/pod-product-compliance
Lightning Source LLC
Chambersburg PA
CBHW030908270326
41929CB00008B/617